Hakluyt's
Voyages
to the
New World

American History Landmarks

Edited by
David Freeman Hawke

Hakluyt's Voyages to the New World

by
Richard Hakluyt

A Selection

The Bobbs-Merrill Company, Inc.
Indianapolis & New York

Richard Hakluyt
1551 or 1552–1616

Copyright © 1972 by The Bobbs-Merrill Company, Inc.
Printed in the United States of America
Library of Congress Catalog Card Number 79-120187
First Printing
Designed by Starr Atkinson

Contents

Editor's Introduction ix

Note on the Text xix

Hakluyt's Voyages to the New World

Preface 3

Part I The Northwest Parts of America

1. The Voyage of Master Hore and Divers Other
   Gentlemen to Newfoundland and Cape Breton
   in the Year 1536 11
2. The Second Voyage of Master Martin Frobisher
   to the West and Northwest Regions in the
   Year 1577 14
3. Notes Framed [ca. 1578] by Master Richard
   Hakluyt of the Middle Temple, Esquire, Given
   to Certain Gentlemen That Went with Master
   Frobisher in His Northwest Discovery, for
   Their Directions 29
4. The Third Voyage of Master Martin Frobisher,
   Pretended for the Discovery of Cathay, by Meta
   Incognita, Anno Do[mini] 1578 34
5. The Voyage of Sir Humphrey Gilbert to
   Newfoundland, Anno 1583 47
6. A Report of Master John Davis Concerning His
   Three Voyages [1585, 1586, 1587] Made for the
   Discovery of the Northwest Passage, Taken Out
   of a Treatise of His Entitled "The World's
   Hydrographical Description" 66

Part II Virginia

1. The Letters Patent Granted by the Queen's
   Majesty to Sir Walter Raleigh, for the

Discovering and Planting of New Lands and
Countries, Anno 1584   73
2. The First Voyage Made to the Coast of Virginia
by M[aster] Philip Amadas and M[aster] Arthur
Barlowe, 1584   79
3. An Extract of M[aster] Ralph Lane's Letter to
M[aster] Richard Hakluyt, Esquire, and Another
Gentleman of the Middle Temple, from
Virginia, 1585   90
4. An Account of the Particular Employments of
the Englishmen Left in Virginia by S[ir]
Richard Grenville under M[aster] Ralph Lane,
Their General, from the Seventeenth of August,
1585, Until the Eighteenth of June, 1586, at
Which Time They Departed the Country   91
5. The Third Voyage to Virginia Made by a Ship
Sent in the Year 1586 for the Relief of the Colony
Planted in Virginia at the Sole Charges of Sir
Walter Raleigh   113
6. The Fourth Voyage made to Virginia with Three
Ships, Anno 1587, Wherein Was Transported the
Second Colony   115
7. A Letter of M[aster] John White to M[aster]
Richard Hakluyt Written in February, 1593   123
8. The Fifth Voyage to Virginia Made by Master
John White in the Year 1590   125

Part III The Caribbean

1. The First Voyage of the Right Worshipful and
Valiant Knight, Sir John Hawkins, Sometimes
Treasurer of Her Majesty's Navy Royal, Made to
the West Indies in the Year 1562   133
2. The Third Troublesome Voyage of the Right
Worshipful Sir John Hawkins, with the *Jesus of
Lübeck,* the *Minion,* and Four Other Ships, to the
Parts of Guinea and Coasts of Tierra Firma
and Nueva España, Anno 1567 and 1568   134
3. The Voyage of Henry Hawks, Merchant, to
Nueva España (in Which Country He Traveled
for the Space of Five Years and Observed Many

Notable Things). Written at the Request of
M[aster] Richard Hakluyt of Eyton in the
County of Hereford, Esquire, 1572   144
4. The First Voyage Attempted and Set Forth by
the Valiant and Expert Captain M[aster]
Francis Drake with a Ship Called the *Dragon*,
and Another Ship and a Pinnace, to Nombre de
Dios and Darien, About the Year 1572   160
5. The Famous Expedition of Sir Francis Drake to
the West Indies, Wherein Were Taken the Cities
of Saint Iago, Santo Domingo, Cartagena, with
the Fort and Town of Saint Augustine in
Florida, in the Years 1585 and 1586   162
6. The Last Voyage of Sir Francis Drake and Sir
John Hawkins, Intended for Some Special
Services on the Islands and Main of the West
Indies, Anno 1595. In Which Voyage Both the
Foresaid Knights Died of Sickness   185

Editor's Introduction

1.

Some men find themselves early in life and build from youth toward an achievement that gives them fame forever. So it was with Richard Hakluyt. When still a lad he became fascinated with those who "go down to the sea in ships and occupy by the great waters," and from then on he moved, consciously or otherwise, steadily toward the work that capped his life—the three large volumes of *The Principal Navigations, Voyages, Traffiques, and Discoveries of the English Nation*, which came forth in their final form, a volume each year, from 1598 to 1600. Seldom, if ever, has a sedate scholar-clergyman done so much to shape both the present and the future of a nation.

There is something preposterous about a mild, retiring preacher emerging out of Elizabethan England as one of the giants of the age. Indeed, Hakluyt's whole life skirts the absurd. He knew more about the New World than any other man of the day, yet he never saw it. Salty phrases dot his writings— "it is high time for us to weigh our anchor, to hoist up our sails"— yet he knew nothing firsthand about a sailor's life. He produced the greatest collection of sea tales ever assembled in the English language without once having ventured upon the ocean. In a hyperbolic age, he had a passion for truth, and once he rode two hundred miles to check the facts about an early and insignificant expedition to America—Master Hore's in 1536— from a lone survivor. He was a visionary and romantic who gave sound advice to businessmen prepared to invest in risky projects overseas. He was a scholar who mingled with ease among courtiers and statesmen and with equal ease among sailors in the rowdy taverns of the port towns where he collected accounts of their latest adventures. Perhaps strangest of all for a minister of the Gospel, he helped give form to the British Empire when it was little more than a dream. Virginia in time might have been settled by Englishmen anyhow, but Hakluyt's prodding did much to hasten the event; and his constant encouragement, privately and in print, of what seemed a doomed experiment helped to assure the eventual establishment of what became the foundation stone of the United States.

Hakluyt as much as any man inspired the settlement of America. Unwittingly, he then went on to become something of an oracle for Americans. Virtually every ship that came to the colonies in the seventeenth century carried a set of the *Voyages,* or at least a copy of the third volume, which dealt with the New World. The accounts by previous visitors to the wilderness helped to guide newcomers along the unknown coast, to acquaint them with the Indians and with the flora and fauna. Hakluyt revealed Virginia before the Jamestown settlers saw it and New England before the Puritans and Pilgrims set foot upon those rocky coasts. His translated reminiscences of French Huguenots who had settled along the South Carolina and Florida coasts encouraged the first English settlers, then living in the West Indies, to emigrate to that region. When colonists finally ventured into the interior of the continent, Spanish explorers' reports unearthed by Hakluyt told them what to expect. Well into the eighteenth century much of what Americans knew of Mexico and South America came from what they had read in the *Voyages.* The name Hakluyt—pronounced, incidentally, "Hack-lit"—became for the colonists a synonym for guidebook to a continent.

To call the *Voyages* a guidebook and leave it at that denigrates Hakluyt's purpose, his achievement, and his influence upon Americans. He wished, he said, to expose the "heroical intents and attempts" of past Englishmen, with the hope of kindling among those of the present a flame that "could never be quenched until such time as their own valor had equaled the fame and glory of their progenitors." That lofty purpose left its mark on the early colonists. Though they had cut adrift from England and lived buried in a wilderness some three thousand miles from their former homes, they remained a people with a past now engaged in a noble enterprise. Their errand in the wilderness was as much to glorify England as to enrich themselves or to worship as they wished. Two of the earliest and greatest books about the initial American experience—William Bradford's *Of Plymouth Plantation* and John Smith's *General History*—reflected Hakluyt's influence on their style and content and their reasons for writing. (Bradford merely referred to Hakluyt in passing, but Smith admitted a larger debt. He plagiarized large sections from that part of the *Voyages* concerning Virginia.) With the same emphasis on "heroical intents and attempts," with the same forthright exposure of failures and successes, and with the same Elizabethan eloquence, both men sought to continue the story Hakluyt had begun. Throughout the seventeenth and into the eighteenth century, whenever Americans wrote about America they continued to use the mold forged by Hakluyt. What he had produced to inspire Englishmen ended, curiously, inspiring Americans.

2.

"The name of Hakluyt has become one to conjure with," George B. Parks, his most successful biographer, has remarked, "but the man remains as obscure as ever in his living and breathing actuality." As with Shakespeare, a contemporary, he has largely vanished in his work. Like one of his Elizabethan sailors viewing an unknown, mist-shrouded coastline, one finds only here and there a landmark on which to take a fairly accurate fix. He was born either in 1551 or 1552, probably in London, most likely the son of a merchant. His father died when Hakluyt was no more than five, and a cousin, a lawyer also named Richard Hakluyt, took charge of his upbringing. He attended Westminster School—"that fruitful nursery," he called it—until 1570, then studied at Christchurch, Oxford. He was ordained in 1578 and remained until death a priest in the Church of England. He lived a comfortable life, respected by the Queen and her ministers, was twice married, had one son, and died in his mid-sixties in 1616—the year of Shakespeare's death—but unlike Shakespeare honored enough in his time to be buried in Westminster Abbey.

At Hakluyt's birth England, so far as Europe was concerned, lay awash off the coast of France in "sluggish security." In the succeeding half century "this sceptered isle" (Shakespeare's phrase) came to excel "all the nations and people of the earth" (Hakluyt's remark, contained in what Howard Mumford Jones calls "one of his most splendid passages"). Hakluyt reveals in a rare autobiographical section that it was a chance encounter with his cousin that enticed him into what for the the time was the center of the "action," to use a word favored by Eliza-bethans. Richard Hakluyt, the lawyer, his cousin's senior by some twenty years, had been deeply involved in England's expansion overseas for some time, no doubt first as a legal adviser, then, as his knowledge broadened, as technical con-sultant on all aspects of international mercantile affairs. He devised operating procedures for the Muscovy Company, drew up instructions for an expert being sent to Persia to discover new techniques for dyeing wool, and suggested itineraries for an agent headed for the Far East. It was his "Notes" on how to choose a suitable plantation site that Sir Humphrey Gilbert carried when he set out in 1578 for the New World with a charter in his pocket from the Queen granting him the right to colonize English claims in the New World.

Meanwhile, at Oxford the younger Hakluyt had been reading "whatsoever printed or written discoveries and voyages I found extant either in the Greek, Latin, Italian, Spanish, Portugal, French, or English languages," and he had also begun to lecture on geography, or cosmography as the specialty, then in its infancy, was called. At first through his cousin, then on his own, he met and talked with the leading mariners and merchants of the day, visiting them both in London and in Bristol before they left and after they returned from overseas. It was surely through his cousin that he became attached to Gilbert's twin interests, the search for the Northwest Passage and the creation of a colony in America. In 1580, two years after he had been ordained, he helped promote Gilbert's cause — some already called him Gilbert's "trumpet" — by arranging for the translation and publication of Cartier's first two voyages to America. Two years later he promoted it still further with a small book entitled *Divers Voyages Touching the Discovery of America and the Islands Adjacent unto the Same . . . .*, which, E.G.R. Taylor has remarked, "formed a very complete manual for readers anxious to form an opinion on the merits of a Northwest Passage and western plantation schemes." Hakluyt coupled the propaganda, if that is the word, with visits to Bristol in an apparently successful effort to promote contributions from merchants for the proposed expedition.

Hakluyt had hoped to travel on Gilbert's next colonizing voyage—it turned out to be his last—but those in government eager to advance English settlement in the New World arranged instead for him to go to France, ostensibly as the ambassador's chaplain, actually to make "diligent inquiry of such things as may yield any light unto our western discovery." There he could read Spanish reports on the New World that were un-available in England, talk to well-informed Dutch spies about Spanish accomplishments, and listen to the experiences of Huguenots who had made several abortive attempts at settle-ment inside both the Spanish and Portuguese spheres of influence in North and South America. The information Hakluyt accumulated during his five years in France made him unquestionably the best-informed Englishman of the time about the New World in general and North America in particular.

During Hakluyt's absence in France, Gilbert's expedition failed to plant a settlement, and on the return trip Gilbert was lost at sea. His charter, which lapsed in 1584, was reissued by the Queen to his half brother, Sir Walter Raleigh, who promptly dispatched a reconnaissance led by Philip Amadas and Arthur Barlowe to search out a site for an American colony. Before the party returned Hakluyt, at Raleigh's request, began *A Discourse of Western Planting,* a lengthy and impressive "collection of certain reasons *to induce her Majesty and the state to take in hand the western voyage and the planting there.*" After Amadas and Barlowe had arrived back in England and reported on the glories of Virginia, as Raleigh chose to call the land in honor of the Virgin Queen, Hakluyt's essay was presented to Eliza-beth. Despite a host of persuasive arguments for establishing overseas colonies—they would promote trade, strengthen the navy, provide raw materials for English industry, offer an outlet for "the fry of wandering beggars of England," advance the Protestant religion, and, above all, undercut the power of

Spain—the hard-pressed Crown refused financial support of Raleigh's endeavor, the time being especially inopportune now that war with Spain seemed imminent.

The rebuff discouraged both Hakluyt and Raleigh and other imperial enthusiasts, but it did not diminish their efforts to promote colonies in America. While Raleigh continued to send out exploratory expeditions to Virginia, which culminated in a full-scale effort to plant a permanent settlement in 1587, Hakluyt, as he moved back and forth between Paris and London on a variety of diplomatic assignments, all the while "waded on still farther and farther in the sweet study of the history of cosmography." He returned for good to England in the winter of 1588, either shortly before or after the Spanish Armada hovered off his homeland's shore. The time had now come, after a quarter of a century of accumulating material, to produce the book toward which all his research had been directed since that day his cousin picked up a wand, pointed at a map of the world, and "began to instruct my ignorance."

3.

The Principall Navigations, Voiages, and Discoveries of the English Nation was first published in 1589 in one large volume, and without the word "Traffiques." The work divided into three parts, the first dealing with those voyages "performed to the south and southeast parts of the world, by which I chiefly mean that part of Asia which is nearest and of the rest hithermost towards us"; the second with those to the north and northeast, principally in search of a Northeast Passage, which resulted in a profitable trade route into Russia; and the third and largest with "the western navigations and travels of ours" into the New World. "I meddle in this work with the navigations only of our nation," he remarked in the dedicatory epistle, more modestly than accurately, for wherever he had found material relevant to his theme, be it in Spanish, Portuguese, Latin, French, or Italian, he had translated and included it.

And he did have a theme. What at first glance seemed a potpourri of mariners' narratives, promotional tracts, business letters, ships' logs, and government documents had been cemented into an English epic by Hakluyt's compulsion to put between book covers all he could find "which might commend our nation for their high courage and singular activity in the search and discovery of the most unknown quarters of the world." Hakluyt pretended to be no more than the collector and editor of this material, yet his modesty had limits. The search for documents "which long have lain miserably scattered in musty corners and wretchedly hidden in misty darkness" had been no easy task, he later said; only "the ardent love of my country devoured all difficulties and, as it were, with a sharp goad provoked me and thrust me forward into this most troublesome and painful action."

Knowledgeable contemporaries realized at once the quality of Hakluyt's achievement. Those who knew firsthand some aspect of the material covered saw that he had for the most part been a scrupulous editor, presenting a report or narrative as he had found it, with few excisions or interpolations. He made no effort to scrub away failures or exaggerate successes. He let the reader evaluate for himself the quality of an account, and where research had revealed discrepant versions, he would present them without comment. He rarely intruded his own views, here or in the 1598-1600 edition, except in the Dedicatory Epistles and Prefaces, where he would plead for a professorship of navigation, warmer support for the settlement of Virginia, or some other project close to his heart.

Nothing like the *Voyages* had ever appeared in English, and yet for all its strangeness it had an instant and wide appeal. For those who relished tales of far-off lands, of heroic exploits, and of adventures at sea it offered reading enough for a month of Sundays. More than that, it was a useful book—as a geography, for example. "There is no chief river, no port, no town, no city, no province of any reckoning in the West Indies that hath not here some good description thereof," Hakluyt later bragged, and what he said of the West Indies could be applied to the known parts of Virginia, of Newfoundland, and of large parts of Russia, the Near East, and the Orient. A neophyte merchant eager to expand into, say, Constantinople or Moscow found the *Voyages* an excellent business manual. A pilot crossing the Atlantic could bolster his confidence by comparing course headings with those given in various of Hakluyt's narratives, and if in doubt about the landfall, the description of an earlier mariner might clarify his location.

The timing of the *Voyages'* appearance contributed to its appeal. It came forth less than a year after the Spanish Armada had retreated in disgrace from England's shores. Hakluyt helped the English evaluate what had been achieved. The victory, he made clear, had not been a fluke produced by luck, a great Queen, and intrepid seamen, but was the result of a long, slowly garnered tradition that had its roots deep in England's past. Several centuries of exploits by English mariners and merchants, hitherto "scattered as several ships," an admirer remarked, "Master Hakluyt hath embodied into a fleet." A fleet, it could be added, sailing toward a single goal—domination of the world's oceans.

In the decade between the first and second editions of the *Voyages,* Hakluyt continued to collect material, so much so that the original one volume expanded into three. His basic organization of material remained the same, but within the old framework great changes had been worked. The addition of the word "Traffiques" to the title pointed up an emphasis on trade. The inclusion of sea battles—the first of the new volumes opened with an account of the Armada—gave a prominence, hitherto lacking, to the navy. A mass of new material from the medieval period now appeared and the cutoff date, which in the first edition had ostensibly been 1500, now moved up to 1600. Material on the New World came to occupy an even larger part in the story. Old accounts whose authenticity Hakluyt had come to doubt—such as John Mandeville's trip to the Far East and David Ingram's overland journey from Mexico to Cape Breton—were deleted.

Hakluyt's obsession with England's life overseas did not cease with the publication of the final volume of the *Voyages* in 1600. When James I in 1606 issued a charter for the colonization of Virginia, Hakluyt numbered among those adventurers who had pledged ten pounds to promote the project. He talked briefly of traveling with those who eventually settled Jamestown, but friends and family or failing health—he was then in his mid-fifties—must have dissuaded him. When he died ten years later the Jamestown colony seemed on a firm footing, and the great drama of the course of empire that he had revealed in the *Voyages* appeared about to enter a new act.

4.

Today the *Voyages'* usefulness has faded away for all save historians, and the work survives mainly as literature, a literature *of* the people produced by men who were part of the "troublesome and painful action." But for the reports they gave Hakluyt, an Edward Hayes or a Ralph Lane or an Arthur Barlowe might otherwise be forgotten. Each of their reports becomes an epic story "infused by its very nature with the mysterious and the remote," Parks has said. "The wonder of the world strikes perpetually across the matter-of-fact pages, the more powerfully because the pages are matter-of-fact." Often their narratives are awkwardly told but, as in all epics, the effort of common men to tell as honestly as they can what it was like to confront the unknown carries a power that overrides the lack of art.

The literary virtues of the *Voyages* do not detract from their value to the historian, whose research has been eased as much as his pleasure increased by Hakluyt's labors. No one writing about the Elizabethans and the New World can avoid constant use of the *Voyages* nor, for that matter, of the volumes periodically issued by the Hakluyt Society — such as David B. Quinn's edition of *The Roanoke Voyages, 1584–1590*—which build with additional source material on the groundwork laid by the master nearly four centuries ago.

And no one attempting a brief selection from Hakluyt's massive collection, which in its most authoritative reprinting (the Glasgow edition of 1903–1905) embraces eleven volumes, can possibly do justice to the scope and variety of its contents. To make the task more manageable, and also more relevant to the American reader toward whom this small volume is aimed, selections have been confined to that part of the *Voyages* dealing with the New World. Some of the most famous narratives—those of Frobisher's second and third voyages and

Gilbert's last one, for example—are included, but some, like Raleigh's great account of the *Revenge*'s defeat, have been omitted because they are outside the American story. Hakluyt's "double order of time and place" has been adhered to; the organization of the material from north to south with a chronological arrangement within each section is that used by Hakluyt. A virtue of this pattern, most apparent in the section on Virginia, is that the reader can sense, as he moves from one narrative to the next, something of the progressive accumulation of knowledge that Elizabethans acquired with each new voyage to America.

An effort has been made to suggest the diversity in Hakluyt's collection, but to include such items as Raleigh's charter for Virginia and Henry Hawks' report on Mexico—the most detailed and accurate, incidentally, that Americans probably knew until the American Revolution and perhaps sometime after—only hints at the *Voyages'* inclusiveness.

And now, as Hakluyt puts it, "it is high time for us to weigh our anchor, to hoist up our sails, to get clear of these boisterous, frosty, and misty seas, and with all speed to direct our course for the mild, lithesome, temperate, and warm Atlantic Ocean."

D.F.H.

Note on the Text

No attempt has been made in this edition to alter the style of any of the authors. The Elizabethan language has been respected, though the punctuation and most spellings have been modernized. Occasionally, words that might confuse or pointlessly distract today's reader, such as "strooken" and "drave," have been changed. The spelling of personal names, the paragraphing, the syntax remain, with few exceptions, Hakluyt's. The spelling of place names has been silently corrected where it closely resembles the modern form; where it does not, the original spelling is kept throughout but the currently accepted form is indicated in brackets at its first appearance. Words and geographical references that might puzzle the reader have been keyed the first time they appear but not thereafter.

The Contents is as Hakluyt gave it in the *Voyages;* where Hakluyt did not include the account in his own Contents, his heading within the text has been used. The authorship of most of these accounts has been provided. Omitted material is indicated by the usual ellipses, except in Hakluyt's Preface, which is made up of scattered extracts from several of his Prefaces and Dedicatory Epistles.

In 1907 the Everyman Library published an eight-volume edition of Hakluyt's *Voyages* that is accurate enough to satisfy all but the most specialized scholar. For the convenience of any reader who might wish to trace a particular report back to Hakluyt's version, the accounts in this volume have been drawn from the Everyman edition as follows:

Hakluyt's Preface comes from Volume I, pages 1–4, 47, 48–49, 39–40, 22, 12. In Volume V are found Hore's voyage, pages 338–341; Frobisher's second voyage, pages 137–153; Hakluyt's "Notes," pages 165–170; Frobisher's third voyage, pages 228–231; 237–241, 242–245, 252–255, 265–267; and Davis's voyages, pages 332–336. From Volume VI come Gilbert's voyage, pages 1–2, 6–7, 8–9, 11–12, 13–14, 16–20, 23–25, 27–29,

31–36, 37–38; Raleigh's letters patent, pages 115–121; first voyage to Virginia, pages 121–132; Lane's letter, page 140; Grenville's account, pages 141–162; third voyage to Virginia, pages 162–164; fourth voyage to Virginia, pages 196, 200–207; White's letter, pages 211–213; and the fifth voyage to Virginia, pages 213–214, 218–228. Hawkins' first and third voyages come from Volume VII, pages 5–6, 53–62. Hawks' voyage is from Volume VI, pages 279, 280–296. And from Volume VII are Drake's first voyage, pages 62–64; Drake's 1585 voyage, pages 77, 78–108; and the Drake-Hawkins voyage of 1595, pages 183–199.

Hakluyt's
Voyages
to the
New World

Preface

I do remember that being a youth, and one of her Majesty's scholars at Westminster, that fruitful nursery, it was my hap to visit the chamber of Master Richard Hakluyt, my cousin, a gentleman of the Middle Temple, at a time when I found lying open upon his board certain books of cosmography with a universal map. He, seeing me somewhat curious in the view thereof, began to instruct my ignorance by showing me the division of the earth into three parts after the old account, and then according to the later and better distribution into more. He pointed with his wand to all the known seas, gulfs, bays, straits, capes, rivers, empires, kingdoms, dukedoms, and territories of each part, with declaration also of their special commodities and particular wants, which by benefit of traffic and intercourse of merchants are plentifully supplied. From the map he brought me to the Bible, and turning to Psalm 107 directed me to the twenty-third and twenty-fourth verses, where I read that they which go down to the sea in ships and occupy by the great waters, they see the works of the Lord and His wonders in the deep, etc. Which words of the Prophet together with my cousin's discourse (things of high and rare delight to my young nature) took in me so deep an impression that I constantly resolved if ever I were preferred to the University, where better time and more convenient place might be ministered for these studies, I would by God's assistance prosecute that knowledge and kind of literature, the doors whereof (after a sort) were so happily opened before me.

According to which my resolution, when, not long after I was removed to Christchurch in Oxford, my exercises of duty first performed, I fell to my intended course and by degrees read over whatsoever printed or written discoveries and voyages I found extant either in the Greek, Latin, Italian, Spanish, Portugal, French, or English languages; and in my public lectures was the first that produced and showed both the old imperfectly composed and the new lately reformed maps, globes, spheres, and other instruments of this art for demon-

3

stration in the common schools, to the singular pleasure and
general contentment of my auditory. In continuance of time
and by reason principally of my insight in this study, I grew
familiarly acquainted with the chiefest captains at sea, the
greatest merchants, and the best mariners of our nation. By
which means having gotten somewhat more than common
knowledge, I passed at length the narrow seas into France
with Sir Edward Stafford, her Majesty's careful and discreet
ligier [ambassador], where during my five years' abode with
him in his dangerous and chargeable residency in her Highness's service, I both heard in speech and read in books other
nations miraculously extolled for their discoveries and notable
enterprises by sea; but the English of all others for their sluggish security and continual neglect of the like attempts, especially in so long and happy a time of peace, either ignominiously
reported or exceedingly condemned.

For stopping the mouths of the reproachers, [I] determined,
notwithstanding all difficulties, to undertake the burden of
that work wherein all others pretended either ignorance, or
lack of leisure, or want of sufficient argument, whereas (to
speak truly) the huge toil and the small profit to ensue were
the chief causes of the refusal. I call the work a burden in consideration that these voyages lay so dispersed, scattered, and
hidden in several hucksters' hands that I now wonder at myself
to see how I was able to endure the delays, curiosity, and
backwardness of many from whom I was to receive my originals.
So that I have just cause to make that complaint of the mali-
ciousness of divers in our time, which Pliny made of the men
of his age: *At nos elaborata iis abscondere atque supprimere
cupimus, et fraudare vitam etiam alienis bonis, etc.*

To harp no longer upon this string, and to speak a word of
that just condemnation which our nation do indeed deserve:
it cannot be denied but, as in all former ages, they have been
men full of activity, stirrers abroad, and searchers of the
remote parts of the world, so in this most famous and peerless
government of her most excellent Majesty, her subjects through
the special assistance and blessing of God in searching the most
opposite corners and quarters of the world and, to speak
plainly, in compassing the vast globe of the earth more than

once, have excelled all the nations and people of the earth. For which of the kings of this land before her Majesty had ever seen their banners in the Caspian Sea? Which of them hath ever dwelt with the Emperor of Persia, as her Majesty hath done, and obtained for her merchants large and loving privileges? Who ever saw before this regiment [reign] an English ligier in the stately porch of the Grand Signor at Constantinople? Who ever found English consuls and agents at Tripolis in Syria, at Aleppo, at Babylon, at Bulsar, and which is more, who ever heard of [an] Englishman at Goa before now? What English ships did heretofore ever anchor in the mighty river of Plate, pass and repass the unpassable (in former opinion) Strait of Magellan, range along the coast of Chile, Peru, and all the backside of Nova Hispania further than any Christian ever passed, traverse the mighty breadth of the South Sea, land upon the Luzons in despite of the enemy, enter into alliance, amity, and traffic with the princes of the Moluccas and the Isle of Java, double the famous Cape of Bona Speranza [Good Hope], arrive most richly laden with the commodities of China, as the subjects of this now flourishing monarchy have done?

Lucius Florus in the very end of his *History de Gestis Romanorum* recordeth as a wonderful miracle that the Seres (which I take to be the people of Cathay, or China) sent ambassadors to Rome to entreat friendship, as moved with the fame of the majesty of the Roman Empire. And have not we as good cause to admire that the kings of the Moluccas and Java Major have desired the favor of her Majesty and the commerce and traffic of her people? Is it not as strange that the born naturals of Japan and the Philippines are here to be seen agreeing with our climate, speaking our language, and informing us of the state of their Eastern habitations? For mine own part, I take it as a pledge of God's further favor both unto us and them; to them especially, unto whose doors I doubt not in time shall be by us carried the incomparable treasure of the truth of Christianity and of the Gospel, while we use and exercise common trade with their merchants.

The subject and matter herein contained is the fourth part of the world, which more commonly than properly is called

America, but by the chiefest authors the New World. New in regard of the new and late discovery thereof made by Christopher Colon, alias Columbus, a Genoese by nation, in the year of grace 1492. And world in respect of the huge extension thereof, which to this day is not thoroughly discovered, neither within the inland nor on the coast, especially toward the north and northwest, although on the hither side it be known unto us for the space of five thousand leagues at the least, compting [computing] and considering the trending of the land, and for three thousand more on the backside in the South Sea from the Strait of Magellan to Cape Mendocino and Nova Albion. So that it seemeth very fitly to be called a New World.

Of this New World and every special part thereof in this my third volume I have brought to light the best and most perfect relations of such as were chief actors in the particular discoveries and searches of the same, giving unto every man his right and leaving everyone to maintain his own credit. The order observed in this work is far more exact than heretofore I could attain unto. For whereas in my two former volumes, I was enforced for lack of sufficient store in divers places to use the method of time only (which many worthy authors on the like occasion are enforced unto); being now more plentifully furnished with matter, I always follow the double order of time and place. Wherefore proposing unto myself the right situation of the New World, I begin at the extreme northern limit and put down successively in one rank or classis, according to the order aforesaid, all such voyages as have been made to the said part. Which coming all together and following orderly one upon another do much more lighten the reader's understanding and confirm his judgment than if they had been scattered in sundry corners of the work. Which method I observe from the highest North to the lowest South. Now where any country hath been but seldom haunted [frequented] or any extraordinary and chief action occurreth, if I find one voyage well written by two several persons, sometimes I make no difficulty to set down both those journals, as finding divers things of good moment observed in the one, which are quite omitted in the other. For commonly a soldier observeth one thing and a mariner another. But this course I take very seldom and sparingly.

And albeit my work do carry the title of the English voyages, as well in regard that the greatest part are theirs and that my travail was chiefly undertaken for preservation of their memorable actions, yet where our own men's experience is defective, there I have been careful to supply the same with the best and chiefest relations of strangers. As in the discovery of the Grand Bay, of the mighty river of St. Lawrence, of the countries of Canada, Hochelaga [Montreal], and Saguenay [southern Quebec], of Florida, and the inland of Cibola, Tiguex, Cicuye [all three are in New Mexico], and Quivira [central Kansas], of the Gulf of California, and the northwestern seacoast to Cape Mendocino and Sierra Nevada. As also of the late and rich discovery of fifteen provinces on the backside of Florida and Virginia, the chiefest whereof is called the kingdom of New Mexico, for the wealth, civil government, and populousness of the same.

Moreover, because since our wars with Spain, by the taking of their ships, and sacking of their towns and cities, most of all their secrets of the West Indies, and every part thereof are fallen into our peoples' hands (which in former time were for the most part unknown unto us), I have used the uttermost of my best endeavor, to get, and having gotten, to translate out of Spanish, and here in this present volume to publish such secrets of theirs as may any way avail us or annoy them, if they drive and urge us by their sullen insolencies to continue our courses of hostility against them, and shall cease to seek a good and Christian peace upon indifferent and equal conditions.

These and the like heroical intents and attempts of our princes, our nobility, our clergy, and our chivalry I have in the first place exposed and set forth to the view of this age with the same intention that the old Romans set up in wax in their palaces the statues or images of their worthy ancestors. Whereof Sallust in his treatise of the war of Jugurtha writeth in this manner: I have often heard (quoth he) how Quintus Maximus, Publius Scipio, and many other worthy men of our city were want to say, when they beheld the images and portraitures of their ancestors, that they were most vehemently inflamed into virtue. Not that the said wax portraiture had any such force at all in itself, but that by the remembering of their worthy acts that flame was kindled in their noble breasts and could never be quenched until such time as their own valor had equaled the fame and glory of their progenitors. So, though not in wax, yet in record of writing have I presented to the noble courages of this English monarchy the like images of their famous predecessors, with hope of like effect in their posterity.

And here by the way: if any man shall think that a universal peace with our Christian neighbors will cut off the employment of the courageous increasing youth of this realm, he is much deceived. For there are other most convenient employments for all the superfluity of every profession in this realm. For, not to meddle with the state of Ireland nor that of Guiana, there is under our noses the great and ample country of Virginia; the inland whereof is found of late to be so sweet and wholesome a climate, so rich and abundant in silver mines, so apt and capable of all commodities which Italy, Spain, and France can afford, that the Spaniards themselves in their own writings printed in Madrid, 1586, and within few months afterward reprinted by me in Paris, and in a secret map of those parts made in Mexico the year before for the king of Spain (which original with many others is in the custody of the excellent mathematician Master Thomas Hariot) as also in their intercepted letters come unto my hand, bearing date 1595, they acknowledge the inland to be better and richer country than Mexico and Nueva Spania itself.

And on the other side their chiefest writers, as Peter Martyr ab Angleria and Francis Lopez de Gomara, the most learned Venetian John Baptista Ramusió, and the French geographers as, namely, [Lancelot Voison La] Popelinière and the rest, acknowledge with one consent that all that mighty tract of land from sixty-seven degrees [North] to the latitude almost of Florida was first discovered out of England by the commandment of King Henry VII, and the south part thereof, before any other Christian people, of late hath been planted with divers English colonies by the royal consent of her sacred Majesty under the broad seal of England, whereof [no] one as yet remaineth, for ought we know, alive in the country. Which action, if upon a good and godly peace obtained, it shall please the Almighty to stir up her Majesty's heart to continue with her favorable countenance (as upon the ceasing of the wars of Granada He stirred up the spirit of Isabella, Queen of Castile, to advance the enterprise of Columbus) with transporting of one or two thousand of her people and such others as upon mine own knowledge will most willingly at their own charges become adventurers in good numbers with their bodies and goods. She shall, by God's assistance, in short space work many great and unlooked-for effects, increase her dominions, enrich her coffers, and reduce many pagans to the faith of Christ. The neglecting hitherto of which last point our adversaries daily in many of their books full bitterly lay unto the charge of the professors of the Gospel. No sooner should we set footing in that pleasant and good land, and erect one or two convenient forts in the continent, or in some island near the main, but every step we tread would yield us new occasion of action, which I wish the gentry of our nation rather to regard than to follow those soft unprofitable pleasures wherein they now too much consume their time and patrimony and hereafter will do much more when as our neighbor wars being appeased they are like to have less employment than now they have unless they be occupied in this or some other the like expedition.

But now it is high time for us to weigh our anchor, to hoist up our sails, to get clear of these boisterous, frosty, and misty seas, and with all speed to direct our course for the mild, lithesome, temperate, and warm Atlantic Ocean, over which the Spaniards and Portugals have made so many pleasant, prosperous, and golden voyages. This being the sum of those things which I thought good to admonish thee of (good Reader), it remaineth that thou take the profit and pleasure of the work, which I wish to be as great to thee as my pains and labor have been in bringing these raw fruits unto this ripeness and in reducing these loose papers into this order. Farewell.

PART ONE

The Northwest Parts of America

1.

The Voyage of Master Hore and Divers Other Gentlemen to Newfoundland and Cape Breton, in the Year 1536 and in the Twenty-eighth Year of King Henry VIII. [Written by Hakluyt.]

One Master Hore of London, a man of goodly stature and of great courage and given to the study of cosmography, in the twenty-eighth year of King Henry VIII and in the year of our Lord 1536 encouraged divers gentlemen and others, being assisted by the King's favor and good countenance, to accompany him in a voyage of discovery upon the northwest parts of America. Wherein his persuasions took such effect that within short space many gentlemen of the Inns of Court and of the Chancery and divers others of good worship, desirous to see the strange things of the world, very willingly entered into the action with him . . . . [Among these gentlemen was] Thomas Butts, the son of Sir William Butts, knight, of Norfolk, which was lately living and from whose mouth I wrote most of this relation . . . .

The whole number that went in the two tall ships . . . , to wit, the *Trinity* and the *Minion,* were about six score persons, whereof thirty were gentlemen, which all we mustered in warlike manner at Gravesend and after the receiving of the sacrament they embarked themselves in the end of April, 1536.

From the time of their setting out from Gravesend they were very long at sea, to wit, above two months, and never touched any land until they came to . . . Cape Breton, shaping their course thence northeastwards until they came to the island of Penguin [off south coast of Newfoundland] which is very full of rocks and stones, whereon they went and found it full of great fowls white and gray, as big as geese, and they saw infinite numbers of their eggs. They drove a great number of the fowls into their boats upon their sails and took up many of their eggs. The fowls they flayed and their skins were very like honeycombs full of holes being flayed off. They dressed and ate them and found them to be very good and nourishing meat. They saw also store of bears both black and white, of whom they killed some and took them for no bad food.

Master Oliver Dawbeny, which . . . was in this voyage and in the *Minion,* told Master Richard Hakluyt of the Middle Temple these things following, to wit, that after their arrival in Newfoundland and having been there certain days at anchor and not having yet seen any of the natural people of the country, the same Dawbeny walking one day on the hatches spied a boat with savages of those parts, rowing down the bay toward them to gaze upon the ship and our people; and taking view of the coming aloof [at a distance], he called to such as were under the hatches and willed them to come up if they would see the natural people of the country, that they had so long and so much desired to see. Whereupon they came up and took view of the savages rowing toward them and their ship, and upon the view they manned out a ship boat to meet them and to take them. But they spying our ship boat making towards them returned with main force and fled into an island that lay up in the bay or river there, and our men pursued them into the island, and the savages fled and escaped. But our men found a fire and the side of a bear on a wooden spit left at the same by the savages that were fled.

There in the same place they found a boot of leather garnished on the outward side of the calf with certain brave [excellent] trails [tails], as it were of raw silk, and also found a certain great warm mitten; and these carried with them, they returned to their ship, not finding the savages nor seeing anything else besides the soil and the things growing in the same, which chiefly were store of fir and pine trees.

And further, the said Master Dawbeny told him, that lying there they grew into great want of victuals and that there they found small relief, [no] more than that they had from the nest of an osprey, that brought hourly to her young great plenty of divers sorts of fishes. But such was the famine that increased amongst them from day to day that they were forced to seek to relieve themselves of raw herbs and roots that they sought on the main. But the famine increasing and the relief of herbs being to little purpose to satisfy their insatiable hunger, in the fields and deserts here and there the fellow killed his mate while he stooped to take up a root for his relief, and cutting out pieces of his body whom he had murdered, broiled the same on the coals and greedily devoured them.

By this mean the company decreased and the officers knew not what was become of them. And it fortuned that one of the company driven with hunger to seek abroad for relief found out in the fields the savor of broiled flesh and fell out with one for that he would suffer him and his fellows to starve, enjoying plenty as he thought. And this matter growing to cruel speeches, he that had the broiled meat burst out into these words: "If thou wouldst needs know, the broiled meat that I had was a piece of such a man's buttock." The report of this brought to the ship, the captain found what became of those that were missing and was persuaded that some of them were neither devoured with wild beasts nor yet destroyed with savages. And hereupon he stood up and made a notable oration, containing how much these dealings offended the Almighty and vouched the Scriptures from first to last, what God had in cases of distress done for them that called upon Him and told them that the power of the Almighty was then no less than in all former time it had been. And added that if it had not pleased God to have holpen them in that distress that it had been better to have perished in body and to have lived everlastingly than to have relieved for a poor time their mortal bodies and to be condemned everlastingly both body and soul to the unquenchable fire of hell. And thus having ended to that effect he began to exhort to repentance and besought all the company to pray that it might please God to look upon their miserable present state and for His own mercy to relieve the same. The famine increasing and the inconvenience of the men that were missing being found, they agreed amongst themselves rather than all should perish to cast lots who should be killed. And such was the mercy of God that the same night there arrived a French ship in that port well furnished with victual, and such was the policy of the English that they became masters of the same, and changing ships and victualing them they set sail to come into England.

In their journey they were so far northwards that they saw mighty islands of ice in the summer season, on which were hawks and other fowls to rest themselves, being weary of flying over far from the main. They saw also certain great white fowls with red bills and red legs, somewhat bigger than herons, which they supposed to be storks. They arrived at Saint Ives in Cornwall about the end of October. From thence they departed unto a certain castle belonging to Sir John Luttrell, where Master Thomas Butts and Master Rastall and other gentlemen of the voyage were very friendly entertained. After that they came to the Earl of Bath at Bath and thence to Bristol, so to London. Master Butts was so changed in the voyage with hunger and misery that Sir William his father and my lady his mother knew him not to be their son until they found a secret mark which was a wart upon one of his knees, as he told me, Richard Hakluyt of Oxford, himself, to whom I rode two hundred miles only to learn the whole truth of this voyage from his own mouth, as being the only man now alive that was in this discovery.

Certain months after those Frenchmen came into England and made complaint to King Henry VIII. The King causing the matter to be examined and finding the great distress of his subjects and the causes of the dealing so with the French was so moved with pity that he punished not his subjects but of his own purse made full and royal recompense unto the French.

In this distress of famine the English did somewhat relieve their vital spirits by drinking at the springs the fresh water out of certain wooden cups, out of which they had drunk their *aqua composita* before.

2.

The Second Voyage of Master Martin Frobisher, Made to the West and Northwest Regions in the Year 1577. With a Description of the Country and People. Written by Master Dionise Settle.

On Whitsunday, being the six and twentieth of May, in the year of our Lord God 1577, Captain Frobisher departed from Blackwall with one of the Queen Majesty's ships called the *Aid,* of nine score tons or thereabouts, and two other little barks likewise, the one called the *Gabriel,* whereof Master [Edward] Fenton, a gentleman of my Lord of Warwick's, was captain, and the other, the *Michael,* whereof Master [Gilbert] Yorke, a gentleman of my Lord Admiral's, was captain; accompanied with seven score gentlemen, soldiers, and sailors, well furnished with victuals and other provision necessary for one half year on this second voyage for the further discovering of the passage to Cathay and other countries thereunto adjacent, by west and northwest navigations. Which passage or way is supposed to be on the north and northwest part of America; and the said America to be an island environed with the sea, where through our merchants may have course and recourse with their merchandise from these our northermost parts of Europe to those oriental coasts of Asia in much shorter time and with greater benefit than any others, to their no little commodity and profit that do or shall frequent the same. Our said captain and general of this present voyage and company having the year before with two little pinnaces to his great danger and no small commendations given a worthy attempt towards the performance thereof is also pressed, when occasion shall be ministered (to the benefit of his prince and native country) to adventure himself further therein. As for this second voyage, it seemeth sufficient that he hath better explored and searched the commodities of those people and countries which in his first voyage the year before he had found out.

Upon these considerations . . . we departed from Blackwall to Harwich, where making an accomplishment of things necessary, the last of May we hoisted up sails and with a merry wind the seventh of June we arrived at the islands called Orcades, or vulgarly Orkney, being in number thirty, subject and adjacent to Scotland, where we made provision of fresh water. In the doing whereof our general licensed the gentlemen and soldiers for their recreation to go on shore. At our landing the people fled from their poor cottages with shrieks and alarms to warn their neighbors of enemies, but by gentle persuasions we reclaimed them to their houses. It seemeth they are often frighted with pirates or some other enemies that move them to such sudden fear. Their houses are very simply builded with pebble stone, without any chimneys, the fire being made in the midst thereof. The good man, wife, children, and other of their family eat and sleep on the one side of the house and the cattle on the other, very beastly and rudely, in respect of civility. They are destitute of wood, their fire is turfs and cowshards. They have corn, bigg [barley], and oats with which they pay their King's rent to the maintenance of his house. They take great quantity of fish, which they dry in the wind and sun. They dress their meat very filthily and eat it without salt. Their apparel is after the rudest sort of Scotland. Their money is all base. Their church and religion is reformed according to the Scots. The fishermen of England can better declare the dispositions of those people than I . . . .

We departed herehence the eighth of June and followed our course between west and northwest until the fourth of July. All which time we had no night, [so] that easily and without any impediment we had when we were so disposed the fruition of our books and other pleasures to pass away the time, a thing of no small moment to such as wander in unknown seas and long navigations, especially when both the winds and raging surges do pass their common and wonted course. This benefit endureth in those parts not six weeks, while the sun is near the Tropic of Cancer, but where the pole is raised to seventy or eighty degrees it continueth much longer.

All along these seas after we were six days sailing from Orkney we met floating in the sea great fir trees, which as we judged were with the fury of great floods rooted up and so driven into the sea. Iceland hath almost no other wood nor fuel but such as they take upon their coasts. It seemeth that these trees are driven from some part of Newfoundland with the current that setteth from the west to the east.

The fourth of July we came within the making of Frisland [Greenland]. From this shore ten or twelve leagues we met great islands of ice of half a mile, some more, some less, in compass, showing above the sea thirty or forty fathoms and as we supposed fast on ground where with our lead we could scarce sound the bottom for depth.

Here, in place of odoriferous and fragrant smells of sweet gums and pleasant notes of musical birds which other countries in more temperate zones do yield, we tasted the most boisterous boreal blasts mixed with snow and hail in the months of June and July, nothing inferior to our untemperate winter. A sudden alteration and especially in a place or parallel where the pole is not elevate above sixty-one degrees, at which height other countries more to the north, yea unto seventy degrees, show themselves more temperate than this doth.

All along this coast ice lieth as a continual bulwark and so defendeth the country that those that would land there incur great danger. Our general, three days together, attempted with the ship boat to have gone on shore, which, for that without great danger he could not accomplish, he deferred it until a more convenient time. All along the coast lie very high mountains covered with snow except in such places where through the steepness of the mountains of force it must needs fall. Four days coasting along this land we found no sign of habitation. Little birds which we judged to have lost the shore by reason of thick fogs which that country is much subject unto came flying into our ships, which causeth us to suppose that the country is both more tolerable and also habitable within than the outward shore maketh show or signification.

From hence we departed the eighth of July and the sixteenth of the same we came with the making of land. Which land our general the year before had named the Queen's Foreland [Resolution Island], being an island as we judge lying near the supposed continent with America; and on the other side, opposite to the same, one other island called Hall's Isle [Loks Land], after the name of the master of the ship, near adjacent to the firmland [terra firma, the mainland], supposed continent with Asia. Between the which two islands there is a large entrance or strait called Frobisher Strait, after the name of our general, the first finder thereof. This said strait is supposed to have passage into the Sea of Sur, which I leave unknown as yet.

It seemeth that either here or not far hence the sea should have more large entrance than in other parts within the frozen or untemperate zone, and that some contrary tide either from the east or west with main force casteth out that great quantity

of ice which cometh floating from this coast even unto Frisland, causing that country to seem more untemperate than
others much more northerly than the same.

I cannot judge that any temperature under the pole . . . can
have power to dissolve such monstrous and huge ice, comparable to great mountains, except by some other force as by
swift currents and tides . . . .

Before we came within the making of these lands we tasted
cold storms, in so much that it seemed we had changed summer
with winter if the length of the days had not removed us from
that opinion.

At our first coming the straits seemed to be shut up with a
long mure of ice which gave no little cause of discomfort unto
us all. But our general (to whose diligence imminent dangers
and difficult attempts seemed nothing, in respect of his willing
mind for the commodity [accommodation] of his Prince and
country) with two little pinnaces prepared of purpose passed
twice through them to the east shore and the islands thereunto
adjacent. And the ship with the two barks lay off and on something further into the sea from the danger of the ice.

Whilst he was searching the country near the shore, some of
the people of the country showed themselves leaping and
dancing with strange shrieks and cries, which gave no little
admiration [astonishment] to our men. Our general, desirous
to allure them unto him by fair means, caused knives and other
things to be proffered unto them, which they would not take
at our hands; but being laid on the ground and the party going
away they came and took up, leaving some things of theirs to
countervail the same. At the length two of them, leaving their
weapons, came down to our general and master, who did the
like to them, commanding the company to stay, and went unto
them; who after certain dumb signs and mute congratulations
began to lay hands upon them, but they deliverly [deftly]
escaped and ran to their bows and arrows and came fiercely
upon them (not respecting the rest of our company which were
ready for their defense) but with their arrows hurt divers of
them. We took the one and the other escaped.

Whilst our general was busied in searching the country and
those islands adjacent on the east shore, the ship and barks,

having great care not to put far into the sea from him for that he had small store of victuals, were forced to abide in a cruel tempest chancing in the night amongst and in the thickest of the ice, which was so monstrous that even the least of a thousand [icebergs] had been of force sufficient to have shivered our ship and barks into small portions if God (who in all necessities hath care upon the infirmity of man) had not provided for this our extremity a sufficient remedy through the light of the night, whereby we might well discern to flee from such imminent dangers, which we avoided with fourteen boards [tacks] in one watch the space of four hours. If we had not incurred this danger amongst these monstrous islands of ice we should have lost our general and master and the most of our best sailors, which were on the shore destitute of victuals. But by the valor of our master gunner, Master [Charles] Jackman, and Andrew Dier, the master's mates, men expert both in navigation and other good qualities, we were all content to incur the dangers afore rehearsed before we would with our own safety run into the seas to the destruction of our said general and his company.

The day following, being the nineteenth of July, our captain returned to the ship with report of supposed riches, which showed itself in the bowels of those barren mountains, wherewith we were all satisfied.

Within four days after we had been at the entrance of the straits, the northwest and west winds dispersed the ice into the sea and made us a large entrance into the straits, so that without any impediment on the nineteenth of July we entered them, and the twentieth thereof our general and master with great diligence sought out and sounded the west shore [the southwestern tip of Baffin Island] and found a fair harbor for the ship and barks to ride in and named it after our master's mate, Jackman's Sound, and brought the ship, barks, and all their company to safe anchor, except one man, which died by God's visitation.

At our first arrival after the ship rode at anchor our general with such company as could well be spared from the ships in marching order entered the land, having special care by exhortations that at our entrance thereinto we should all with one voice kneeling upon our knees chiefly thank God for our safe arrival. Secondly, beseech Him that it would please His divine Majesty long to continue our Queen for whom he [the general] and all the rest of our company in this order took possession of the country. And thirdly, that by our Christian study and endeavor those barbarous people trained up in paganism and infidelity might be reduced to the knowledge of true religion and to the hope of salvation in Christ our Redeemer. With other words very apt to signify his willing mind and affection toward his Prince and country, whereby all suspicion of an undutiful subject may credibly be judged to be utterly exempted from his mind. All the rest of the gentlemen and others deserve worthily herein their due praise and commendation.

These things in this order accomplished, our general commanded all the company to be obedient in things needful for our own safeguard to Master Fenton, Master Yorke, and Master [George] Best, his lieutenant, while he was occupied in other necessary affairs concerning our coming thither.

After this order we marched through the country with ensign displayed so far as was thought needful and now and then heaped up stones on high mountains and other places in token of possession, as likewise to signify unto such as hereafter may chance to arrive there, that possession is taken in the behalf of some other prince by those who first found out the country.

Whoso maketh navigations to those countries hath not only extreme winds and furious seas to encounter withal but also many monstrous and great islands of ice, a thing both rare, wonderful, and greatly to be regarded.

We were forced sundry times while the ship did ride here at anchor to have continual watch with boats and men ready with hawsers to knit fast unto such ice as with the ebb and flood were tossed to and fro in the harbor and with force of oars to hale them away for endangering the ship.

Our general certain days searched this supposed continent with America; and not finding the commodity to answer his expectation, after he had made trial thereof he departed thence with two little barks and men sufficient to the east shore being the supposed continent of Asia, and left the ship with most of the gentlemen, soldiers, and sailors until such time as he either thought good to send or come for them.

The stones of this supposed continent with America be altogether sparkled and glister in the sun like gold; so likewise doth the sand in the bright water, yet they verify the old proverb: all is not gold that glistereth.

On this west shore we found a dead fish floating [a narwhal], which had in his nose a horn straight and torqued [spiraled], of length two yards lacking two inches, being broken in the top where we might perceive it hollow, into the which some of our sailors putting spiders they presently died. I saw not the trial thereof, but it was reported unto me of a truth, by virtue whereof we supposed it to be the sea unicorn.

After our general had found out good harbor for the ship and barks to anchor in and also such store of supposed gold ore as he thought himself satisfied withal he returned to the *Michael* whereof Master Yorke aforesaid was captain, accompanied with our master and his mate. Who coasting along the west shore not far from whence the ship rode, they perceived a fair harbor, and willing to sound the same, at the entrance thereof they espied two tents of seals' skins, unto which the captain, our said master, and the other company resorted. At the sight of our men the people fled into the mountains. Nevertheless they went to their tents, where leaving certain trifles of ours, as glasses, bells, knives, and such like things they departed, not taking anything of theirs except one dog. They did in like manner leave behind them a letter, pen, ink, and paper, whereby our men whom the captain lost the year before, and in that peoples' custody, might (if any of them were alive) be advertised of our presence and being there.

On the same day, after consultation, . . . all the gentlemen and others likewise that could be spared from the ship under the conduct and leading of Master [Richard] Philpot (unto to whom, in our general's absence and his lieutenant, Master Best, all the rest were obedient) went ashore, determining to see if by fair means we could either allure them to familiarity or otherwise take some of them and so attain to some knowledge of those men whom our general lost the year before.

At our coming back again to the place where their tents were before, they had removed their tents further into the said bay or sound, where they might if they were driven from the land flee with their boats into the sea. We parting ourselves into

two companies and compassing a mountain came suddenly
upon them by land, who espying us, without any tarrying fled
to their boats, leaving the most part of their oars behind them
for haste and rowed down the bay where our two pinnaces met
them and drove them to shore. But if they had had all their
oars, so swift are they in rowing, it had been lost time to have
chased them.

When they were landed they fiercely assaulted our men with
their bows and arrows, who wounded three of them with our
arrows. And perceiving themselves thus hurt they desperately
leapt off the rocks into the sea and drowned themselves. Which
if they had not done but had submitted themselves or if by any
means we could have taken them alive (being their enemies
as they judged) we would both have saved them and also have
sought remedy to cure their wounds received at our hands. But
they altogether void of humanity and ignorant what mercy
meaneth in extremeties look for no other than death. And
perceiving they should fall into our hands, thus miserably by
drowning rather desired death than otherwise to be saved by
us. The rest perceiving their fellows in this distress, fled into
the high mountains. Two women not being so apt to escape as
the men were, the one for her age and the other being encumbered with a young child, we took. The old wretch, whom
divers of our sailors supposed to be either a devil or a witch,
had her buskins plucked off to see if she were cloven footed, and
for her ugly hue and deformity we let her go. The young woman
and the child we brought away. We named the place where
they were slain Bloody Point and the bay or harbor Yorke
Sound after the name of one of the captains of the two barks.

Having this knowledge both of their fierceness and cruelty,
and perceiving that fair means as yet is not able to allure them
to familiarity, we disposed ourselves, contrary to our inclina-
tion, something to be cruel, returned to their tents and made a
spoil of the same, where we found an old shirt, a doublet, a
girdle, and also shoes of our men, whom we lost the year before.
On nothing else unto them belonging could we set our eyes.

Their riches are not gold, silver, or precious drapery but
their said tents and boats made of the skins of red deer and seal
skins; also dogs like unto wolves but for the most part black,

with other trifles, more to be wondered at for their strangeness than for any other commodity needful for our use.

Thus returning to our ship the third of August, we departed from the west shore supposed firm with America after we had anchored there thirteen days. And so the fourth thereof we came to our general on the east shore and anchored in a fair harbor named Anne Warwick's Sound, unto which is annexed an island both named after the Countess of Warwick, Anne Warwick's Sound and Isle.

In this isle our general thought good for this voyage to freight both the ship and bark with such stone or supposed gold mineral as he judged to countervail the charges of his first and this his second navigation to these countries.

In the meantime of our abode here some of the country people came to show themselves unto us sundry times on the main shore near adjacent to the said isle. Our general, desirous to have some news of his men whom he lost the year before, with some company with him repaired with the ship boat to common [confer], or sign with them for familiarity, whereunto he is persuaded to bring them. They at the first show made tokens that three of his five men were alive and desired pen, ink, and paper and that within three or four days they would return and (as we judged) bring those of our men which were living with them.

They also made signs or tokens of their king, whom they called Cacough, and how he was carried on men's shoulders and a man far surmounting any of our company in bigness and stature.

With these tokens and signs of writing, pen, ink, and paper was delivered them, which they would not take at our hands but being laid upon the shore and the party gone away they took up. Which likewise they do when they desire anything for change of theirs, laying for that which is left so much as they think will countervail the same and not coming near together. It seemeth they have been used to this trade or traffic with some other people adjoining or not far distant from their country.

After four days some of them showed themselves upon the firmland but not where they were before. Our general very glad thereof, supposing to hear of our men, went from the island with the boat and sufficient company with him. They seemed very glad and allured him about a certain point of the land, behind which they might perceive a company of the crafty villains to lie lurking, whom our general would not deal withal, for that he knew not what company they were, and so with few signs dismissed them and returned to his company.

Another time as our said general was coasting the country with two little pinnaces whereby at our return he might make the better relation thereof, three of the crafty villains with a white skin allured us to them. Once again our general for that he hoped to hear of his men went towards them. At our coming near the shore whereon they were, we might perceive a number of them lie hidden behind great stones, and those three in sight laboring by all means possible that some would come on land. And perceiving we made no haste by words nor friendly signs which they used by clapping of their hands and being without weapons and but three in sight they sought further means to provoke us thereunto. One alone laid flesh on the shore, which we took up with the boat hook as necessary victuals for the relieving of the man, woman, and child whom we had taken, for that as yet they could not digest our meat. Whereby they perceived themselves deceived of their expectation, for all their crafty allurements. Yet once again to make (as it were) a full show of their crafty natures and subtle sleights to the intent thereby to have entrapped and taken some of our men, one of them counterfeited himself impotent and lame of his legs, who seemed to descend to the waterside with great difficulty. And to cover his craft more one of his fellows came down with him, and in such places where he seemed unable to pass he took him on his shoulders, set him by the waterside, and departed from him leaving him (as it should seem) all alone, who playing his counterfeit pageant very well thought thereby to provoke some of us to come on shore, not fearing but that one of us might make our party good with a lame man.

Our general having compassion of his impotency thought good (if it were possible) to cure him thereof. Wherefore he caused a soldier to shoot at him with his caliver [a light musket], which grazed before his face. The counterfeit villain deliverly fled without any impediment at all, and got him to his bow and arrows and the rest from their lurking holes with their weapons, bows, arrows, slings, and darts. Our general caused some calivers to be shot off at them, whereby some being hurt they might hereafter stand in more fear of us.

This was all the answer for this time we could have of our men or of our general's letter. Their crafty dealing at these three several times being thus manifest unto us may plainly show their disposition in other things to be correspondent. We judged that they used these strategems thereby to have caught some of us for the delivering of the man, woman, and child whom we had taken.

They are men of a large corporature and good proportion. Their color is not much unlike the sunburnt countryman who laboreth daily in the sun for his living.

They wear their hair something long, and cut before either with stone or knife, very disorderly. Their women wear their hair long and knit up with two loops showing forth on either side of their faces and the rest foltered [folded?] upon a knot. Also some of their women race [scrape] their faces proportionally as chin, cheeks, and forehead, and the wrists of their hands, whereupon they lay a color which continueth dark azurine.

They eat their meat all raw, both flesh, fish, and fowl, or something parboiled with blood and a little water which they drink. For lack of water they will eat ice that is hard frozen as pleasantly as we will do sugar candy or other sugar.

If they for necessity's sake stand in need of the premises [aforesaid matters], such grass as the country yieldeth they pluck up and eat, not daintily or salletwise [as a salad] to allure their stomachs' appetite but for necessity's sake without either salt, oils, or washing, like brute beasts devouring the same. They neither use table, stool, or tablecloth for comines [meals]. But when they are imbrued with blood, knuckle deep, and their knives in like sort, they use their tongues as apt instruments to lick them clean; in doing whereof they are assured to lose none of their victuals.

They frank [shut up and feed] or keep certain dogs not much unlike wolves, which they yoke together as we do oxen and horses to a sled or trail and so carry their necessaries over the ice and snow from place to place. . . . And when those dogs are not apt for the same use, or when with hunger they are constrained for lack of other victuals, they eat them, so that they are as needful for them in respect of their bigness as our oxen are for us.

They apparel themselves in the skins of such beasts as they kill, sewed together with the sinews of them. All the fowl which they kill they skin and make thereof one kind of garment or other to defend them from the cold.

They make their apparel with hoods and tails, which tails they give when they think to gratify any friendship showed unto them; a great sign of friendship with them. The men have them not so side [long] as the women.

The men and women wear their hose [breeches] close to their legs from the waist to the knee without any open before as well the one kind as the other. Upon their legs they wear hose of leather with the fur side inward, two or three pair at once and especially the women. In those hose they put their knives, needles, and other things needful to bear about. They put a bone with their hose which reacheth from the foot to the knee, whereupon they draw their said hose and so in place of garter they are holden from falling down about their feet.

They dress their skins very soft and supple with the hair on. In cold weather or winter they wear the fur side inward and in summer outward. Other apparel they have none but the said skins.

Those beasts, fishes, and fowls which they kill are their meat, drink, apparel, houses, bedding, with many other necessaries whereof they stand in need and almost all their riches.

Their houses are tents made of seal skins, pitched up with four fir quarters [two-by-fours] four square meeting at the top and the skins sewed together with sinews and laid thereupon. They are so pitched up that the entrance into them is always south or against the sun.

They have other sorts of houses which we found not to be inhabited, which are raised with stones and whale bones and a skin laid over them to withstand the rain or other weather. The entrance of them being not much unlike an oven's mouth, whereto I think they resort for a time to fish, hunt, and fowl and so leave them until the next time they come thither again.

Their weapons are bows, arrows, darts, and slings. Their bows are of wood of a yard long, sinewed at the back with strong sinews, not glued to but fast girded and tied on. Their bow strings are likewise sinews. Their arrows are three pieces notched with bone and ended with bone, with those two ends and the wood in the midst; they pass not in length half a yard or little more. They are feathered with two feathers, the pen end being cut away and the feathers laid upon the arrows with the broad side to the wood; insomuch that they seem when they are tied on to have four feathers. They have also three sorts of heads to those arrows: one sort of stone or iron, proportioned like to a heart; the second sort of bone, much like unto a stopped head with a hook on the same; the third sort of bone likewise made sharp at both sides and sharp pointed. They are not made very fast but lightly tied to or else set in a notch, that upon small occasion the arrows leave these heads behind them, and they are of small force except they be very near when they shoot.

Their darts are made of two sorts, the one with many forks of bone in the fore end and likewise in the midst. Their proportions are not much unlike our toasting irons but longer; these they cast out of an instrument of wood very readily. The other sort is greater than the first aforesaid, with a long bone made sharp on both sides not much unlike a rapier, which I take to be their most hurtful weapon.

They have two sorts of boats made of leather set out on the inner side with quarters of wood artificially tied together with thongs of the same. The greater sort are not much unlike our wherries, wherein sixteen or twenty men may sit; they have for a sail dressed the guts of such beasts as they kill very fine and thin, which they sew together. The other boat is but for one man to sit and row in with one oar.

Their order of fishing, hunting, and fowling are with these said weapons, but in what sort or how they use them we have no perfect knowledge as yet.

I can suppose their abode or habitation not to be here, for that neither their houses or apparel are of such force to withstand the extremity of cold that the country seemeth to be infected withal. Neither do I see any signs likely to perform the same.

Those houses, or rather dens, which stand there have no sign of footway or anything else trodden, which is one of the chiefest tokens of habitation. And those tents which they bring with them when they have sufficiently hunted and fished they remove to other places. And when they have sufficiently stored them of such victuals as the country yieldeth or bringeth forth, they return to their winter stations or habitations. This conjecture do I make for the infertility which I conjecture to be in that country.

They have some iron whereof they make arrowheads, knives, and other little instruments to work their boats, bows, arrows, and darts withal, which are very unapt to do anything withal but with great labor.

It seemeth that they have conversation [commerce] with some other people of whom for exchange they should receive the same. They are greatly delighted with anything that is bright or giveth a sound.

What knowledge they have of God or what idol they adore we have no perfect intelligence. I think them rather anthropophagi or devourers of man's flesh than otherwise, for that there is no flesh or fish which they find dead (smell it never so filthily) but they will eat it as they find it without any other dressing. A loathsome thing either to the beholders or hearers.

There is no manner of creeping beast hurtful except some spiders (which as many affirm are signs of great store of gold) and also certain stinging gnats which bite so fiercely that the place where they bite shortly after swelleth and itcheth very sore.

They make signs of certain people that wear bright plates of gold in their foreheads and other places of their bodies.

The countries on both sides the straits lie very high with rough stony mountains and great quanity of snow thereon. There is very little plain ground and no grass except a little which is much like unto moss that groweth on soft ground, such as we get turfs in. There is no wood at all. To be brief, there is nothing fit or profitable for the use of man which that country with root yieldeth or bringeth forth. Howbeit there is great quantity of deer, whose skins are like unto asses, their heads or horns do far exceed as well in length as also in breadth any in these our parts or countries. Their feet likewise are as great as our oxen's which we measured to be seven or eight inches in breadth.

There are also hares, wolves, fishing bears, and sea fowl of sundry sorts.

As the country is barren and unfertile, so are they rude and of no capacity to culture the same to any perfection, but are contented by their hunting, fishing, and fowling with raw flesh and warm blood to satisfy their greedy paunches, which is their only glory. . . .

The twenty-fourth of August, after we had satisfied our minds with freight sufficient for our vessels though not our covetous desires with such knowledge of the country, people, and other commodities as are before rehearsed, we departed there hence. The seventeenth of September we fell with the Lands End of England and so sailed to Milford Haven, from whence our general rode to the Court for order to what port or haven to conduct the ship.

We lost our two barks in the way homeward, the one the twenty-ninth of August, the other the thirty-first of the same month, by occasion of great tempest and fog. Howbeit God restored the one to Bristol and the other made his course by Scotland to Yarmouth. In this voyage we lost two men, one in the way by God's visitation and the other homeward cast overboard with a surge of the sea. . . .

Countries new discovered where commodity is to be looked for do better accord with a new name given by the discoverers than an uncertain name by a doubtful author.

Our general named sundry islands, mountains, capes, and harbors after the names of divers noblemen and other gentlemen his friends, as well on the one shore as also on the other.

3.

Notes Framed [ca. 1578] by Master Richard Hakluyt of the Middle Temple, Esquire, Given to Certain Gentlemen That Went with Master Frobisher in His Northwest Discovery, for Their Directions, and Not Unfit to Be Committed to Print, Considering the Same May Stir Up Considerations of These and Such Other Things Not Unmeet in Such New Voyages as May Be Attempted Hereafter.

That the first seat [settlement] be chosen on the seaside so as (if it may be) you may have your own navy within bay, river, or lake, within your seat safe from the enemy. And so as the enemy shall be forced to lie in open road abroad without, to be dispersed with all winds and tempests that shall arise. Thus seated you shall be least subject to annoy of the enemy, so may you by your navy within, pass out to all parts of the world, and so may the ships of England have access to you to supply all wants, so may your commodities be carried away also. This seat is to be chosen in temperate climate, in sweet air, where you may possess always sweet water, wood, sea coals [mineral coal], or turf, with fish, flesh, grain, fruits, herbs, and roots, or so many of those, as may suffice every necessity for the life of such as shall plant there. And for the possessing of mines of gold, of silver, copper, quicksilver, or of any such precious thing, the wants of those needful things may be supplied from some other place by sea, etc.

Stone to make lime of,
Slate stone to tile withal
   or such clay as maketh tile,
Stone to wall withal if brick
   may not be made,
Timber for building easily to
   be conveyed to the place,
Reed to cover houses or such
   like, if tile or slate be not.

are to be looked for as
things without which
no city may be made nor
people in civil sort be
kept together.

The people there to plant and to continue are either to live without traffic, or by traffic and by trade of merchandise. If they shall live without sea traffic, at the first they become naked by want of linen and woolen, and very miserable by infinite wants that will otherwise ensue, and so will they be forced of themselves to depart, or else easily they will be consumed by the Spaniards, by the French, or by the natural inhabitants of the country, and so the enterprise becomes reproachful to our nation, and a let [hindrance] to many other good purposes that may be taken in hand.

And by trade of merchandise they cannot live, except the sea or the land there may yield commodity. And therefore you ought to have most special regard of that point, and so to plant,

that the natural commodities of the place and seat, may draw
to you access of navigation for the same, or that by your own
navigation you may carry the same out, and fetch home the
supply of the wants of the seat.

Such navigation so to be employed shall, besides the supply
of wants, be able to encounter with foreign force.

And for that in the ample vent [market] of such things as
are brought to you out of England by sea, standeth a matter of
great consequence, it behooveth that all humanity and courtesy
and much forbearing of revenge to the inland people be used,
so shall you have firm amity with your neighbors, so shall
you have their inland commodities to maintain traffic, and so
shall you wax rich and strong in force. Divers and several commodities of the inland are not in great plenty to be brought
to your hands, without the aid of some portable or navigable
river, or ample lake, and therefore to have the help of such a
one is most requisite. And so is it of effect for the dispersing
of your own commodities in exchange into the inlands.

Nothing is more to be endeavored with the inland people
than familiarity. For so may you best discover all the natural
commodities of their country, and also all their wants, all
their strengths, all their weaknesses, and with whom they
are in war, and with whom considerate in peace and amity,
etc., which known, you may work many great effects of
greatest consequence.

And in your planting, the consideration of the climate and
of the soil be matters that are to be respected. For if it be so
that you may let in the salt sea water, not mixed with the fresh
into flats, where the sun is of the heat that it is at La Rochelle,
in the bay of Portugal, or in Spain, then may you procure a
man of skill, and so you have won one noble commodity for
the fishing, and for trade of merchandise by making of salt.

Or if the soil and climate be such as may yield you the grape
as good as that at Bordeaux, as that in Portugal, or as that about
Seville in Spain, or that in the islands of the Canaries, then
there resteth but a workman to put in execution to make wines,
and to dress raisins of the sun and other, etc.

Or if you find a soil of the temperature of the south part of
Spain or Barbary in the which you find the olive tree to grow,
then you may be assured of a noble merchandise for this realm,

considering that our great trade of clothing doeth require oil, and weighing how dear of late it is become by the vent they have of that commodity in the West Indies, and if you find the wild olive there it may be grafted.

Or if you can find the berry of cochineal, with which we color stammel [coarse woolen fabric], or any root, berry, fruit, wood, or earth fit for dyeing, you win a notable thing fit for our state of clothing. This cochineal is natural in the West Indies on that firm [continent].

Or if you have hides of beasts fit for sole leather, etc., it will be a merchandise right good, and the savages there yet cannot tan leather after our kind, yet excellently after their own manner.

Or if the soil shall yield figs, almonds, sugar canes, quinces, oranges, lemons, potatoes, etc., there may arise some trade and traffic by figs, almonds, sugar, marmelade, sucket [preserved fruit], etc.

Or if great woods be found, if they be of cypress, chests may be made; if they be of some kind of trees, pitch and tar may be made; if they be of some other, then they may yield rosin, turpentine, etc., and all for trade and traffic, and casks for wine and oil may be made; likewise ships and houses, etc.

And because traffic is a thing so material, I wish that great observation be taken what every soil yieldeth naturally, in what commodity soever, and what it may be made to yield by endeavor, and to send us notice home, that thereupon we may devise what means may be thought of to raise trades.

Now admit that we might not be suffered by the savages to enjoy any whole country or any more than the scope of a city, yet if we might enjoy traffic and be assured of the same, we might be much enriched, our navy might be increased, and a place of safety might there be found, if change of religion or civil wars should happen in this realm, which are things of great benefit. But if we may enjoy any large territory of apt soil, we might so use the matter, as we should not depend upon Spain for oils, sacks [white wines], raisins, oranges, lemons, Spanish skins, etc. Nor upon France for woad, bay salt, and Gascoyne wines, nor on Eastland [lands bordering the Baltic Sea] for flax, pitch, tar, masts, etc. So we should not so exhaust our treasure, and so exceedingly enrich our doubtful friends, as we do, but should purchase the commodities that we want for half the treasure that now we do. But should by our own industries and the benefits of the soil there cheaply purchase oils, wines, salt, fruits, pitch, tar, flax, hemp, masts, boards, fish, gold, silver, copper, tallow, hides, and many other commodities. Besides if there be no flats to make salt on, if you have plenty of wood you may make it in sufficient quantity for common uses at home there.

If you can keep a safe haven, although you have not the friendship of the near neighbors, yet you may have traffic by sea upon one shore or other, upon that firm in time to come, if not present.

If you find great plenty of timber on the shore side or upon any portable river, you were best to cut down of the same the first winter, to be seasoned for ships, barks, boats, and houses.

And if near such wood there be any river or brook upon which a sawing mill may be placed, it would do great service, and therefore consideration would be had of such a place.

And if such port and chosen place of settling were in possession and after fortified by art, although by the land side our Englishmen were kept in, and might not enjoy any traffic with the next neighbors, nor any victual. Yet might they victual themselves of fish to serve very necessity, and enter into amity with the enemies of their next neighbors, and so have vent of their merchandise of England and also have victual, or by means hereupon to be used to force the next neighbors to amity. And keeping a navy at the settling place, they should find out along the tract of the land to have traffic, and at divers islands also. And so this first seat might in time become a stapling place of the commodities of many countries and territories, and in time this place might become of all the provinces round about the only governor. And if the place first chosen should not so well please our people, as some other more lately found out, there might be an easy remove, and that might be razed, or rather kept for others of our nation to avoid an ill neighbor, etc.

If the soils adjoining to such convenient haven and settling places be found marshy and boggy, then men skillful in draining are to be carried thither. For art may work wonderful effects therein, and make the soil rich for many uses.

To plant upon an island in the mouth of some notable river,

or upon the point of the land entering into the river, if no such island be, were to great end. For if such river were navigable or portable far into the land, then would arise great hope of planting in fertile soils, and traffic on the one or on the other side of the river, or on both, or the linking in amity with one or other petty king contending there for dominion.

Such rivers found, both barges and boats may be made for the safe passage of such as shall pierce the same. These are to be covered with doubles of coarse linen artifically wrought, to defend the arrow or the dart of the savage from the rower.

Since every soil of the world by art may be made to yield things to feed and clothe man, bring in your return a perfect note of the soil without and within, and we shall devise if need require to amend the same, and to draw it to more perfection. And if you find not fruits in your planting place to your liking, we shall . . . furnish you with such kinds of plants to be carried thither the winter after your planting as shall the very next summer following yield you some fruit, and the year next following, as much as shall a town as big as Calice [Calais], and that shortly after shall be able to yield you great store of strong durable good cider to drink, and these trees shall be able to increase you within less than seven years as many trees presently to bear, as may suffice the people of divers parishes, which at the first settling may stand you in great stead, if the soil have not the commodity of fruits of goodness already. And because you ought greedily to hunt after things that yield present relief, without trouble of carriage thither, therefore I make mention of these, thus specially, to the end you may have it specially in mind.

4.

The Third Voyage of Captain Frobisher, Pretended [Intended] for the Discovery of Cathay, by Meta Incognita [southern Baffin Island], Anno Do[mini] 1578.
[Written by Captain George Best.]

The general being returned from the second voyage, immediately after his arrival in England repaired with all haste to the Court, being then at Windsor, to advertise her Majesty of his prosperous proceeding and good success in this last voyage and of the plenty of gold ore, with other matters of importance which he had in these septentrional parts discovered. He was courteously entertained and heartily welcomed of many noble men, but especially for his great adventure commended of her Majesty, at whose hands he received great thanks and most gracious countenance, according to his deserts. Her Highness also greatly commended the rest of the gentlemen in this service for their great forwardness in this so dangerous an attempt, but especially she rejoiced very much that among them there was so good order of government, so good agreement, every man so ready in his calling to do whatsoever the general should command. Which due commendation graciously of her Majesty remembered gave so great encouragement to all her captains and gentlemen that they, to continue her Highness's so good and honorable opinion of them, have since neither spared labor, limb, nor life to bring this matter (so well begun) to a happy and prosperous end.

And finding that the matter of the gold ore had appearance and made show of great riches and profit and the hope of the passage to Cathay by this last voyage greatly increased, her Majesty appointed special commissioners chosen for this purpose, gentlemen of great judgment, art, and skill, to look thoroughly into the cause for the true trial and due examination thereof and for the full handling of all matters thereunto appertaining. And because that place and country hath never heretofore been discovered and therefore had no special name by which it might be called and known, her Majesty named it very properly Meta Incognita, as a mark and bound utterly hitherto unknown.

The commissioners after sufficient trial and proof made of the ore and having understood by sundry reasons and substantial grounds the possibility and likelihood of the passage, advertised her Highness that the cause was of importance and the voyage greatly worthy to be advanced again. Whereupon preparation was made of ships and all other things necessary with such expedition as the time of the year then required. And because it was assuredly made account of that the commodity of mines there already discovered would at the least countervail in all respects the adventurers' charge and give further hope and likelihood of greater matters to follow, it was thought needful, both for the better guard of those parts already found and for further discovery of the inland and secrets of those countries, and also for further search of the passage to Cathay (whereof the hope continually more and more increaseth) that certain numbers of chosen soldiers and discreet men for those purposes should be assigned to inhabit there. Whereupon there was a strong fort or house of timber artificially framed and cunningly devised by a notable learned man here at home in ships to be carried thither, whereby those men that were appointed to winter and stay there the whole year might as well be defended from the danger of the snow and cold air as also fortified from the force or offense of those country people, which perhaps otherwise with too great multitudes might oppress them.

And to this great adventure and notable exploit many well minded and forward young gentlemen of our country willingly have offered themselves. And first Captain Fenton, lieutenant general for Captain Frobisher and in charge of the company with him there, Captain Best, and Captain Philpot, unto whose good discretions the government of that service was chiefly commended, who as men not regarding peril in respect of the profit and common wealth of their country, were willing to abide the first brunt and adventure of those dangers among a savage and brutish kind of people in a place hitherto ever thought for extreme cold not habitable. The whole number of men which had offered and were appointed to inhabit Meta Incognita all the year were one hundred persons, whereof forty should be mariners for the use of ships, thirty miners for gathering the gold ore together for the next year, and thirty soldiers for the better guard of the rest, within which last number are included the gentlemen, goldfiners, bakers, carpenters, and all necessary persons. To each of the captains was assigned one ship, as well for the further searching of the coast and country there, as for to return and bring back their companies again, if the necessity of the place so urged or by miscarrying of the fleet the next year they might be disappointed of their further provision. Being therefore thus furnished with all necessaries, there were ready to depart upon the said voyage fifteen sail of good ships, whereof the whole number was to return again with their loading of gold ore in the end of the summer, except those three ships which should be left for the use of those captains which should inhabit there the whole year. And being in so good readiness, the general with all the captains came to the Court, then lying at Greenwich, to take their leave of her Majesty, at whose hands they all received great encouragement and gracious countenance. Her Highness besides other good gifts and greater promises bestowed on the general a fair chain of gold and the rest of the captains kissed her hand, took their leave, and departed every man towards their charge. . . .

[THE ARRIVAL]

The second day of July, early in the morning, we had sight of Queen's Foreland, and bare in with the land all the day, and passing through great quantity of ice, by night were entered somewhat within the straits, perceiving no way to pass further in, the whole place being frozen over from the one side to the other, and as it were with many walls, mountains, and bulwarks of ice, choked up the passage and denied us entrance . . . .

And the cause why this year we have been more encumbered with ice than at other times before may be by reason of the easterly and southerly winds which brought us more timely thither now than we looked for. Which blowing from the sea directly upon the place of our straits hath kept in the ice [bergs] and not suffered them to be carried out by the ebb to the main sea, where they would in more short time have been dissolved. And all these fleeting ice are not only so dangerous in that they wind and gather so near together that a man may pass sometimes ten or twelve miles as it were upon one firm island of ice, but also for that they open and shut together again in such sort with the tides and sea-gate that whilst one ship followeth the other with full sails the ice which was open unto the foremost will join and close together before the latter can come to follow the first, whereby many times our ships were brought into great danger, as being not able so suddenly to take in our sails or stay the swift way of our ships.

We were forced many times to stem and strike great rocks of ice, and so as it were make way through mighty mountains. By which means some of the fleet where they found the ice to open entered in and passed so far within the danger thereof with continual desire to recover their port that it was the greatest wonder of the world that they ever escaped safe or were ever heard of again. For even at this present we missed two of the fleet, that is, the *Judith,* wherein was the lieutenant general, Captain Fenton, and the *Michael,* whom both we supposed had been utterly lost, having not heard any tidings of them in more than twenty days before.

And one of our fleet named the bark *Dennis,* being of a hundred-ton burden, seeking way in amongst these ice received such a blow with a rock of ice that she sunk down therewith in the sight of the whole fleet. Howbeit having signified her danger by shooting off a piece of great ordnance, new succor of other ships came so readily unto them that the men were all saved with boats.

Within this ship that was drowned there was parcel of our house which was to be erected for them that should stay all the winter in Meta Incognita.

This was a more fearful spectacle for the fleet to behold, for that the outrageous storm which presently followed threatened them the like fortune and danger. For the fleet being thus compassed (as aforesaid) on every side with ice, having left much behind them through which it was not possible to pass there arose a sudden terrible tempest at the southeast which blowing from the main sea directly upon the place of the straits brought together all the ice a seaboard of us upon our backs and thereby debarred us of turning back to recover sea room again, so that being thus compassed with danger on every side sundry men with sundry devices sought the best way to save themselves. Some of the ships where they could find a place more clear of ice and get a little berth of sea room did take in their sails and there lay adrift. Others fastened and moored anchor upon a great island of ice and rode under the lee thereof, supposing to be better guarded thereby from the outrageous winds and the danger of the lesser fleeting ice. And again some were so fast shut up and compassed in amongst an infinite number of great countries and islands of ice that they were fain to submit themselves and their ships to the mercy of the unmerciful ice, and strengthened the sides of their ships with junks [fenders] of cables, beds, masts, planks, and such like, which being hanged overboard on the sides of their ships might the better defend them from the outrageous sway and strokes of the said ice. But as in greatest distress men of best valor are best to be discerned, so it is greatly worthy of commendation and noting with what invincible mind every captain encouraged his company and with what incredible labor the painful mariners and poor miners (unacquainted with such extremities) to the everlasting renown of our nation did overcome the brunt of these so great and extreme dangers. For some even without board upon the ice and some within board upon the sides of their ships having poles, pikes, pieces of timber, and oars in their hands stood almost day and night without any rest bearing off the force and breaking the sway of the ice with such incredible pain and peril that it was wonderful to behold, which otherwise no doubt had striken quite through and through the sides of their ships, notwithstanding our former provision for planks of timber of more than three inches thick and other things of greater force and bigness, by the surging of the sea and billows with the ice were shivered and cut in sunder at the sides of our ships so that it will seem more than credible to be reported of. And yet (that which is more) it is faithfully and plainly to be proved, and that by many substantial witnesses, that our ships, even those of greatest burdens, with the meeting of contrary waves of the sea were heaved up between islands of ice a foot well near out of the sea above their watermark, having their knees and timbers within board both bowed and broken therewith.

And amidst these extremes whilst some labored for defense of the ships and sought to save their bodies, other some of more milder spirit sought to save the soul by devout prayer and meditation to the Almighty, thinking indeed by no other means possible than by a divine miracle to have their deliverance. So that there was none that were either idle or not well occupied, and he that held himself in best security had (God knoweth) but only bare hope remaining for his best safety.

Thus all the gallant fleet and miserable men without hope
of ever getting forth again distressed with these extremities
remained here all the whole night and part of the next day,
excepting four ships, that is, the *Anne Francis,* the *Moone,*
the *Francis of Foy,* and the *Gabriel,* which being somewhat
a seaboard of the fleet and being fast ships by a wind, having
a more scope of clear, tried it out all the time of the storm under
sail, being hardly able to bear a coast of each.

And albeit by reason of the fleeting ice which were dispersed
here almost the whole sea over, they were brought many times
to the extremest point of peril, mountains of ice ten thousand
times scaping them scarce one inch, which to have striken
had been their present destruction, considering the swift course
and way of the ships and the unwieldiness of them to stay and
turn as a man would wish. Yet they esteemed it their better
safety with such peril to seek sea room than without hope of
ever getting liberty to lie striving against the stream and
beating amongst the icy mountains, whose hugeness and
monstrous greatness was such that no man would credit but
such as to their pains saw and felt it. And these four ships by
the next day at noon got out to sea and were first clear of the ice
who now enjoying their own liberty began anew to sorrow
and fear for their fellows' safeties. And devoutly kneeling about
the mainmast they gave unto God humble thanks not only for
themselves but besought Him likewise highly for their friends'
deliverance. And even now whilst amidst these extremities
this gallant fleet and valiant men were together overlabored
and forwatched with the long and fearful continuance of the
foresaid dangers, it pleased God with His eyes of mercy to
look down from heaven to send them help in good time, giving
them the next day a more favorable wind at the west northwest,
which did not only disperse and drive forth the ice before them,
but also gave them liberty of more scope and sea room and
they were by night of the same day following perceived of the
other four ships, where (to their greatest comfort) they enjoyed
again the fellowship one of another. Some in mending the
sides of their ships, some in setting up their topmasts, and
mending their sails and tacklings. Again, some complaining
of their false stem born away, some in stopping their leaks,

some in recounting their dangers past, spent no small time and labor. So that I dare well avouch there were never men more dangerously distressed nor more mercifully by God's providence delivered. And hereof both the torn ships and the fore-wearied bodies of the men arrived do bear most evident mark and witness. And now the whole fleet plied off to seaward, resolving there to abide until the sun might consume or force of wind disperse these ice from the place of their passage. And being a good berth off the shore they took in their sails and lay adrift.

The seventh of July as men nothing yet dismayed we cast about towards the inward and had sight of land, which rose in form like the northerland of the straits, which some of the fleet and those not the worst mariners judged to be the North Foreland. Howbeit other some were of contrary opinion. But the matter was not well to be discerned by reason of the thick fog which a long time hung upon the coast and the new falling snow which yearly altereth the shape of the land and taketh away oftentimes the mariners' marks. And by reason of the dark mists which continued by the space of twenty days together this doubt grew the greater and the longer perilous. For whereas indeed we thought ourselves to be upon the northeast side of Frobisher's Straits we were now carried [into Hudson Strait] to the southwestwards of the Queen's Foreland and being deceived by a swift current coming from the northeast were brought to the southwestwards of our said course many miles more than we did think possible could come to pass . . . .

[THE NORTHWEST PASSAGE]

The general albeit with the first perchance he found out the error and that this was not the old straits yet he persuaded the fleet always that they were in their right course and known straits. Howbeit I suppose he rather dissembled his opinion therein than otherwise, meaning by that policy (being himself led with an honorable desire of further discovery) to induce the fleet to follow him to see a further proof of that place. And as some of the company reported he hath since confessed that if it had not been for the charge and care he had of the fleet and fraughted ships he both would and could have gone through to the South Sea, called Mar del Sur, and dissolved the long doubt of the passage which we seek to find to the rich country of Cathay.

Of which Mistaken Straits, considering the circumstance we have great cause to confirm our opinion to like and hope well of the passage in this place. For the foresaid bay or sea the further we sailed therein the wider we found it, with great likelihood of endless continuance. And where in other places we were much troubled with ice, as in the entrance of the same, so after we had sailed fifty or sixty leagues therein we had no let of ice or other thing at all, as in other places we found.

Also this place seemeth to have a marvelous great indraft and draweth unto it most of the drift ice, and other things which do fleet [float, drift] in the sea either to the north or eastwards of the same as by good experience we have found . . . .

And some mariners do affirm that they have diligently observed that there runneth in this place nine hours flood to three ebb, which may thus come to pass by force of the said current. For whereas the sea in most places of the world doth more or less ordinarily ebb and flow once every twelve hours with six hours ebb and six hours flood, so also would it do there were it not for the violence of this hastening current, which forceth the flood to make appearance to begin before his ordinary time one hour and a half and also to continue longer than his natural course by another hour and a half, until the force of the ebb be so great that it will no longer be resisted. According to the saying, *naturam expellas furac licet, usque recurrit:* although nature and natural courses be forced and resisted never so much, yet at last they will have their own sway again.

Moreover, it is not possible that so great course of floods and current, so high swelling tides with continuance of so deep waters, can be digested here without unburdening themselves into some open sea beyond this place, which argueth the more likelihood of the passage to be hereabouts. Also we suppose these great indrafts do grow and are made by the reverberation and reflection of that same current which at our coming by Ireland met and crossed us . . . , which coming from the Bay of Mexico, passing by and washing the southwest parts of Ireland, reboundeth over to the northeast parts of the world, as Norway, Iceland, etc., where not finding any passage to an open sea but rather being there increased by a new access and another current meeting with it from the Scythian Sea, passing the Bay of Saint Nicholas [both on northern coast of Russia] westward, it doth once again rebound back by the coasts of Greenland and from thence upon Frobisher's Straits, being to the south-westwards of the same.

And if that principle of philosophy be true that *inferiora corpora reguntur a superioribus*, that is, if inferior bodies be governed, ruled, and carried after the manner and course of the superiors, then the water being an inferior element must needs be governed after the superior heaven and so follow the course of primum mobile from east to west.

But every man that hath written or considered anything of this passage hath more doubted the return by the same way by reason of a great downfall of water which they imagine to be thereabout (which we also by experience partly find) than any mistrust they have of the same passage at all. For we find (as it were) a great downfall in this place but yet not such but that we may return although with much ado. For we were more easily carried in one hour than we could get forth again in three. Also by another experience at another time we found this current to deceive us in this sort; that whereas we supposed it to be fifteen leagues off, and lying a hull, we were brought within two leagues of the shore contrary to all expectation.

Our men that sailed furthest in the same Mistaken Straits (having the mainland upon their starboard side) affirm that they met with the outlet or passage of water which cometh through Frobisher's Straits and followeth as all one into this passage.

Some of our company also affirm that they had sight of a continent upon their larboard side being sixty leagues within the supposed straits. Howbeit except certain islands in the entrance hereof we could make no part perfect thereof. All the foresaid tract of land seemeth to be more fruitful and better stored of grass, deer, wild fowl as partridges, larks, seamews, gulls, wilmots, falcons, and tassel-gentles, ravens, bears, hares, foxes, and other things than any other part we have yet dis-

covered and is more populous. And here Luke Ward, a gentleman of the company, traded merchandise and did exchange
knives, bells, looking glasses, etc., with those country people,
who brought him fowl, fish, bears' skins, and such like as their
country yieldeth for the same. Here also they saw of those
greater boats of the country with twenty persons in a piece.

Now after the general had bestowed these many days here
not without many dangers, he returned back again. And
by the way sailing alongst this coast (being the backside of
the supposed continent of America) and the Queen's Foreland he perceived a great sound to go through into Frobisher's Straits. . . .

[THE HOUSE AND THE ORE]

The general, after his arrival in the Countess [of Warwick]
Sound, spent no time in vain, but immediately at his first
landing called the chief captains of his council together, and
consulted with them for the speedier execution of such things
as then they had in hand. As first for searching and finding out
good mineral for the miners to be occupied on. Then to give
good orders to be observed of the whole company on shore.
And lastly, to consider for the erecting up of the fort and
house for the use of them which were to abide there the
whole year. . . .

The first of August every captain by order from the general
and his council was commanded to bring ashore unto the
Countess's Island all such gentlemen, soldiers, and miners as
were under their charge, with such provision as they had of
victuals, tents, and things necessary for the speedy getting
together of mine and freight for the ships.

The muster of the men being taken and the victuals with all
other things viewed and considered, every man was set to his
charge, as his place and office required. The miners were
appointed where to work and the mariners discharged
their ships.

Upon the second of August were published and proclaimed
upon the Countess of Warwick's Island with sound of trumpet
certain orders by the general and his council appointed to be
observed of the company during the time of their abiding there.

In the meantime, whilst the mariners plied their work, the captains sought out new mines, the goldfiners made trial of the ore, the mariners discharged their ships, the gentlemen for example sake labored heartily and honestly encouraged the inferior sort to work. . . .

The ninth of August the general with the captains of his council assembled together and began to consider and take order for the erecting up of the house or fort for them that were to inhabit there the whole year and that presently the masons and carpenters might go in hand therewith. First, therefore, they perused the bills of lading, what every man received into his ship, and found that there was arrived only the east side and the south side of the house, and yet not that perfect and entire; for many pieces thereof were used for fenders in many ships and so broken in pieces whilst they were distressed in the ice. Also after due examination had and true account taken, there was found want of drink and fuel to serve one hundred men, which was the number appointed first to inhabit there, because their gravest store was in the ships which were not yet arrived. Then Captain Fenton seeing the scarcity of the necessary things aforesaid was contented and offered himself to inhabit there with sixty men. Whereupon they caused the carpenters and masons to come before them and demanded in what time they would take upon them to erect up a less house for sixty men. They required eight or nine weeks if there were timber sufficient, whereas now they had but six and twenty days in all to remain in that country. Wherefore it was fully agreed upon and resolved by the general and his council that no habitation should be there this year. And therefore they willed Master [Edward] Selman, the register, to set down this decree with all their consents for the better satisfying of her Majesty, the lords of the Council, and the adventurers. . . .

The thirtieth of August the *Anne Francis* was brought aground and had eight great leaks mended which she had received by means of the rocks and ice. This day the masons finished a house which Captain Fenton caused to be made of lime and stone upon the Countess of Warwick's Island to the end we might prove against the next year, whither the snow could overwhelm it, the frost break it up, or the people dismember the same. And the better to allure those brutish and uncivil people to courtesy against other times of our coming we left therein divers of our country toys, as bells, and knives, wherein they specially delight, one for the necessary use and the other for the great pleasure thereof. Also pictures of men and women in lead, men on horseback, looking glasses, whistles, and pipes. Also in the house was made an oven and bread left baked therein for them to see and taste.

We buried the timber of our pretended fort. Also here we sowed peas, corn, and other grain to prove the fruitfulness of the soil against the next year.

Master Wolfall on Winter's Furnace [mine site] preached a godly sermon, which being ended he celebrated also a communion upon the land, at the partaking whereof was the captain of the *Anne Francis* and many other gentlemen and soldiers, mariners, and miners with him. The celebration of the divine mystery was the first sign, seal, and confirmation of Christ's name, death, and passion ever known in these quarters. The said Master Wolfall made sermons and celebrated the communion at sundry other times in several and sundry ships because the whole company could never meet together at any one place. The fleet now being in some good readiness for their lading, the general calling together the gentlemen and captains to consult told them that he was very desirous that some further discovery should be attempted and that he would not only by God's help bring home his ships laden with ore but also meant to bring some certificate of a further discovery of the country, which thing to bring to pass (having sometime therein consulted) they found very hard and almost invincible. And considering that already they had spent some time in searching out the trending and fashion of the Mistaken Straits, therefore it could not be said but that by this voyage they have notice of a further discovery and that the hope of the passage thereby is much furthered and increased, as appeared before in the discourse thereof.

Yet notwithstanding if any means might be further devised, the captains were contented and willing as the general should appoint and command to take any enterprise in hand. Which after long debating was found a thing very impossible and that rather consultation was to be had of returning homeward, especially for these causes following. First, the dark foggy mists, the continual falling snow and stormy weather which they commonly were vexed with and now daily ever more and more increased, have no small argument of the winter's drawing near. And also the frost every night was so hard congealed within the sound that if by evil hap they should be long kept in with contrary winds, it was greatly to be feared that they should be shut up there fast the whole year, which being utterly unprovided would be their utter destruction. Again, drink was so scant throughout all the fleet by means of the great leakage that not only the provision which was laid in for the habitation was wanting and wasting, but also each ship's several provision spent and lost, which many of our company to their great grief found in their return since, for all the way homewards they drank nothing but water. And the great cause of this leakage and wasting was for that the great timber and sea coal which lay so weighty upon the barrels broke, bruised, and rotted the hoops in sunder. Yet notwithstanding these reasons alleged the general himself (willing the rest of the gentlemen and captains every man to look to his several charge and lading that against a day appointed they should be all in a readiness to set homeward) went in a pinnace and discovered further northward in the straits and found that by Bear's Sound and Hall's Island the land was not firm as it was first supposed but all broken islands in manner of an archipelago; and so with other secret intelligence, upon his arrival at the Countess's Sound he began to take order for their returning homeward and first caused certain articles to be proclaimed for the better keeping of orders and courses in their return, which articles were delivered to every captain. . . .

5.

A Report of the Voyage and Success Thereof, Attempted in the Year of Our Lord 1583 by Sir Humphrey Gilbert, Knight, with Other Gentlemen Assisting Him in That Action, Intended to Discover and to Plant Christian Inhabitants in Place

Convenient Upon Those Large and Ample
Countries Extended Northward from the Cape of
Florida, Lying Under Very Temperate Climes,
Esteemed Fertile and Rich in Minerals, yet Not
in the Actual Possession of Any Christian Prince.
Written by Master Edward Hayes, Gentleman,
and Principal Actor in the Same Voyage,
Who Alone Continued unto the End, and by
God's Special Assistance Returned Home
with His Retinue Safe and Entire.

Many voyages have been pretended, yet hitherto never
any thoroughly accomplished by our nation of exact discovery
into the bowels of those main, ample, and vast countries, extended infinitely into the north from thirty degrees, or rather
from twenty-five degrees of septentrional latitude. Neither
hath a right way been taken of planting a Christian habitation
and regiment upon the same, as well may appear both by the
little we yet do actually possess therein, and by our ignorance
of the riches and secrets within those lands, which unto this
day we know chiefly by the travel and report of other nations,
and most of the French, who albeit they cannot challenge
such right and interest unto the said countries as we, neither
these many years have had opportunity nor means so great
to discover and to plant (being vexed with the calamities of
intestine [internal] wars) as we have had by the inestimable
benefit of our long and happy peace. Yet have they both ways
performed more and had long since attained a sure possession
and settled government of many provinces in those northerly
parts of America, if their many attempts into those foreign and
remote lands had not been impeached by their garboils [dis-
turbances] at home.

The first discovery of these coasts (never heard of before)
was well begun by John Cabot, the father, and Sebastian Cabot,
his son, an Englishman born, who were the first finders out of
all that great tract of land stretching from the cape of Florida
unto those islands which we now call the Newfoundland, all

which they brought and annexed unto the crown of England. Since when, if with like diligence the search of inland countries had been followed, as the discovery upon the coast and outparts thereof was performed by those two men, no doubt her Majesty's territories and revenue had been mightily enlarged and advanced by this day. And which is more, the seed of Christian religion had been sowed amongst those pagans, which by this time might have brought forth a most plentiful harvest and copious congregation of Christians; which must be the chief intent of such as shall make any attempt that way, or else whatsoever is builded upon other foundation shall never obtain happy success nor continuance. . . .

I will now proceed to make relation briefly, yet particularly, of our voyage undertaken with Sir Humphrey Gilbert.

When first Sir Humphrey Gilbert undertook the western discovery of America and had procured from her Majesty [in 1578] a very large commission to inhabit and possess at his choice all remote and heathen lands not in the actual possession of any Christian prince, the same commission exemplified with many privileges such as in his discretion he might demand, very many gentlemen of good estimation drew unto him to associate him in so commendable an enterprise, so that the preparation was expected to grow unto a puissant fleet, able to encounter a king's power by sea. Nevertheless, amongst a multitude of voluntary men their dispositions were divers, which bred a jar [dissension] and made a division in the end, to the confusion of that attempt even before the same was begun. And when the shipping was in a manner prepared and men ready upon the coast to go aboard, at that time some broke consort and followed courses degenerating from the voyage before pretended. Others failed of their promises contracted and the greater number were dispersed, leaving the general with few of his assured friends with whom he adventured to sea, where having tasted of no less misfortune, he was shortly driven to retire home with the loss of a tall ship and (more to his grief) of a valiant gentleman, Miles Morgan.

Having buried only in a preparation a great mass of substance, whereby his estate was impaired, his mind yet not dismayed he continued his former designment and purpose to revive this enterprise, good occasion serving. Upon which determination standing long, without means to satisfy his desire, at last he granted certain assignments out of his commission to sundry persons of mean ability, desiring the privilege of his grant to plant and fortify in the north parts of America about the river of Canada, to whom if God gave good success in the north parts (where then no matter of moment was expected) the same (he thought) would greatly advance the hope of the south and be a furtherance unto his determination that way. And the worst that might happen in that course might be excused without prejudice unto him by the former supposition, that those north regions were of no regard, but chiefly a possession taken in any parcel of those heathen countries by virtue of his grant did invest him of territories extending every way two hundred leagues. Which induced Sir Humphrey Gilbert to make those assignments, desiring greatly their expedition, because his commission did expire after six years, if in that space he had not gotten actual possession.

Time went away without anything done by his assigns. Insomuch that at last he must resolve himself to take a voyage in person for more assurance to keep his patent in force, which then almost was expired, or within two years.

In furtherance of his determination, amongst others, Sir George Peckham, knight, showed himself very zealous to the action, greatly aiding him both by his advice and in the charge. Other gentlemen to their ability joined unto him, resolving to adventure their substance and lives in the same cause. Who beginning their preparation from that time, both of shipping, munition, victual, men, and things requisite, some of them continued the charge two years complete without intermission. Such were the difficulties and cross accidents opposing these proceedings, which took not end in less than two years, many of which circumstances I will omit.

The last place of our assembly before we left the coast of England was in Cawsand Bay near unto Plymouth. Then [we] resolved to put unto the sea with shipping and provision, such as we had before our store yet remaining, but chiefly the time and season of the year were too far spent. . . .

[THE CROSSING]

We resolved to begin our course northward and to follow directly as we might the trade way unto Newfoundland. From whence after our refreshing and reparation of wants, we intended without delay (by God's permission) to proceed into the south, not omitting any river or bay which in all that large tract of land appeared to our view worthy of search. Immediately we agreed upon the manner of our course and orders to be observed in our voyage, which were delivered unto the captains and masters of every ship a copy in manner following:

Every ship had delivered two billets or scrolls, the one sealed up in wax, the other left open, in both which were included several watchwords. That open, serving upon our own coast or the coast of Ireland; the other sealed, was promised on all hands not to be broken up until we should be clear of the Irish coast, which from thenceforth did serve until we arrived and met altogether in such harbors of the Newfoundland as were agreed for our rendezvous. The said watchwords being requisite to know our consorts whensoever by night, either by fortune of weather our fleet dispersed should come together again or one should hail another, or if by ill watch and steerage one ship should chance to fall aboard of another in the dark.

The reason of the billet sealed was to keep secret that watchword while we were upon our own coast, lest any of the company stealing from the fleet might betray the same, which known to the enemy he might board us by night without mistrust, having our own watchword. . . .

Orders thus determined, and promises mutually given to be observed, every man withdrew himself unto his charge. The anchors being already weighed and our ships under sail, having a soft gale of wind we began our voyage upon Tuesday, the eleventh day of June in the year of our Lord 1583, having in our fleet at our departure from Cawsand Bay these ships, whose names and burdens, with the names of the captains and masters of them, I have also inserted as follows:

1. The *Delight,* alias the *George,* of burden 120 tons, was admiral, in which went the general and William Winter, captain in her and part owner, and Richard Clarke, master.

2. The bark *Raleigh,* set forth by Master Walter Raleigh, of the burden of 200 tons, was then vice-admiral, in which went Master Butler, captain, Robert Davis of Bristol, master.

3. The *Golden Hinde,* of burden 40 tons, was then rear-admiral, in which went Edward Hayes, captain and owner, and William Cox of Limehouse, master.

4. The *Swallow,* of burden 40 tons; in her was Captain Maurice Browne.

5. The *Squirrel,* of burden 10 tons, in which went Captain William Andrews and one Cade, master.

We were in number in all about 260 men, among whom we had of every faculty good choice, as shipwrights, masons, carpenters, smiths, and such like requisite to such an action; also mineral men and refiners. Besides, for solace of our people and allurement of the savages, we were provided of music in good variety, not omitting the least toys, as morris dancers, hobbyhorse, and many like conceits to delight the savage people, whom we intended to win by all fair means possible. And to that end we were indifferently furnished of all petty haberdashery wares to barter with those simple people . . . .

[NEWFOUNDLAND]

Before we came to Newfoundland, about fifty leagues on this side, we pass the [Grand] Bank, which are high ground rising within the sea and under water, yet deep enough and without danger, being commonly not less than twenty-five and thirty fathom water upon them. The same (as it were some vein of mountains within the sea) do run along and from the Newfoundland, beginning northward about fifty-two or fifty-three degrees of latitude, and do extend into the south infinitely. The breadth of this Bank is somewhere more and somewhere less, but we found the same about ten leagues over, having sounded both on this side thereof and the other toward Newfoundland, but found no ground with almost two hundred fathom of line, both before and after we had passed the Bank. The Portugals and French chiefly have a notable trade of fishing upon this Bank, where are sometimes a hundred or more sails of ships, who commonly begin the fishing in April and have ended by July. That fish is large, always wet, having no land near to dry, and is called cor [cod] fish.

During the time of fishing, a man shall know without sounding when he is upon the Bank by the incredible multitude of sea-fowl hovering over the same, to prey upon the offals and garbage of fish thrown out by fishermen and floating upon the sea.

Upon Tuesday the eleventh of June we forsook the coast of England. So again Tuesday the thirtieth of July (seven weeks after) we got sight of land, being immediately embayed in the Grand Bay, or some other great bay, the certainty whereof we could not judge, so great haze and fog did hang upon the coast as neither we might discern the land well nor take the sun's height. But by our best computation we were then in the fifty-one degrees of latitude.

Forsaking this bay and uncomfortable coast (nothing appearing unto us but hideous rocks and mountains, bare of trees and void of any green herb), we followed the coast to the south, with weather fair and clear.

We had sight of an island named Penguin [Funk Island] of a fowl there breeding in abundance almost incredible, which cannot fly, their wings not able to carry their body, being very large (not much less than a goose) and exceeding fat; which the Frenchmen used to take without difficulty upon that island and to barrel them up with salt. But for lingering of time we had made us there the like provision. . . .

Having taken place convenient in the road [at Saint John's], we let fall anchors, the captains and masters repairing aboard our admiral, whither also came immediately the masters and owners of the fishing fleet of Englishmen, to understand the general's intent and cause of our arrival there. They were all satisfied when the general had shown his commission and purpose to take possession of those lands to the behalf of the Crown of England and the advancement of Christian religion in those paganish regions, requiring but their lawful aid for repairing of his fleet and supply of some necessaries, so far as conveniently might be afforded him, both out of that and other harbors adjoining. In lieu whereof, he made offer to gratify them with any favor and privilege which upon their better advice [consideration] they should demand, the like being not to be obtained hereafter for greater price. So, craving expedition of his demand, minding to proceed further south without long detention in those parts, he dismissed them after promise given of their best endeavor to satisfy speedily his so reasonable request. The merchants with their masters departed, they caused forthwith to be discharged all the great ordnance of their fleet in token of our welcome.

It was further determined that every ship of our fleet should deliver unto the merchants and masters of that harbor a note of all their wants; which done, the ships as well English as strangers were taxed at an easy rate to make supply. And besides, commissioners were appointed, part of our own company and part of theirs, to go into other harbors adjoining (for our English merchants command all there) to levy our provision; whereunto the Portugals (above other nations) did most willingly and liberally contribute, insomuch as we were presented (above our allowance) with wines, marmalades, most fine rusk or biscuit, sweet oils, and sundry delicacies. Also we wanted not of fresh salmons, trouts, lobsters, and other fresh fish brought daily unto us. Moreover, as the manner is in their fishing every week to choose their admiral anew, or rather they succeed in orderly course and have weekly their admiral's feast solemnized, even so the general, captains, and masters of our fleet were continually invited and feasted. To grow short, in our abundance at home the entertainment had been delightful, but after our wants and tedious passage through the ocean it seemed more acceptable and of greater contentation by how much the same was unexpected in that desolate corner of the world, where at other times of the year wild beasts and birds have only the fruition of all those countries, which now seemed a place very populous and much frequented.

The next morning, being Sunday and the fourth of August, the general and his company were brought on land by English merchants, who showed unto us their accustomed walks unto a place they call "the garden." But nothing appeared more than Nature itself without art, who confusedly hath brought forth roses abundantly, wild, but odoriferous and to sense very comfortable. Also the like plenty of raspberries, which do grow in every place.

Monday following the general had his tent set up, who, being accompanied with his own followers, summoned the merchants and masters, both English and strangers, to be present at his taking possession of those countries. Before whom openly was read and interpreted unto the strangers his commission, by virtue whereof he took possession in the same harbor of Saint John's and two hundred leagues every way, invested the Queen's Majesty with the title and dignity thereof, had delivered unto him (after the custom of England) a rod and a turf of the same soil, entering possession also for him, his heirs and assigns forever; and signified unto all men that from that time forward they should take the same land as a territory appertaining to the Queen of England and himself authorized under her Majesty to possess and enjoy it and to ordain laws for the government thereof, agreeable (so near as conveniently might be) unto the laws of England, under which all people coming thither hereafter, either to inhabit or by way of traffic, should be subjected and governed. And especially at the same time for a beginning he proposed and delivered three laws to be in force immediately, that is to say: the first for religion, which in public exercise should be according to the Church of England; the second for maintenance of her Majesty's right and possession of those territories, against which if anything were attempted prejudicial, the party or parties offending should be adjudged and executed as in case of high treason according to the laws of England; the third, if any person should utter words sounding to the dishonor of her Majesty he should lose his ears and have his ship and goods confiscate.

These contents published, obedience was promised by general voice and consent of the multitude, as well of Englishmen as strangers, praying for continuance of this possession and government begun. After this the assembly was dismissed. And afterward were erected not far from that place the arms of England engraven in lead and infixed upon a pillar of wood. Yet further and actually to establish this possession taken in the right of her Majesty and to the behoof of Sir Humphrey Gilbert, knight, his heirs and assigns forever, the general granted in fee-farm divers parcels of land lying by the water-side, both in this harbor of Saint John's and elsewhere, which was to the owners a great commodity, being thereby assured (by their proper inheritance) of grounds convenient to dress and to dry their fish, whereof many times before they did fail, being prevented by them that came first into the harbor. For which grounds they did covenant to pay a certain rent and service unto Sir Humphrey Gilbert, his heirs or assigns forever, and yearly to maintain possession of the same by themselves or their assigns.

Now remained only to take in provision granted according as every ship was taxed which did fish upon the coast adjoining. In the meanwhile the general appointed men unto their charge: some to repair and trim the ships; others to attend in gathering together our supply and provisions; others to search the commodities and singularities of the country to be found by sea or land and to make relation unto the general what either themselves could know by their own travel and experience or by good intelligence of Englishmen or strangers who had longest frequented the same coast. Also some observed the elevation of the pole and drew plats of the country exactly graded. And by that I could gather by each man's several relation, I have drawn a brief description of the Newfoundland, with the commodities by sea or land already made, and such also as are in possibility and great likelihood to be made. Nevertheless, the cards and plats that were drawing, with the due gradation of the harbors, bays, and capes, did perish with the admiral; wherefore in the description following I must omit the particulars of such things.

A BRIEF RELATION OF THE NEWFOUNDLAND AND THE COMMODITIES THEREOF

That which we do call the Newfoundland and the Frenchmen Baccalaos is an island, or rather (after the opinion of some) it consists of sundry islands and broken lands, situate in the north regions of America upon the gulf and entrance of the great river called Saint Lawrence in Canada. Into the which navigation may be made both on the south and north side of this island. The land lies south and north, containing in length between three and four hundred miles, accounting from Cape Race (which is in forty-six degrees twenty-five minutes) unto the Grand Bay in fifty-two degrees of septentrional latitude. The island round about has very many goodly bays and harbors, safe roads for ships, the like not to be found in any part of the known world. . . .

For amongst other charges given to inquire out the singularities of this country, the general was most curious in the search of metals, commanding the mineral-man and refiner especially to be diligent. The same was a Saxon born, honest and religious, named Daniel, who after search brought at first some sort of ore, seeming rather to be iron than other metal. The next time he found ore, which with no small show of contentment he delivered unto the general, using protestation that if silver were the thing which might satisfy the general and his followers, there it was, advising him to seek no further; the peril whereof he undertook upon his life (as dear unto him as the Crown of England unto her Majesty, that I may use his own words) if it fell not out accordingly.

Myself at this instant liker to die than to live, by a mischance, could not follow this confident opinion of our refiner to my own satisfaction, but afterward demanding our general's opinion therein, and to have some part of the ore, he replied: "Content yourself, I have seen enough, and were it but to satisfy my private humor I would preceed no further. The promise unto my friends and necessity to bring also the south countries within compass of my patent near expired, as we have already done these north parts, do only persuade me further. And touching the ore, I have sent it aboard, whereof I would have no speech to be made so long as we remain within harbor, here being both Portugals, Biscayans, and Frenchmen not far off, from whom must be kept any bruit or muttering of such matter. When we are at sea, proof shall be made; if it be to our desire, we may return the sooner hither again." Whose answer I judged reasonable and contenting me well, wherewith I will conclude this narration and description of the Newfoundland and proceed to the rest of our voyage, which ended tragically.

While the better sort of us were seriously occupied in repairing our wants and contriving of matters for the commodity of our voyage, others of another sort and disposition were plotting of mischief, some casting to steal away our shipping by night, watching opportunity by the general's and captain's lying on the shore, whose conspiracies discovered, they were prevented. Others drew together in company and carried away out of the harbors adjoining a ship laden with fish, setting the poor men on shore. A great many more of our people stole into the woods to hide themselves, attending time and means to return home by such shipping as daily departed from the coast. Some were sick of fluxes and many dead; and, in brief, by one means or other our company was diminished and many by the general licensed to return home. Insomuch as after we had reviewed our people, resolved to see an end of our voyage, we grew scant of men to furnish all our shipping. It seemed good, therefore, unto the general to leave the *Swallow* with such provision as might be spared for transporting home the sick people.

The captain of the *Delight*, or admiral, returned into England, in whose stead was appointed Captain Maurice Browne, before captain of the *Swallow*, who also brought with him into the *Delight* all his men of the *Swallow*, which before have been noted of outrage perpetrated and committed upon fishermen there met at sea.

The general made choice to go in his frigate, the *Squirrel* (whereof the captain also was among them that returned into England), the same frigate being most convenient to discover upon the coast and to search into every harbor or creek, which a great ship could not do. Therefore the frigate was prepared with her nettings and fights [protective screens] and overcharged with bases [small cannon] and such small ordnance, more to give a show than with judgment to foresee unto the safety of her and the men, which afterward was an occasion also of their overthrow.

Now having made ready our shipping, that is to say, the *Delight*, the *Golden Hinde*, and the *Squirrel*, and put aboard our provision, which was wines, bread or rusk, fish wet and dry, sweet oils, besides many other, as marmalades, figs, lemons barreled, and such like. Also we had other necessary provisions for trimming our ships, nets and lines to fish withal, boats or pinnaces fit for discovery. In brief, we were supplied of our wants commodiously, as if we had been in a country or some city populous and plentiful of all things.

We departed from this harbor of Saint John's upon Tuesday the twentieth of August, which we found by exact observation to be in forty-seven degrees forty minutes. And the next day by night we were at Cape Race twenty-five leagues from the same harbor. . . .

THE MANNER HOW OUR ADMIRAL WAS LOST

Upon Tuesday, the twenty-seventh of August, toward the evening, our general caused them in his frigate to sound, who found white sand at thirty-five fathom, being then in latitude about forty-four degrees.

Wednesday toward night the wind came south, and we bare with the land all the night west-northwest. . . .

The evening was fair and pleasant, yet not without token of storm to ensue, and most part of this Wednesday night, like the swan that sings before death, they in the admiral, or *Delight,* continued in sounding of trumpets, with drums and fifes; also winding the cornets, hautboys; and, in the end of their jollity, left with the battle and ringing of doleful knells.

Towards the evening also we caught in the *Golden Hinde* a very mighty porpoise, with a harping-iron, having first stricken divers of them and brought away part of their flesh sticking upon the iron, but could recover only that one. These also, passing through the ocean in herds, did portend storm. I omit to recite frivolous reports by them in the frigate of strange voices the same night, which scared some from the helm.

Thursday the twenty-ninth of August the wind rose and blew vehemently at south and by east, bringing withal rain and thick mist, so that we could not see a cable length before us. . . .

In this distress we had vigilant eye unto the admiral, whom we saw cast away without power to give the men succor; neither could we espy any of the men that leaped overboard to save themselves, either in the same pinnace or cock, or upon rafters and such-like means presenting themselves to men in those extremities, for we desired to save the men by every possible means. But all in vain, since God had determined their ruin; yet all that day and part of the next we beat up and down as near unto the wreck as was possible for us, looking out if by good hap we might espy any of them.

This was a heavy and grievous event, to lose at one blow our chief ship, freighted with great provision, gathered together with much travel [travail], care, long time, and difficulty. But more was the loss of our men, which perished to the number almost of a hundred souls. . . .

Our people lost courage daily after this ill success; the weather continuing thick and blustering with increase of cold, winter drawing on, which took from them all hope of amendment, settling an assurance of worse weather to grow upon us every day. The lee side of us lay full of dangers and unto us unknown. But above all, provision waxed scant and hope of supply was gone with loss of our admiral.

Those in the frigate were already pinched with spare allowance and want of clothes chiefly. Whereupon they besought the general to return for England before they all perished. And to them of the *Golden Hinde* they made signs of their distress, pointing to their mouths and to their clothes thin and ragged. Then immediately they also of the *Golden Hinde* grew to be of the same opinion and desire to return home.

The former reasons having also moved the general to have compassion of his poor men, in whom he saw no want of good will but of means fit to perform the action they came for, resolved upon retire. And calling the captain and master of the *Hinde,* he yielded them many reasons, enforcing this unexpected return, withal protesting himself greatly satisfied with that he had seen and knew already.

Reiterating these words: "Be content, we have seen enough, and take no care of expense past. I will set you forth royally the next spring if God send us safe home. Therefore, I pray you let us no longer strive here where we fight against the elements."

Omitting circumstances, how unwillingly the captain and master of the *Hinde* condescended to this motion, his own company can testify. Yet comforted with the general's promises of a speedy return at spring, and induced by other apparent reasons proving an impossibility to accomplish the action at that time, it was concluded on all hands to retire.

So upon Saturday in the afternoon the thirty-first of August we changed our course and returned back for England, at which very instant, even in the winding about, there passed along between us and towards the land which we now forsook a very lion to our seeming, in shape, hair, and color, not swimming after the manner of a beast by moving of his feet, but rather sliding upon the water with his whole body (excepting the legs) in sight, neither yet diving under and again rising above the water as the manner is of whales, dolphins, tunny, porpoises, and all other fish, but confidently showing himself above water without hiding. Notwithstanding, we presented ourselves in open view and gesture to amaze [terrify] him, as all creatures will be commonly at a sudden gaze and sight of men. Thus he passed along, turning his head to and fro, yawning and gaping wide, with ugly demonstration of long teeth and glaring eyes, and to bid us a farewell (coming right against the *Hinde*) he sent forth a horrible voice, roaring or bellowing as doth a lion, which spectacle we all beheld so far as we were able to discern the same, as men prone to wonder at every strange thing, as this doubtless was, to see a lion in the ocean sea or fish in shape of a lion. What opinion others had thereof, and chiefly the general himself, I forbear to deliver. But he took it for *bonum omen*, rejoicing that he was to war against such an enemy, if it were the Devil. . . .

This Monday the general came aboard the *Hinde* to have the surgeon of the *Hinde* to dress his foot, which he hurt by treading upon a nail, at what time we comforted each other with hope of hard success [luck] to be all past and of the good to come. So, agreeing to carry out lights always by night, that we might keep together, he departed into his frigate, being by no means to be entreated to tarry in the *Hinde*, which had been more for his security. Immediately after followed a sharp storm, which we overpassed for that time, praised be God.

The weather fair, the general came aboard the *Hinde* again to make merry together with the captain, master, and company, which was the last meeting and continued there from morning until night. During which time there passed sundry discourses touching affairs past and to come, lamenting greatly the loss of his great ship, more of the men, but most of all of his books and notes, and what else I know not, for which he was out of measure grieved, the same doubtless being some matter of more importance than his books, which I could not draw from him; yet by circumstance I gathered the same to be the ore which Daniel the Saxon had brought unto him in the Newfoundland. Whatsoever it was, the remembrance touched him so deep as, not able to contain himself, he beat his boy in great rage, even at the same time, so long after the miscarrying of the great ship, because upon a fair day when we were calmed upon the coast of the Newfoundland near unto Cape Race he sent his boy aboard the admiral to fetch certain things, amongst which this, being chief, was yet forgotten and left behind. After which time he could never conveniently send again aboard the great ship, much less he doubted her ruin so near at hand.

Herein my opinion was better confirmed diversly and by sundry conjectures, which maketh me the greater hope of this rich mine. For whereas the general had never before good conceit of these north parts of the world, now his mind was wholly fixed upon the Newfoundland. And as before he refused not to grant assignments liberally to them that required the same into these north parts, now he became contrarily affected, refusing to make any so large grants, especially of Saint John's, which certain English merchants made suit for, offering to employ their money and travel upon the same. Yet neither by his own suit nor of others of his own company, whom he seemed willing to pleasure, it could be obtained.

Also laying down his determination in the spring following for disposing of his voyage then to be reattempted, he assigned the captain and master of the *Golden Hinde* unto the South discovery and reserved unto himself the North, affirming that this voyage had won his heart from the South and that he was now become a northern man altogether.

Last, being demanded what means he had at his arrival in England to compass the charges of so great preparation as he intended to make the next spring (having determined upon two fleets, one for the South, another for the North). "Leave that to me," he replied. "I will ask a penny of no man. I will bring good tidings unto her Majesty, who will be so gracious to lend me ten thousand pounds, willing us therefore to be of good cheer." For he did thank God, he said, with all his heart, for that he had seen the same being enough for us all, and that we needed not to seek any further. And these last words he would often repeat, with demonstration of great fervency of mind, being himself very confident, and settled in belief of inestimable good by his voyage, which the great number of his followers nevertheless mistrusted altogether, not being made partakers of those secrets which the general kept unto himself. Yet all of them that are living may be witnesses of his words and protestations, which sparingly I have delivered.

Leaving the issue of this good hope unto God, who knoweth the truth only and can at His good pleasure bring the same to light, I will hasten to the end of this tragedy, which must be knit up in the person of our general. And as it was God's ordinance upon him, even so the vehement persuasion and entreaty of his friends could nothing avail to divert him from a willful resolution of going through in his frigate, which was overcharged upon their decks with fights, nettings, and small artillery, too cumbersome for so small a boat that was to pass through the ocean sea at that season of the year, when by course we might expect much storm of foul weather, whereof indeed we had enough.

But when he was entreated by the captain, master, and other his well willers of the *Hinde,* not to venture in the frigate, this was his answer: "I will not forsake my little company going homeward, with whom I have passed so many storms and perils." And in very truth, he was urged to be so over hard, by hard reports given of him, that he was afraid of the sea, albeit this was rather rashness than advised resolution to prefer the wind of a vain report to the weight of his own life.

Seeing he would not bend to reason, he had provision out of the *Hinde* such as was wanting aboard his frigate. And so we committed him to God's protection, and set him aboard his pinnace, we being more than three hundred leagues onward of our way home.

By that time we had brought the islands of Azores south of us, yet we then keeping much to the north, until we had got into the height and elevation of England. We met with very foul weather, and terrible seas, breaking short and high, pyramid-wise. The reason whereof seemed to proceed either of hilly grounds high and low within the sea (as we see hills and dales upon the land) upon which the seas do mount and fall; or else the cause proceedeth of diversity of winds, shifting often in sundry points. All which having power to move the great ocean, which again is not presently settled, so many seas do encounter together, as there had been diversity of winds. Howsoever it cometh to pass, men which all their lifetime had occupied the sea, never saw more outrageous seas. We had also upon our mainyard an apparition of a little fire by night, which seamen do call Castor and Pollux. But we had only one, which they take an evil sign of more tempest. The same is usual in storms.

Monday, the ninth of September, in the afternoon, the frigate was near cast away, oppressed by waves, yet at that time recovered. And giving forth signs of joy, the general sitting abaft with a book in his hand, cried out unto us in the *Hinde* (so oft as we did approach within hearing): "We are as near to heaven by sea as by land." Reiterating the same speech, well beseeming a soldier resolute in Jesus Christ, as I can testify he was.

The same Monday night, about twelve of the clock, or not long after, the frigate being ahead of us in the *Golden Hinde*, suddenly her lights were out, whereof, as it were in a moment, we lost the sight, and withal our watch cried the general was cast away, which was too true. For in that moment, the frigate was devoured and swallowed up of the sea. Yet still we looked out all that night, and ever after, until we arrived upon the coast of England, omitting no small sail at sea unto which we gave not the tokens between us agreed upon to have perfect knowledge of each other if we should at any time be separated.

In great torment of weather and peril of drowning, it pleased God to send safe home the *Golden Hinde*, which arrived in Falmouth the twenty-second day of September, being Sunday, not without as great danger escaped in a flaw [storm], coming from the southeast with such thick mist that we could not discern land to put in right with the haven.

From Falmouth we went to Dartmouth and lay there at anchor before the range while the captain went aland, to inquire if there had been any news of the frigate, which sailing well might happily have been there before us. Also to certify Sir John Gilbert, brother unto the general, of our hard success, whom the captain desired (while his men were yet aboard him and were witnesses of all occurrences in that voyage) it might please him to take the examination of every person particularly in discharge of his and their faithful endeavor. Sir John Gilbert refused so to do, holding himself satisfied with report made by the captain; and not altogether despairing of his brother's safety, offered friendship and courtesy to the captain and his company, requiring to have his bark brought into the harbor. In furtherance whereof, a boat was sent to help to tow her in. . . .

Thus have I delivered the contents of the enterprise and last action of Sir Humphrey Gilbert, knight, faithfully, for so much as I thought meet to be published. Wherein may always appear (though he be extinguished) some sparks of his virtues, he remaining firm and resolute in a purpose by all pretense honest and godly, as was this, to discover, possess, and to reduce unto the service of God and Christian piety, those remote and heathen countries of America not actually possessed by Christians and most rightly appertaining unto the Crown of England. Unto the which, as his zeal deserveth high commendation, even so he may justly be taxed of temerity and presumption (rather) in two respects.

First, when yet there was only probability, not a certain and determinate place of habitation selected, neither any demonstration of commodity there in esse [in being] to induce his followers, nevertheless he both was too prodigal of his own patrimony and too careless of other men's expenses to employ both his and their substance upon a ground imagined good. The which falling, very like his associates were promised, and made it their best reckoning to be saved some other way, which pleased not God to prosper in his first and great preparation.

Secondly, when by his former preparation he was enfeebled of ability and credit to perform his designments, as it were impatient to abide in expectation [of] better opportunity and means, which God might raise, he thrust himself again into the action, for which he was not fit, presuming the cause pretended on God's behalf would carry him to the desired end. Into which, having thus made reentry, he could not yield again to withdraw, though he saw no encouragement to proceed lest his credit, foiled in his first attempt, in a second should utterly be disgraced. Between extremities he made a right adventure, putting all to God and good fortune, and, which was worst, refused not to entertain every person and means whatsoever, to furnish out this expedition, the success whereof hath been declared.

But such is the infinite bounty of God, who from every evil deriveth good. For besides that fruit may grow in time of our traveling into those northwest lands, the crosses, turmoils, and afflictions, both in the preparation and execution of this voyage, did correct the intemperate humors which before we noted to be in this gentleman, and made unsavory and less delightful his other manifold virtues.

Then as he was refined and made nearer drawing unto the image of God, so it pleased the divine will to resume him unto Himself, whither both his and every other high and noble mind have always aspired.

6.

A Report of John Davis of His Three Voyages [1585, 1586, 1587] Made for the Discovery of the Northwest Passage, Taken Out of a Treatise of His Entitled "The World's Hydrographical Description."

Now there only resteth the north parts of America upon which coast myself have had most experience of any in our age. For thrice I was that way employed for the discovery of this notable passage by the honorable care and some charge of Sir Francis Walsingham, knight, principal secretary to her Majesty, with whom divers noble men and worshipful merchants of London joined in purse and willingness for the futherance of that attempt, but when his honor died the

voyage was friendless and men's minds alienated from ad-
venturing therein.

In my first voyage, not experienced of the nature of those
climates and having no direction either by chart, globe, or
other certain relation in what altitude that passage was to be
searched, I shaped a northerly course . . . and in that my
northerly course I fell upon the shore which in ancient time
was called Greenland, five hundred leagues distant from the
Durseys [on Irish coast] west-northwest northerly, the land
being very high and full of mighty mountains all covered with
snow, no view of wood, grass, or earth to be seen and the shore
two leagues off into the sea so full of ice as that no shipping
could by any means come near the same. The loathsome view
of the shore and irksome noise of the ice was such as that it
bred strange conceits among us, so that we supposed the place
to be waste and void of any sensible or vegetable creatures,
whereupon I called the same Desolation. So coasting this shore
towards the south in the latitude of sixty degrees, I found it to
trend towards the west. I still followed the leading thereof in
the same height and after fifty or sixty leagues it failed and lay
directly north, which I still followed, and in thirty leagues
sailing upon the west side of this coast by me named Desolation we were past all the ice and found many green and pleasant
isles bordering upon the shore, but the hills of the main were
still covered with great quantities of snow. I brought my ship
among those isles and there moored to refresh ourselves in our
weary travel in the latitude of sixty-four degrees or thereabout.
The people of the country having espied our ships came down
unto us in their canoes and holding up their right hand to the
sun and crying "Yliaout," would strike their breasts. We doing
the like, the people came aboard our ships, men of good stature,
unbearded, small eyed, and of tractable conditions, by whom
as signs would permit we understood that towards the north
and west there was a great sea. And using the people with
kindness in giving them nails and knives, which of all things
they most desired, we departed. And finding the sea [Davis
Strait] free from ice, supposing ourselves to be past all danger,
we shaped our course west-northwest, thinking thereby to
pass for China. But in the latitude of sixty-six degrees we fell

with another shore [Cumberland Peninsula of Baffin Island],
and there found another passage of twenty leagues broad
directly west into the same, which we supposed to be our
hoped [for] strait. We entered into the same thirty or forty
leagues, finding it neither to widen nor straighten. Then
considering that the year was spent (for this was the fine [end]
of August), not knowing the length of the strait and dangers
thereof, we took it our best course to return with notice of our
good success for this small time of search. And so returning
in a sharp fret of westerly winds the twenty-ninth of September
we arrived at Dartmouth.

And acquainting Master Secretary Walsingham with the rest
of the honorable and worshipful adventurers of all our proceedings, I was appointed again the second year to search the bottom of this strait, because by all likelihood it was the place
and passage by us labored for. In this second attempt the
merchants of Exeter and other places of the west became adventurers in the action, so that being sufficiently furnished for six
months and having direction to search these straits until we
found the same to fall into another sea upon the west side of
this part of America, we should again return. For then it was
not to be doubted but shipping with trade might safely be
conceived to China and the parts of Asia. We departed from
Dartmouth and arriving upon the south part of the coast of
Desolation, coasted the same upon his west shore to the latitude of sixty-six degrees, and there anchored among the isles
bordering upon the same, where we refreshed ourselves.
The people of this place came likewise unto us, by whom I
understood through their signs that towards the north the sea
was large. At this place the chief ship whereupon I trusted,
called the *Mermaid* of Dartmouth, found many occasions of
discontentment and being unwilling to proceed she there
forsook me. Then considering how I had given my faith and
most constant promise to my worshipful good friend, Master
William Sanderson, who of all men was the greatest adventurer
in that action and took such care for the performance thereof
that he hath to my knowledge at one time disbursed as much
money as any five others whatsoever, out of his own purse,
when some of the company have been slack in giving in their

adventure, and also knowing that I should lose the favor of Master Secretary Walsingham if I should shrink from his direction, in one small bark of thirty tons, whereof Master Sanderson was the owner, alone without farther company I proceeded on my voyage and arriving at these straits followed the same eighty leagues until I came among many islands [along Cumberland Peninsula] where the water did ebb and flow six fathom upright and where there had been great trade of people to make train. But by such things as there we found, we knew that they were not Christians of Europe that had used that trade. In fine, by searching with our boat we found small hope to pass any farther that way, and therefore recovered the sea and coasted the shore towards the south, and in so doing (for it was too late to search towards the north) we found another great inlet near forty leagues broad where the water entered in with violent swiftness. This we also thought might be a passage, for no doubt the north parts of America are all islands by ought that I could perceive therein. But because I was alone in a small bark of thirty tons and the year spent, I entered not into the same, for it was now the seventh of September. But coasting the [Labrador] shore towards the south we saw an incredible number of birds. Having divers fishermen aboard our bark they all concluded that there was a great school of fish. We, being unprovided of fishing furniture, with a long spike nail made a hook and fastened the same to one of our sounding lines. Before the bait was changed we took more than forty great cods, the fish swimming so abundantly thick about our bark as is incredible to be reported, of which with a small portion of salt that we had we preserved some thirty couple or thereabouts, and so returned for England. And having reported to Master Secretary Walsingham the whole success of this attempt, he commanded me to present unto the most honorable Lord High Treasurer of England some part of that fish. Which when his lordship saw and heard at large the relation of this second attempt, I received favorable countenance from his honor, advising me to prosecute the action, of which his lordship conceived a very good opinion. The next year, although divers of the adventurers fell from the action, as all the western merchants and most of those in London, yet some of the adventurers both honorable and worshipful continued their willing favor and charge, so that by this means the next year two ships were appointed for the fishing and one pinnace for the discovery.

Departing from Dartmouth through God's merciful favor I arrived at the place of fishing and there according to my direction I left the two ships to follow that business, taking their faithful promise not to depart until my return unto them, which should be in the fine of August. And so in the bark I proceeded for the discovery. But after my departure in sixteen days the two ships had finished their voyage and so presently departed for England without regard of their promise. Myself not distrusting any such hard measure proceeded for the discovery, and followed my course in the free and open sea between north and northwest to the latitude of sixty-seven degrees, and there I might see America west from me and Greenland, which I called Desolation, east. Then when I saw the land of both sides I began to distrust it would prove but a gulf. Notwithstanding, desirous to know the full certainty I proceeded and in sixty-eight degrees the passage enlarged, so that I could not see the western shore. Thus I continued to the latitude of seventy-three degrees in a great sea free from ice, coasting the western shore of Desolation. The people came continually rowing out unto me in their canoes—twenty, forty, and one hundred at a time—and would give me fishes dried, salmon, salmon peal, cod, caplin, lump, stone base, and such like, besides divers kinds of birds as partridge, pheasant, gulls, sea birds, and other kinds of flesh. I still labored by signs to know from them what they knew of any sea toward the north. They still made signs of a great sea, as we understood them. Then I departed from the coast, thinking to discover the north parts of America. And after I had sailed towards the west forty leagues, I fell upon a great bank of ice [in Baffin Bay]. The wind being north and blew much, I was constrained to coast the same toward the south, not seeing any shore west from me. Neither was there any ice towards the north but a great sea, free, large, very salt and blue, and of an unsearchable depth. So coasting towards the south I came to the place where I left the ships to fish but found them not. Then being forsaken and left in this

distress, referring myself to the merciful providence of God
I shaped my course for England and unhoped for of any, God
alone relieving me, I arrived at Dartmouth.

By this last discovery it seemed most manifest that the
passage was free and without impediment toward the north.
But by reason of the Spanish fleet and unfortunate time of
master secretary's death, the voyage was omitted and never
since attempted. The cause why I use this particular relation
of all my proceedings for this discovery is to stay this objection:
why hath not Davis discovered this passage, being thrice that
ways employed? How far I proceeded and in what form this
discovery lieth doth appear upon the globe which Master
Sanderson to his very great charge hath published, for which
he deserveth great favor and commendations.

PART TWO

Virginia

The Voyages and Navigations of the English Nation to Virginia, and the Several Discoveries thereof Chiefly at the Charges of the Honorable Sir Walter Raleigh, Knight, from Thirty-three to Forty Degrees of Latitude. Together with the Success of the English Colonies there Planted. As likewise a Description of the Country, with the Inhabitants, and the Manifold Commodities. Whereunto Are Annexed the Patents, Letters, Discourses, etc., to This Part Belonging.

1.

The Letters Patent Granted by the Queen's Majesty to M[aster] Walter Raleigh, Now Knight, for the Discovering and Planting of New Lands and Countries, to Continue the Space of Six Years and No More.

Elizabeth by the grace of God of England, France, and Ireland, Queen, defender of the faith, etc. To all people to whom these presents shall come, greeting. Know ye that of our especial grace, certain science, and mere motion, we have given and granted and by these presents for us, our heirs and successors do give and grant to our trusty and well-beloved servant, Sir Walter Raleigh, esquire, and to his heirs and assigns forever, free liberty and license from time to time, and at all times forever hereafter, to discover, search, find out, and view such remote, heathen, and barbarous lands, countries, and territories not actually possessed of any Christian prince, nor inhabited by Christian people, as to him, his heirs and assigns, and to every or any of them shall seem good, and the same to have, hold, occupy, and enjoy to him, his heirs and assigns forever, with all prerogatives, commodities, jurisdictions, royalties, privileges, franchises, and preeminences, thereto or there-

73

abouts both by sea and land, whatsoever we by our letters patent may grant, and as we or any of our noble progenitors have heretofore granted. And the said Walter Raleigh, his heirs and assigns, and all such as from time to time, by license of us, our heirs and successors, shall go or travel thither to inhabit or remain there to build and fortify, at the discretion of the said Walter Raleigh, his heirs and assigns, the statutes or acts of Parliament made against fugitives or against such as shall depart, remain, or continue out of our realm of England without license, or any other statute, act, law, or any ordinance whatsoever to the contrary, in any wise notwithstanding.

And we do likewise by these presents of our especial grace, mere motion, and certain knowledge, for us, our heirs, and successors give and grant full authority, liberty, and power to the said Walter Raleigh, his heirs and assigns, and every of them that he and they and every or any of them shall and may at all and every time and times hereafter have, take, and lead in the said voyage and travel thitherward or to inhabit there with him or them, and every or any of them, such and so many of our subjects as shall willingly accompany him or them and every or any of them. And to whom also we do by these presents give full liberty and authority in that behalf and also to have, take, and employ and use sufficient shipping and furniture for the transportations and navigations in that behalf, so that none of the same persons or any of them be such as hereafter shall be restrained by us, our heirs, or successors.

And further that the said Walter Raleigh, his heirs and assigns, and every of them, shall have, hold, occupy, and enjoy to him, his heirs and assigns, and every of them forever, all the soil of all such lands, territories, and countries so to be discovered and possessed as aforesaid, and of all such cities, castles, towns, villages, and places in the same, with the right, royalties, franchises, and jurisdictions, as well marine as other within the said lands or countries or the seas thereunto adjoining to be had or used with full power to dispose thereof and of every part in fee simple or otherwise, according to the order of the laws of England, as near as the same conveniently may be at his and their will and pleasure, to any persons then being or that shall remain within the allegiance of us, our heirs and successors, for all services, duties, and demands, the fifth part of all the ore of gold and silver that from time to time and at all times after such discovery, subduing, and possessing, shall be there gotten and obtained. All which lands, countries, and territories shall forever be holden of the said Walter Raleigh, his heirs and assigns of us, our heirs and successors by homage and by the said payment of the said fifth part reserved only for all services.

And moreover we do by these presents for us, our heirs and successors give and grant license to the said Walter Raleigh, his heirs and assigns, and every of them that be, and they and every or any of them shall and may from time to time and at all times forever hereafter for his and their defense encounter and expulse, repel, and resist as well by sea as by land and by all other ways whatsoever all and every such person and persons whatsoever as without the especial liking and license of the said Walter Raleigh, and of his heirs and assigns shall attempt to inhabit within the said countries or any of them or within the space of two hundred leagues near to the place or places within such countries as aforesaid (if they shall not be before planted or inhabited within the limits as aforesaid with the subjects of any Christian prince being in amity with us) where the said Walter Raleigh, his heirs or assigns, or any of them or his or their or any of their associates or company, shall within six years (next ensuing) make their dwellings or abidings or that shall enterprise or attempt at any time hereafter unlawfully [to] annoy either by sea or land the said Walter Raleigh, his heirs or assigns, or any of them or his or their, or any of his or their companies. Giving and granting by these presents further power and authority to the said Walter Raleigh, his heirs and assigns and every of them from time to time and at all time forever hereafter to take and surprise by all manner of means whatsoever all and every those persons or persons with their ships, vessels, and other goods and furniture which without the license of the said Walter Raleigh or his heirs or assigns, as aforesaid, shall be found trafficking into any harbor or harbors, creek or creeks, with the limits aforesaid (the subjects of our realms and dominions and all other persons in amity with us trading to the Newfoundlands for fishing as heretofore

they have commonly used or being driven by force of a tempest
or shipwreck only excepted), and those persons and every of
them with their ships, vessels, goods, and furniture to detain
and possess as of good and lawful prize, according to the
discretion of him the said Walter Raleigh, his heirs and assigns
and every or any of them. And for uniting in more perfect
league and amity of such countries, lands, and territories so
to be possessed and inhabited as aforesaid with our realms
of England and Ireland and the better encouragement of men to
these enterprises, we do by these presents grant and declare
that all such countries so hereafter to be possessed and inhabited as is aforesaid from thenceforth shall be of the allegiance
to us, our heirs and successors. And we do grant to the said
Walter Raleigh, his heirs and assigns, and to all and every of
them and to all and every other person and persons being of
our allegiance, whose names shall be noted or entered in some
of our courts of record within our realm of England, that with
the assent of the said Walter Raleigh, his heirs or assigns, shall
in his journeys for discovery or in the journeys for conquest
hereafter travel to such lands, countries, and territories as
aforesaid and to their and to every of their heirs within our
said realms of England or Ireland or in any other place within
our allegiance and which hereafter shall be inhabiting within
any of the lands, countries, and territories with such license
(as aforesaid) shall and may have all the privileges of free
denizens and persons native of England and within our
allegiance in such like ample manner and form as if they were
born and personally resident within our said realm of England,
and law, custom, or usage to the contrary notwithstanding.

And forasmuch as upon the finding out, discovering, or
inhabiting of such remote lands, countries, and territories as
aforesaid it shall be necessary for the safety of all men that shall
adventure themselves in these journeys or voyages to deter-
mine to live together in Christian peace and civil quietness,
each with other, whereby everyone may with more pleasure
and profit enjoy that whereunto they shall attain with great
pain and peril, we for us, our heirs and successors are likewise
pleased and contented and by these presents do give and grant
to the said Walter Raleigh, his heirs and assigns forever, that

he and they and every or any of them shall and may from time
to time forever hereafter, within the said mentioned remote
lands and countries in the way by the seas thither and from
thence have full and mere [sole] power and authority to correct,
punish, pardon, govern, and rule by their and every or any
of their good discretions and policies, as well in causes capital
or criminal as civil, both marine and other, all such our subjects
as shall from time to time adventure themselves in the said
journeys or voyages or that shall at any time hereafter inhabit
any such lands, countries, or territories as aforesaid or that
shall abide within two hundred leagues of any of the said place
or places where the said Walter Raleigh, his heirs or assigns,
or any of them or any of his or their associates or companies
shall inhabit within six years next ensuing the date hereof,
according to such statutes, laws, and ordinances as shall be
by him the said Walter Raleigh, his heirs and assigns and every
or any of them devised or established for the better government
of the said people as aforesaid. So always as the said statutes,
laws, and ordinances may be, as near as conveniently as may
be, agreeable to the form of the laws, statutes, government,
or policy of England, and also so as they be not against the true
Christian faith now professed in the Church of England, nor
in any wise to withdraw any of the subjects or people of those
lands or places from the allegiance of us, our heirs and successors as their immediate sovereign under God.

And further we do by these presents for us, our heirs, and
successors give and grant full power and authority to our trusty
and well-beloved councillor Sir William Cecil, knight, Lord
Burghley, our High Treasurer of England to the Lord Treasurer
of England for us, our heirs and successors for the time being,
and to the Privy Council of us, our heirs and successors or any
four or more of them for the time being, that he, they, or any
four or more of them shall and may from time to time and at all
times hereafter under his or their hands or seals by virtue of
these presents, authorize and license the said Walter Raleigh,
his heirs and assigns and every or any of them by him and by
themselves or by their or any of their sufficient attorneys,
deputies, officers, ministers, factors, and servants to embark
and transport out of our realm of England and Ireland and the

dominions thereof all or any of his or their goods, and all or any the goods of his and their associates and companies, and every or any of them with such other necessaries and commodities of any our realms as to the said Lord Treasurer or four or more of the Privy Council of us our heirs and for the time being (as aforesaid) shall be from time to time by his or their wisdoms or discretions thought meet and convenient for the better relief and supportation of him, the said Walter Raleigh, his heirs and assigns, and every or any of them and of his or their or any of their associates and companies, any act, statute, law, or any thing to the contrary in any wise notwithstanding.

Provided always and our will and pleasure is and we do hereby declare to all Christian kings, princes, and states, that if the said Walter Raleigh, his heirs or assigns, or any of them, or any other by their license or appointment shall at any time or times hereafter rob or spoil by sea or by land or do any act of unjust or unlawful hostility to any of the subjects of us, our heirs or successors or to any of the subjects of any the kings, princes, rulers, governors, or estates being then in perfect league and amity with us, our heirs and successors, and that upon such injury or upon just complaint of any such prince, ruler, governor, or estate, or their subjects we, our heirs and successors, shall make open proclamation within any of the ports of our realm of England that the said Walter Raleigh, his heirs and assigns, and adherents, or any to whom these our letters patent may extend, shall within the terms to be limited by such proclamation make full restitution and satisfaction of all such injuries done; so as both we and the said princes or other so complaining may hold us and themselves fully contented. And that if the said Walter Raleigh, his heirs and assigns, shall not make or cause to be made satisfaction accordingly within such time so to be limited, that then it shall be lawful to us, our heirs and successors, to put the said Walter Raleigh, his heirs, and assigns, and adherents, and all the inhabitants of the said places to be discovered (as is aforesaid) or any of them out of our allegiance and protection, and that from and after such time of putting out of protection of the said Walter Raleigh, his heirs, assigns, and adherents, and others so to be put out, and the said places within their habitation, possession, and rule shall be out of our allegiance and protection and free for all princes and others to pursue with hostility, as being not our subjects nor by us to be holden as any of ours, nor to our protection, or dominion, or allegiance any way belonging. For that express mention of the clear yearly value of the certainty of the premises or any part thereof or of any other gift or grant by us or any [of] our progenitors or predecessors to the said Walter Raleigh before this time made in these presents be not expressed or any other grant, ordinance, provision, proclamation, or restraint to the contrary thereof before this time given, ordained, or provided, or any other thing, cause, or matter whatsoever in any wise notwithstanding.

In witness whereof we have caused these our letters to be made patents. Witness ourselves, at Westminster the five and twentieth day of March, in the six and twentieth year [1584] of our reign.

2.

The First Voyage to the Coasts of America, with Two Barks, Wherein Were Captains M[aster] Philip Amadas and M[aster] Arthur Barlowe, Who Discovered Part of the Country Now Called Virginia, Anno 1584. Written by One of the Said Captains [Barlowe] and Sent to Sir Walter Raleigh, Knight, at Whose Charge and Direction the Said Voyage Was Set Forth.

The twenty-seventh day of April, in the year of our redemption 1584, we departed the west of England, with two barks well furnished with men and victuals, having received our last and perfect directions by your letters, confirming the former instructions, and commandments delivered by yourself at our leaving the river of Thames. And I think it a matter both unnecessary, for the manifest discovery of the country, as also for tediousness sake, to remember unto you the diurnal of our course, sailing thither and returning. Only I have presumed to present unto you this brief discourse, by which you may judge how profitable this land is likely to succeed, as well to yourself (by whose direction and charge, and by whose servants this our discovery hath been performed) as also to her Highness, and the Commonwealth, in which we hope your wisdom will be satisfied, considering that as much by us hath been brought to light as by those small means, and number of men we had, could any way have been expected or hoped for.

The tenth of May we arrived at the Canaries, and the tenth of June in this present year, we were fallen with the islands of the West Indies, keeping a more southeasterly course than was needful, because we doubted that the current of the Bay of Mexico, disbogging [emerging] between the cape of Florida and Havana, had been of greater force than afterwards we found it to be. At which islands we found the air very unwholesome, and our men grew for the most part ill-disposed; so that having refreshed ourselves with sweet water and fresh victual, we departed the twelfth day of our arrival there. These islands, with the rest adjoining, are so well known to yourself, and to many others, as I will not trouble you with the remembrance of them.

The second of July we found shoal water, where we smelt so sweet and so strong a smell as if we had been in the midst of some delicate garden abounding with all kind of odoriferous flowers, by which we were assured that the land could not be far distant. And keeping good watch, and bearing but slack sail, the fourth of the same month we arrived upon the coast [somewhere between Cape Fear and Cape Lookout, North Carolina], which we supposed to be a continent and firmland, and we sailed along the same a hundred and twenty English miles before we could find any entrance or river issuing into the sea. The first that appeared unto us we entered [near Oregon Inlet], though not without some difficulty, and cast anchor about three harquebus [light handgun] shot within the haven's mouth, on the left hand of the same. And after thanks given to God for our safe arrival thither, we manned our boats, and went to view the land next adjoining, and to take possession of the same in the right of the Queen's most excellent Majesty, as rightful Queen and Princess of the same, and after delivered the same over to your use, according to her Majesty's grant and letters patent, under her Highness's great seal.

Which being performed, according to the ceremonies used in such enterprises, we viewed the land about us, being, whereas we first landed, very sandy and low towards the water's side, but so full of grapes as the very beating and surge of the sea overflowed them, of which we found such plenty—as well there as in all places else, both on the sand and on the green soil on the hills, as in the plains, as well on every little shrub, as also climbing towards the tops of high cedars—that I think in all the world the like abundance is not to be found. And myself having seen those parts of Europe that most abound, find such difference as were incredible to be written.

We passed from the seaside towards the tops of those hills next adjoining, being but of mean height, and from thence we beheld the sea on both sides to the north and to the south, finding no end any of both ways. This land lay stretching itself to the west, which after we found to be but an island of twenty miles long, and not above six miles broad. Under the bank or hill whereon we stood, we beheld the valleys replenished with goodly cedar trees, and having discharged our harquebus shot, such a flock of cranes (the most part white) arose under us, with such a cry redoubled by many echoes, as if an army of men had shouted all together.

This island had many goodly woods full of deer, conies, hares, and fowls, even in the midst of summer in incredible abundance. The woods are not such as you find in Bohemia, Moscovia, or Hercynia [in the Caucasus], barren and fruitless, but the highest and reddest cedars of the world, far bettering the cedars of the Azores, of the Indies, or Libanus, pines, cyprus, sassafras, the lentisk, or the tree that beareth the mastic, the tree that beareth the rind of black cinnamon, of which Master [John] Winter brought from the Straits of Magellan, and many other of excellent smell and quality.

We remained by the side of this island two whole days before we saw any people of the country. The third day we espied one small boat rowing towards us, having in it three persons. This boat came to the island side, four harquebus shot from our ships, and there two of the people remaining, the third came along the shoreside towards us, and we being then all within board, he walked up and down upon the point of the land next unto us. Then the master and the pilot of the admiral [flagship], Simon Ferdinando, and the Captain Philip Amadas, myself, and others rowed to the land, whose coming this fellow attended, never making any show of fear or doubt. And after he had spoken of many things not understood by us, we brought him with his own good liking, aboard the ships, and gave him a shirt, a hat, and some other things, and made him taste of our wine and our meat, which he liked very well. And after having viewed both barks, he departed, and went to his own boat again, which he had left in a little cove or creek adjoining. As soon as he was two bow shot into the water, he fell to fishing, and in less than half an hour he had laden his boat as deep as it could swim, with which he came again to the point of the land, and there he divided his fish into two parts, pointing one part to the ship, and the other to the pinnace. Which, after he had (as much as he might) requited the former benefits received, he departed out of our sight.

The next day there came unto us divers boats, and in one of them the king's brother, accompanied with forty or fifty men, very handsome and goodly people, and in their behavior as mannerly and civil as any of Europe. His name was Granganimeo, and the king is called Wingina, the country Wingandacoa, and now, by her Majesty, Virginia. The manner of his coming was in this sort: he left his boats altogether as the first man did a little from the ships by the shore, and came along to the place over against the ships, followed with forty men. When he came to the place, his servants spread a long mat upon the ground, on which he sat down, and at the other end of the mat four others of his company did the like, and the rest of his men stood round about him, somewhat afar off. When we came to the shore to him with our weapons, he never moved from his place, nor any of the other four, nor never mistrusted any harm to be offered from us, but sitting still he beckoned us to come and sit by him, which we performed. And being set he made all signs of joy and welcome, striking on his head and his breast and afterwards on ours to show we were all one, smiling and making show the best he could of all love and familiarity. After he had made a long speech unto us, we presented him with divers things, which he received very joyfully and thankfully. None of the company durst speak one word all the time. Only the four which were at the other end spoke one in the other's ear very softly.

The king is greatly obeyed and his brothers and children reverenced. The king himself in person was at our being there sore wounded in a fight which he had with the king of the next country. [He is] called Wingina, and was shot in two places through the body, and once clean through the thigh, but yet he recovered. By reason whereof and for that he lay at the chief town of the country, being six days' journey off, we saw him not at all.

After we had presented this his brother with such things as we thought he liked, we likewise gave somewhat to the others that sat with him on the mat. But presently he arose and took all from them and put it into his own basket, making signs and tokens that all things ought to be delivered unto him and the rest were but his servants and followers. A day or two after this we fell to trading with them, exchanging some things that we had for chamois, buff [buffalo or bison], and deer skins. When we showed him all our packet of merchandise, of all things that he saw a bright tin dish most pleased him, which he presently took up and clapped it before his breast, and after made a hole in the brim thereof and hung it about his neck, making signs that it would defend him against his enemies' arrows. For those people maintain a deadly and terrible war with the people and king adjoining. We exchanged our tin dish for twenty skins, worth twenty crowns or twenty nobles, and a copper kettle for fifty skins, worth fifty crowns. They offered us good exchange for our hatchets and axes and for knives, and would have given anything for swords, but we would not depart with any.

After two or three days the king's brother came aboard the ships and drank wine and ate of our meat and of our bread and liked exceedingly thereof. And after a few days overpassed, he brought his wife with him to the ships, his daughter and two or three children. His wife was very well favored, of mean stature and very bashful. She had on her back a long cloak of leather, with the fur side next to her body, and before her a piece of the same. About her forehead she had a band of white coral, and so had her husband many times. In her ears she had bracelets of pearls hanging down to her middle (whereof we delivered your worship a little bracelet), and those were of the bigness of good peas. The rest of her women of the better sort had pendants of copper hanging in either ear, and some of the children of the king's brother and other noble men have five or six in either ear. He himself had upon his head a broad plate of gold or copper, for being unpolished we knew not what metal it should be, neither would he by any means suffer us to take it off his head, but feeling it, it would bow very easily. His apparel was as his wife's, only the women wear their hair long on both sides and the men but on one. They are of color yellowish and their hair black for the most part, and yet we saw children that had very fine auburn and chestnut-colored hair.

After that these women had been there, there came down from all parts great store of people, bringing with them leather, coral, divers kinds of dyes very excellent, and exchanged with us. But when Granganimeo, the king's brother, was present, none durst trade but himself. Except such as wear red pieces of copper on their heads like himself. For that is the difference between the noblemen and the governors of countries and the meaner sort. And we both noted there, and you have understood since by these men which we brought home, that no people in the world carry more respect to their king, nobility, and governors than these do. The king's brother's wife, when she came to us (as she did many times) was followed with forty or fifty women always. And when she came into the ship, she left them all on land, saving her two daughters, her nurse, and one or two more. The king's brother always kept this order, as many boats as he would come withal to the ships, so many fires would he make on the shore afar off, to the end we might understand with what strength and company he approached.

Their boats are made of one tree, either of pine or pitch trees, a wood not commonly known to our people, nor found growing in England. They have no edge tools to make them withal. If they have any they are very few, and those it seems they had twenty years since, which, as those two men declared, was out of a wreck which happened upon their coast of some Christian ship, being beaten that way by some storm and outrageous weather, whereof none of the people were saved but only the ship or some part of her being cast upon the sand, out of whose sides they drew the nails and the spikes, and with those they made their best instruments. The manner of making their boats is thus: they burn down some great tree, or take such as are windfallen, and putting gum and rosin upon one side thereof, they set fire into it, and when it hath burnt it hollow, they cut out the coal with their shells, and everywhere they would burn it deeper or wider they lay on gums, which burn away the timber, and by this means they fashion very fine boats, and such as will transport twenty men. Their oars are like scoops, and many times they set with long poles, as the depth serveth.

The king's brother had great liking of our armor, a sword, and divers other things which we had; and offered to lay a great box of pearl in gage for them. But we refused it for this time, because we would not make them know that we esteemed thereof until we had understood in what places of the country the pearl grew, which now your worship doth very well understand.

He was very just of his promise. For many times we delivered him merchandise upon his word but ever he came within the day and performed his promise. He sent us every day a brace or two of fat bucks, conies, hares, fish, the best of the world. He sent us divers kinds of fruits, melons, walnuts, cucumbers, gourds, peas, and divers roots, and fruits very excellent good, and of their country corn, which is very white, fair, and well tasted, and groweth three times in five months. In May they sow, in July they reap; in June they sow, in August they reap; in July they sow, in September they reap. Only they cast the corn into the ground, breaking a little of the soft turf with a wooden mattock, or pickax. Ourselves proved the soil, and put some of our peas in the ground, and in ten days they were of fourteen inches high. They have also beans very fair of divers colors and wonderful plenty. Some growing naturally and some in their gardens, and so have they both wheat and oats.

The soil is the most plentiful sweet, fruitful, and wholesome of all the world. There are above fourteen several sweet-smelling timber trees, and the most part of their underwoods are bays and such like. They have those oaks that we have but far greater and better. After they had been divers times aboard our ships, myself, with seven more, went twenty mile into the river that runneth toward the city of Skicoak [near Great Bridge, Virginia], which river they call Occam [Croatan and Albemarle sounds]. And the evening following we came to an island, which they call Roanoke, distant from the harbor by which we entered seven leagues. And at the north end thereof was a village of nine houses, built of cedar and fortified round about with sharp trees to keep out their enemies, and the entrance into it made like a turnpike [a spiked barrier] very artificially [artfully, skillfully]. When we came towards it, standing near unto the water's side, the wife of Granganimeo, the king's brother, came running out to meet us very cheerfully and friendly; her husband was not then in the village. Some of her people she commanded to draw our boat on shore for the beating of the billow. Others she appointed to carry us on their backs to the dry ground, and others to bring our oars into the house for fear of stealing. When we were come into the outer room, having five rooms in her house, she caused us to sit down by a great fire, and after took off our clothes and washed them, and dried them again. Some of the women plucked off our stockings and washed them, some washed our feet in warm water, and she herself took great pains to see all things ordered in the best manner she could, making haste to dress some meat for us to eat.

After we had thus dried ourselves, she brought us into the inner room, where she set on the board standing along the house some wheat like frumenty; sodden [stewed] venison and roasted; fish sodden, boiled, and roasted; melons raw and sodden; roots of divers kinds, and divers fruits. Their drink is commonly water, but while the grape lasteth they drink wine, and for want of casks to keep it, all the year after they drink water, but it is sodden with ginger in it, and black cinnamon, and sometimes sassafras and divers other wholesome and medicinable herbs and trees. We were entertained with all love and kindness, and with as much bounty (after their manner) as they could possibly devise. We found the people most gentle, loving, and faithful, void of all guile and treason, and such as live after the manner of the golden age. The people only care how to defend themselves from the cold in their short winter, and to feed themselves with such meat as the soil affordeth. Their meat is very well sodden and they make broth very sweet and savory. Their vessels are earthen pots, very large, white, and sweet, their dishes are wooden platters of sweet timber. Within the place where they feed was their lodging, and within that their idol, which they worship, of whom they speak incredible things.

While we were at meat there came in at the gates two or three men with their bows and arrows from hunting, whom when we espied we began to look one towards another, and offered to reach our weapons. But as soon as she espied our mistrust, she was very much moved, and caused some of her men to run out, and take away their bows and arrows and break them, and withal beat the poor fellows out of the gate again. When we departed in the evening and would not tarry all night, she was very sorry, and gave us into our boat our supper half dressed, pots and all, and brought us to our boat side, in which we lay all night, removing the same a pretty distance from the shore. She, perceiving our jealousy, was much grieved, and sent divers men and thirty women to sit all night on the bank side by us, and sent us into our boats five mats to cover us from the rain, using very many words to entreat us to rest in their houses. But because we were few men, and if we had miscarried the voyage had been in very great danger, we durst not adventure anything, though there was no cause of doubt. For a more kind and loving people there cannot be found in the world, as far as we have hitherto had trial.

Beyond this island there is the mainland, and over against this island falleth into this spacious water the great river called Occam by the inhabitants, on which standeth a town called Pomeiock [near Lake Landing, North Carolina], and six days' journey from the same is situate their greatest city, called Skicoak, which this people affirm to be very great. But the savages were never at it, only they speak of it by the report of their fathers and other men, whom they have heard affirm it to be above one hour's journey about.

Into this river falleth another great river, called Cipo [Pamlico], in which there is found great store of mussels in which are pearls. Likewise there descendeth into this Occam another

river, called Nomopana [western end of Albemarle Sound],
on the one side whereof standeth a great town called Chawanook [near Harrellsville, on the Chowan River], and the lord
of that town and country is called Pooneno. This Pooneno is
not subject to the king of Wingandacoa but is a free lord.
Beyond this country is there another king, whom they call
Menatonon, and these three kings are in league with each other.
Towards the southwest, four days' journey is situate a town
called Secotan [near Bonnerton], which is the southernmost
town of Wingandacoa, near unto which, six and twenty years
past there was a ship cast away, whereof some of the people
were saved, and those were white people, whom the country
people preserved.

And after ten days remaining in an out island uninhabited
called Wocokon [south of Ocracoke Inlet], they with the help
of some of the dwellers of Secotan fastened two boats of the
country together and made masts unto them and sails of their
shirts, and having taken into them such victuals as the country
yielded, they departed after they had remained in this our
island three weeks. But shortly after it seemed they were cast
away, for the boats were found upon the coast, cast aland in
another island adjoining. Other than these, there was never
any people appareled, or white of color, either seen or heard
of amongst these people, and these aforesaid were seen only
of the inhabitants of Secotan, which appeared to be very true,
for they wondered marvelously when we were amongst them
at the whiteness of our skins, ever coveting to touch our breasts,
and to view the same. Besides they had our ships in marvelous
admiration, and all things else were so strange unto them as
it appeared that none of them had ever seen the like. When we
discharged any piece, were it but a harquebus, they would
tremble thereat for very fear, and for the strangeness of the
same. For the weapons which themselves use are bows and
arrows. The arrows are but of small canes, headed with a sharp
shell or tooth of a fish, sufficient enough to kill a naked man.
Their swords be of wood hardened. Likewise they use wooden
breastplates for their defense. They have besides a kind of club,
in the end whereof they fasten the sharp horns of a stag or other
beast. When they go to wars they carry about with them their

idol, of whom they ask counsel, as the Romans were wont of the oracle of Apollo. They sing songs as they march towards the battle instead of [playing] drums and trumpets. Their wars are very cruel and bloody, by reason whereof, and of their civil dissensions which have happened of late years amongst them, the people are marvelously wasted, and in some places the country left desolate.

Adjoining to this country aforesaid called Secotan beginneth a country called Pomovik [probably between Pamlico and Neuse rivers], belonging to another king whom they call Piamacum, and this king is in league with the next king adjoining towards the setting of the sun, and the country Newsiok, situate upon a goodly river called Neuse. These kings have mortal war with Wingina, king of Wingandacoa. But about two years past there was a peace made between King Piamacum and the lord of Secotan, as these men which we have brought with us to England have given us to understand. But there remaineth a mortal malice in the Secotans, for many injuries and slaughters done upon them by this Piamacum. They invited divers men and thirty women of the best of this country to their town to a feast. And when they were altogether merry, and praying before their idol (which is nothing else but a mere illusion of the devil), the captain or lord of the town came suddenly upon them, and slew them every one, reserving the women and children. And these two have oftentimes since persuaded us to surprise Piamacum's town, having promised and assured us that there will be found in it great store of commodities. But whether their persuasion be to the end they may be revenged of their enemies or the love they bear to us, we leave that to the trial hereafter.

Beyond this island called Roanoke are main islands very plentiful of fruits and other natural increases, together with many towns and villages along the side of the continent, some bounding upon the islands and some stretching up further into the land.

When we first had sight of this country, some thought the first land we saw to be the continent. But after we entered into the haven, we saw before us another mighty long sea. For there lieth along the coast a tract of islands, two hundred miles in length, adjoining to the ocean sea, and between the islands, two or three entrances. When you are entered between them (these islands being very narrow for the most part, as in most places six miles broad, in some places less, in few more) then there appeareth another great sea, containing in breadth in some places forty and in some fifty, in some twenty miles over, before you come unto the continent. And in this enclosed sea there are above a hundred islands of divers bigness, whereof one is sixteen miles long, at which we were, finding it a most pleasant and fertile ground, replenished with goodly cedars and divers sweet woods, full of currants, of flax, and many other notable commodities, which we at that time had no leisure to view. Besides this island there are many, as I have said, some of two, of three, of four, of five miles, some more, some less, most beautiful and pleasant to behold, replenished with deer, conies, hares, and divers beasts, and about them the goodliest and best fish in the world, and in greatest abundance.

Thus, sir, we have acquainted you with the particulars of our discovery made this present voyage as far forth as the shortness of the time we there continued would afford us [to] take view of. And so contenting ourselves with this service at this time, which we hope hereafter to enlarge, as occasion and assistance shall be given, we resolved to leave the country and to apply ourselves to return to England, which we did accordingly, and arrived safely in the west of England about the midst of September. . . .

3.

An Extract of Master Ralph Lane's Letter to M[aster] Richard Hakluyt, Esquire, and Another Gentleman of the Middle Temple, from Virginia.

In the meanwhile, you shall understand that since Sir Richard Grenville's departure from us, as also before, we have discovered the main to be the goodliest soil under the cope [vault] of heaven, so abounding with sweet trees that bring such sundry rich and pleasant gums, grapes of such greatness, yet wild, as France, Spain, nor Italy have no greater, so many sorts of apothecary drugs, such several kinds of flax, and one kind like silk, the same gathered of a grass as common there as grass is here. And now within these few days we have found here maize or guinea wheat, whose ear yieldeth corn for bread, four hundred upon one ear, and the cane maketh very good and perfect sugar; also *terra samia,* otherwise *terra sigillata* [two types of earth valued for their healing properties]. Besides that, it is the goodliest and most pleasing territory of the world; for the continent is of a huge and unknown greatness, and very well peopled and towned, though savagely, and the climate so wholesome that we had not one sick since we touched the land here. To conclude, if Virginia had but horses and kine [cattle] in some reasonable proportion, I dare assure myself, being inhabited with English, no realm in Christendom were comparable to it.

For this already we find that what commodities soever Spain, France, Italy, or the East parts do yield unto us, in wines of all sorts, in oils, in flax, in rosins, pitch, frankincense, currants, sugars, and such like, these parts do abound with the growth of them all; but, being savages that possess the land, they know no use of the same. And sundry other rich commodities that no parts of the world, be they West or East Indies, have, here we find great abundance of. The people naturally are most courteous, and very desirous to have clothes, but especially of coarse cloth rather than silk; coarse canvas they also like well of, but copper carrieth the price of all, so it be made red. Thus good Master Hakluyt and M. H., I have joined you both in one letter of remembrance, as two that I love dearly well, and commending me most heartily to you both, I commit you to the tuition of the Almighty. From the new fort in Virginia, this third of September, 1585.

Your most assured friend,
RALPH LANE

4.
An Account of the Particularities of the Employments of the Englishmen Left in Virginia

by Sir Richard Grenville under the Charge of
Master Ralph Lane, General of the Same, from the
Seventeenth of August, 1585, Until the Eighteenth
of June, 1586, at Which Time They Departed the
Country. Sent [by Lane] and Directed
to Sir Walter Raleigh.

That I may proceed with order in this discourse, I think it requisite to divide it into two parts. The first shall declare the particularities of such parts of the country within the main, as our weak number and supply of things necessary did enable us to enter into the discovery of.

The second part shall set down the reasons generally moving us to resolve on our departure at the instant with the general, Sir Francis Drake, and our common request for passage with him, when the barks, pinnaces, and boats with the masters and mariners meant by him to be left in the country for the supply of such as for a further time meant to have stayed there, were carried away with tempest and foul weather. In the beginning whereof shall be declared the conspiracy of Pemisapan, with the savages of the main to have cut us off, etc.

THE FIRST PART DECLARING THE
PARTICULARITIES OF THE COUNTRY OF VIRGINIA.

First, therefore touching the particularities of the country, you shall understand that our discovery of the same hath been extended from the island of Roanoke (the same having been the place of our settlement or inhabitation) into the south, into the north, into the northwest, and into the west.

The uttermost place to the southward of any discovery was Secotan, being by estimation four score miles distant from Roanoke. The passage from thence was through a broad sound within the main, the same being without kenning [range of sight] of land and yet full of flats and shoals. We had but one boat with four oars to pass through the same, which boat could not carry above fifteen men with their furniture, baggage, and victual for seven days at the most. And as for our pinnace, besides that she drew too deep water for that shallow sound, she would not stir for an oar. For these and other reasons (winter also being at hand) we thought good wholly to leave the discovery of those parts until our stronger supply.

To the northward [starting up Currituck Sound] our furtherest discovery was to the Chesepians, distant from Roanoke about 130 miles. The passage to it [at or near Cape Henry] was very shallow and most dangerous, by reason of the breadth of the sound and the little succor that upon any flaw was there to be had.

But the territory [vicinity of Norfolk County, Virginia] and soil of the Chesepians (being distant fifteen miles from the shore) was for pleasantness of seat, for temperature of climate, for fertility of soil, and for the commodity of the sea, besides multitude of bears (being an excellent good victual) with great woods of sassafras and walnut trees, not to be excelled by any other whatsoever.

There be sundry king, whom they call werowances, and countries of great fertility adjoining to the same, [to the west and southwest of Norfolk County] as the Mandoages, Tripanicks, and Opossians, which all came to visit the colony of the English, which I had for a time appointed to be resident there.

To the northwest the farthest place of our discovery was to Chawanook, distant from Roanoke about 130 miles. Our passage thither lieth through a broad sound, but all fresh water, and the channel of a great depth, navigable for good shipping but out of the channel full of shoals.

The towns about the water's side situated by the way are those following: Passaquenoke, the woman's town; Chepanoc; Weapomeiok; Muscamunge [all four along north shore of Albemarle Sound]; and Metackwem [probably near Edenhouse, North Carolina]; all these being under the jurisdiction of the king of Weapomeiok [North Carolina counties north of Albemarle Sound], called Okisco. From Muscamunge we enter into the river and jurisdiction of Chawanook. There the river beginneth to straighten until it come to Chawanook and then groweth to be as narrow as the Thames between Westminster and Lambeth.

Between Muscamunge and Chawanook upon the left hand as we pass thither is a goodly high land, and there is a town which we called the blind town but the savages called it Ohanoak, and hath a very goodly cornfield belonging unto it. It is subject to Chawanook.

Chawanook itself is the greatest province and seigniory lying upon that river, and the very town itself is able to put seven hundred fighting men into the field, besides the force of the province itself.

The king of the said province is called Menatonon, a man impotent in his limbs but otherwise for a savage a very grave and wise man and of a very singular good discourse in matters concerning the state, not only of his own country and the disposition of his own men but also of his neighbors round about him as well far as near, and of the commodities that each country yieldeth. When I had him prisoner with me for two days that we were together he gave me more understanding and light of the country than I had received by all the searches and savages that before I or any of my company had had conference with. It was in March last past, 1586. Amongst other things he told me that going three days' journey in a canoe up his river of Chawanook and then descending to the land you are within four days' journey to pass overland northeast to a certain king's country whose province lieth upon the sea, but his place of greatest strength is an island situate, as he described unto me, in a bay, the water round about the island very deep.

Out of this bay he signified unto me that this king had so great quantity of pearl, and doeth so ordinarily take the same, as that not only his own skins that he weareth and the better sort of his gentlemen and followers are full set with the said pearl, but also his beds and houses are garnished with them, and that he hath such quantity of them that it is a wonder to see.

He showed me that the said king was with him at Chawanook two years before and brought him certain pearl but the same of the worst sort, yet was he fain to buy them of him for copper at a dear rate, as he thought. He gave me a rope of the same pearl, but they were black and naught [worthless], yet many of them were very great and a few amongst a number very orient [lustrous], and round, all which I lost with other things of mine, coming aboard Sir Francis Drake's fleet. Yet he told me that the said king had great store of pearl that were white, great, and round, and that his black pearl his men did take out of shallow water, but the white pearl his men fished for in very deep water.

It seemed to me by his speech that the said king had traffic with white men that had clothes as we have for these white pearl, and that was the reason that he would not depart with other than with black pearls to those of the same country.

The king of Chawanook promised to give me guides to go overland into that king's country whensoever I would, but he advised me to take good store of men with me and good store of victual, for he said that king would be loath to suffer any strangers to enter into his country, and especially to meddle with the fishing for any pearl there, and that he was able to make a great many of men into the field, which he said would fight very well.

Hereupon I resolved with myself that, if your supply had còme before the end of April and that you had sent any store of boats, or men to have had them made in any reasonable time, with a sufficient number of men and victuals to have found us until the new corn were come in, I would have sent a small bark with two pinnaces about by sea to the northward to have found out the bay he spoke of and to have sounded the bar, if there were any, which should have ridden there in the said bay about that island, while I with all the small boats I could make and with two hundred men would have gone up to the head of the river of Chawanook with the guides that Mena-tonon would have given me, which I would have been assured should have been of his best men, for I had his best beloved son prisoner with me, who also should have kept me company in a handlock [handcuff] with the rest, foot by foot, all the voyage overland.

My meaning was further at the head of the river in the place of my descent where I would have left my boats to have raised a sconce [a small fort or earthwork] with a small trench and a palisado upon the top of it, in the which and in the guard of my boats I would have left five and twenty or thirty men; with the rest would I have marched with as much victual as every man could have carried, with their furniture, mattocks, spades, and axes, two days' journey. In the end of my march upon some convenient plot would I have raised another sconce according to the former, where I would have left fifteen or twenty. And if it would have fallen out conveniently, in the way I would have raised my said sconce upon some cornfield, that my company might have lived upon it.

And so I would have holden this course of ensconcing every two days' march until I had been arrived at the bay or port he spoke of; which finding to be worth the possession I would have raised a main fort, both for the defense of the harbor and our shipping also, and would have reduced our whole habitation from Roanoke and from the harbor and port there (which by proof is very naught) unto this other before mentioned, from whence in the four days' march before specified could I at all times return with my company back unto my boats riding under my sconce, very near whereunto directly from the west runneth a most notable river, and in all those parts most famous called the river of Moratoc [Roanoke]. This river openeth into the broad sound of Weapomeiok. And whereas the river of Chawanook, and all the other sounds and bays, salt and fresh, show no current in the world in calm weather but are moved altogether with the wind, this river of Moratoc hath so violent a current from the west and southwest that it made me almost of opinion that with oars it would scarce be navigable. It passeth with many creeks and turnings and for the space of thirty miles rowing and more it is as broad as the Thames betwixt Greenwich and the Isle of Dogs, in some place more and in some less. The current runneth as strong, being entered so high into the river as at London Bridge upon a vale of water.

And for that not only Menatonon but also the savages of Moratoc themselves do report strange things of the head of that river, and that from Moratoc itself, which is a principal town upon that river, it is thirty days', as some of them say, and some say forty days' voyage to the head thereof, which head they say springeth out of a main rock in that abundance that forthwith it maketh a most violent stream. And further, that this huge rock standeth so near unto a sea that many times in storms (the wind coming outwardly from the sea) the waves thereof are beaten into the said fresh stream, so that the fresh water for a certain space groweth salt and brackish.

I took a resolution with myself, having dismissed Menatonon upon a ransom agreed for, and sent his son into the pinnace to Roanoke, to enter presently so far into that river [Roanoke] with two double wherries and forty persons one or other, as I could have victual to carry us, until we could meet with more either of the Moratocs or of the Mangoaks, which is another kind of savage, dwelling more to the westward of the said river. But the hope of recovering more victual from the savages made me and my company as narrowly to escape starving in that discovery before our return as ever men did that missed the same.

For Pemisapan, who had changed his name of Wingina upon the death of his brother Granganimeo, had given both the Choanists and Mangoaks word of my purpose touching them, I having been enforced to make him privy to the same, to be served by him of a guide to the Mangoaks, and yet he did never rest to solicit continually my going upon them, certifying me of a general assembly even at that time made by Menatonon at Chawanook of all his werowances and allies to the number of three thousand bows, preparing to come upon us at Roanoke, and that the Mangoaks also were joined in the same confederacy, who were able of themselves to bring as many more to the enterprise. And true it was that at that time the assembly was holden at Chawanook about us, as I found at my coming thither, which being unlooked for did so dismay them as it made us have the better hand at them. But this confederacy against us of the Choanists and Mangoaks was altogether and wholly procured by Pemisapan himself, as Menatonon confessed unto me, who sent them continual word that our purpose was fully bent to destroy them. On the other side he told me that they had the like meaning towards us.

He in like sort having sent word to the Mangoaks of mine intention to pass up into their river and to kill them (as he said), both they and the Moratocs, with whom before we were entered into a league and they had ever dealt kindly with us, abandoned their towns along the river and retired themselves with their crenepos [women] and their corn within the main. Insomuch as having passed three days' voyage up the river we could not meet a man nor find a grain of corn in any of their towns. Whereupon considering with myself that we had but two days' victual left and that we were then 160 miles from home, besides casualty of contrary winds or storms and suspecting treason of our own savages in the discovery of our voyage intended, though we had no intention to be hurtful to any of them, otherwise than for our copper to have had corn of them, I at night upon the corps of guard before the putting forth of sentinels, advertised the whole company of the case we stood in for victual and of mine opinion that we were betrayed by our own savages and of purpose drawn forth by them upon vain hope to be in the end starved, seeing all the country fled before us, and therefore while we had those two days' victual left, I thought it good for us to make our return homeward and that it were necessary for us to get the other side of the sound of Weapomeiok in time, where we might be relieved upon the weirs of Chipanum [Chepanoc] and the women's town, although the people were fled.

Thus much I signified unto them as the safest way. Nevertheless, I did refer it to the greatest number of voices whether we should adventure the spending of our whole victual in some further view of that most goodly river in hope to meet with some better hap or otherwise to retire ourselves back again. And for that they might be the better advised, I willed them to deliberate all night upon the matter and in the morning at our going aboard to set our course according to the desires of the greatest part. Their resolution fully and wholly was (and not three found to be of the contrary opinion) that whiles there was left but one half pint of corn for a man, we should not leave the search of that river and that there were in the company two mastiffs upon the pottage of which with sassafras leaves (if the worst fell out) the company would make shift to live two days, which time would bring them down the current to the mouth of the river, and to the entry of the sound, and in two days more at the farthest they hoped to cross the sound and to be relieved by the weirs which two days would fast rather than be drawn back a foot till they had seen the Mangoaks, either as friends or foes. This resolution of theirs did not a little please me since it came of themselves, although for mistrust of that which afterwards did happen I pretended to have been rather of the contrary opinion.

And that which made me most desirous to have some doings with the Mangoaks either in friendship or otherwise to have had one or two of them prisoners, was, for that it is a thing most notorious to all the country, that there is a province to the which the said Mangoaks have recourse and traffic up that river of Moratoc, which hath a marvelous and most strange mineral. This mine is so notorious amongst them as not only to the savages dwelling up the said river and also to the savages of Chawanook and all them to the westward but also to all them of the main. The country's name is of fame and is called Chaunis Temoatan [location, real or imagined, is questionable].

The mineral they say is wassador, which is copper, but they call by the name of wassador every metal whatsoever. They say it is of the color of our copper, but our copper is better than theirs. And the reason is for that it is redder and harder, whereas that of Chaunis Temoatan is very soft and pale. They say that they take the said metal out of a river that falleth very swift from high rocks and hills, and they take it in shallow water. The manner is this: they take a great bowl, by their description as great as one of our targets, and wrap a skin over the hollow part thereof, leaving one part open to receive in the mineral. That done, they watch the coming down of the current and the change of the color of the water, and then suddenly chop down the said bowl with the skin and receive into the same as much ore as will come in, which is ever as much as their bowl will hold, which presently they cast into a fire and forthwith it melteth and doeth yield in five parts at the first melting, two parts of metal for three parts of ore. Of this metal the Mangoaks have so great store, by report of all the savages adjoining, that they beautify their houses with great plates of the same. And this to be true, I received by report of all the country, and particularly by young Skiko, the king of Chawanook's son, my prisoner, who also himself had been prisoner with the Mangoaks and set down all the particularities to me before mentioned. But he had not been at Chaunis Temoatan himself, for he said it was twenty days' journey overland from the Mangoaks to the said mineral country and that they passed through certain other territories between them and the Mangoaks before they came to the said country.

Upon report of the premises which I was very inquisitive in all places where I came to take very particular information of, by all the savages that dwelt towards those parts, and especially Menatonon himself, who in everything did very particularly inform me and promised me guides of his own men, who should pass over with me even to the said country of Chaunis Temoatan (for overland from Chawanook to the Mangoaks is but one day's journey from sun rising to sun setting, whereas by water it is seven days with the soonest). These things, I say, made me very desirous by all means possible to recover the Mangoaks and to get some of that their copper for an assay, and therefore I willingly yielded to their resolution. But it fell out very contrary to all expectation and likelihood, for after two days' travel and our whole victual spent, lying on shore all night, we could never see man, only fires we might perceive made alongst the shore where we were to pass, and up into the country, until the very last day. In the evening whereof about three of the clock we heard certain savages call as we thought, "Manteo," who was also at that time with me in the boat, whereof we all being very glad, hoping of some friendly conference with them and making him to answer them, they presently began a song, as we thought, in token of our welcome to them. But Manteo presently betook him to his piece [weapon] and told me that they meant to fight with us. Which word was not so soon spoken by him and the light horsemen ready to put to shore but there lighted a volley of their arrows amongst them in the boat, but did no hurt (God be thanked) to any man. Immediately, the other boat lying ready with their shot to scour the place for our hand weapons to land upon, which was presently done, although the land was very high and steep. The savages forthwith quitted the shore and betook themselves to flight. We landed, and having fair and easily followed for a small time after them, who had wooded themselves we know not where, the sun drawing then towards the setting, and being then assured that the next day if we would pursue them, though we might happen to meet with them, yet we should be assured to meet with none of their victual, which we then had good cause to think of, therefore choosing for the company a convenient ground in safety to lodge in for the night, making a strong corps of guard and putting

out good sentinels, I determined the next morning before the
rising of the sun to be going back again, if possibly we might
recover the mouth of the river, into the broad sound, which at
my first motion I found my whole company ready to assent
unto. For they were now come to their dogs' porridge that they
had bespoken for themselves if that befell them which did, and
I before did mistrust we should hardly escape. The end was,
we came the next day by night to the river's mouth within four
or five miles of the same, having rowed in one day down the
current as much as in four days we had done against the same.
We lodged upon an island, where we had nothing in the world
to eat but pottage of sassafras leaves, the like whereof for a meat
was never used before as I think. The broad sound we had to
pass the next day all fresh and fasting. That day the wind blew
so strongly, and the billow so great that there was no possibility
of passage without sinking of our boats. This was upon Easter
eve, which was fasted very truly. Upon Easter day in the morning the wind coming very calm we entered the sound and by
four of the clock we were at Chipanum, whence all the savages
that we had left there were fled but their weirs did yield us
some fish, as God was pleased not utterly to suffer us to be lost;
for some of our company of the light horsemen were far spent.
The next morning we arrived at our home Roanoke.

I have set down this voyage somewhat particularly to the end
it may appear unto you (as true it is) that there wanted no great
good will from the most to the least amongst us to have perfited
[accomplished] this discovery of the mine. For that the discovery of a good mine by the goodness of God or a passage to
the South Sea, or some way to it, and nothing else can bring
this country in request [demand] to be inhabited by our nation.
And with the discovery of either of the two above showed, it
will be the most sweet and healthfullest climate, and therewithal the most fertile soil (being manured) in the world; and
then will sassafras and many other roots and gums there found
make good merchandise and lading for shipping, which otherwise of themselves will not be worth the fetching.

Provided also that there be found out a better harbor than yet
there is, which must be to the northward, if any there be, which
was mine intention to have spent this summer in the search of,

and of the mine of Chaunis Temoatan. The one I would have
done if the barks that I should have had of Sir Francis Drake
by his honorable courtesy had not been driven away by storm;
the other if your supply of more men and some other necessaries
had come to us in any convenient sufficiency. For this river of
Moratico promiseth great things, and by the opinion of Master
Hariot the head of it by the description of the country either
riseth from the Bay of Mexico or else from very near unto the
same that openeth out into the South Sea.

And touching the mineral, thus doeth Master Youghan affirm
that though it be but copper, seeing the savages are able to
melt it, it is one of the richest minerals in the world.

Wherefore a good harbor found to the northward, as before
said, and from thence four days overland to the river of Choanoak [Chowan] sconces being raised, from whence again overland through the province of Choanoak one day's voyage to the
first town of the Mangoaks up the river of Moratico by the way,
as also upon the said river for the defense of our boats like
sconces being set, in this course of proceeding you shall clear
yourself from all those dangers and broad shallow sounds before
mentioned, and gain within four days' travel into the heart of the
main two hundred miles at the least and so pass your discovery
into that most notable country, and to the likeliest parts of the
main with far greater felicity than otherwise can be performed.

Thus, sir, I have though simply yet truly set down unto you
what my labor with the rest of the gentlemen and poor men of
our company (not without both pain and peril, which the Lord
in His mercy many ways delivered us from) could yield unto
you, which might have been performed in some more perfection
if the Lord had been pleased that only that which you had provided for us had at the first been left with us or that He had not
in His eternal providence now at the last set some other course
in these things than the wisdom of a man could look into, which
truly the carrying away by a most strange and unlooked for
storm of all our provision, with barks, master, mariners, and
sundry also of mine own company, all having been so courteously supplied by the general, Sir Francis Drake, the same
having been most sufficient to have performed the greatest
part of the premises must ever make me to think the hand of

God only (for some His good purpose to myself yet unknown) to have been in the matter.

THE SECOND PART TOUCHING THE CONSPIRACY OF PEMISAPAN, THE DISCOVERY OF THE SAME, AND, AT THE LAST, OF OUR REQUEST TO DEPART WITH SIR FRANCIS DRAKE FOR ENGLAND.

Ensenore, a savage, father to Pemisapan, being the only friend to our nation that we had amongst them, and about the king, died the twentieth of April, 1586. He alone had before opposed himself in their consultations against all matters proposed against us, which both the king and all the rest of them after Granganimeos's death were very willing to have preferred. And he was not only by the mere providence of God during his life a means to save us from hurt, as poisonings and such like, but also to do us very great good and singularly in this.

The king was advised and of himself disposed as a ready mean to have assuredly brought us to ruin in the month of March, 1586. Himself also with all his savages to have run away from us and to have left his ground in the island unsowed; which if he had done there had been no possibility in common reason (but by the immediate hands of God) that we could have been preserved from starving out of hand. For at that time we had no weirs for fish, neither could our men skill of the making of them, neither had we one grain of corn for seed to put into the ground.

In mine absence on my voyage that I had made against the Chaonists and Mangoaks, they had raised a bruit among themselves that I and my company were part slain and part starved by the Chaonists and Mangoaks. One part of this tale was too true—that I and mine were like to be starved—but the other false.

Nevertheless, until my return it took such effect in Pemisapan's breast and in those against us that they grew not only into contempt of us but also (contrary to their former reverend opinion in show of the Almighty God of heaven and Jesus Christ whom we serve and worship, whom before they would acknowledge and confess the only God) now they began to blaspheme and flatly to say that our Lord God was not God, since He suffered us to sustain much hunger and also to be killed of the Renapoaks, for so they call by that general name all the inhabitants of the whole main, of what province whatsoever. . . .

But even in the beginning of this bruit I returned, which when he saw contrary to his expectation, and the advertisement that he had received, that not only myself and my company were all safe but also by report of his own three savages which had been with me besides Manteo in that voyage, that is to say, Tetepano, his sister's husband Eracano, and Cossine, that the Chanoists and Mangoaks (whose name and multitude besides their valor is terrible to all the rest of the provinces) durst not for the most part of them abide [withstand] us, and that those that did abide us were killed, and that we had taken Menatonon prisoner, and brought his son that he best loved to Roanoke with me, it did not a little assuage all devices against us. On the other side, it made Ensenore's opinions to be received again with great respects. For he had often before told them, and then renewed those his former speeches, both to the king and the rest, that we were the servants of God and that we were not subject to be destroyed by them; but contrariwise, that they amongst them that sought our destruction should find their own and not be able to work ours, and that we being dead men were able to do them more hurt than now we could do being alive; an opinion very confidently at this day holden by the wisest amongst them, and of their old men, as also, that they have been in the night being one hundred miles from any of us, in the air shot at and struck by some men of ours that by sickness had died among them; and many of them hold opinion that we be dead men returned into the world again and that we do not remain dead but for a certain time, and that then we return again.

All these speeches then again grew in full credit with them, the king, and all, touching us, when he saw the small troop returned again, and in that sortie from those whose very names were terrible unto them. But that which made up the matter on our side for that time was an accident, yea rather (as all the rest was) the good providence of the Almighty for the saving of us, which was this:

Within certain days after my return from the said journey, Menatonon sent a messenger to visit his son, the prisoner with me, and sent me certain pearls for a present or rather, as Pemisapan told me, for the ransom of his son, and therefore I refused them. But the greatest cause of his sending them was to signify unto me that he had commanded Okisko, king of Weapomeiok, to yield himself servant and homager to the great werowance of England, and after her to Sir Walter Raleigh; to perform which commandement received from Menatonon, the said Okisko jointly with this Menatonon's messenger sent four and twenty of his principalest men to Roanoke to Pemisapan to signify that they were ready to perform the same, and so had sent those his men to let me know that from that time forward he and his successors were to acknowledge her Majesty their only sovereign, and next unto her, as is aforesaid.

All which being done and acknowledged by them all in the presence of Pemisapan's father, and all his savages in council then with him, it did for the time thoroughly (as it seemed) change him in disposition toward us. Insomuch as forthwith Ensenore won this resolution of him—that out of hand he should go about and withal to cause his men to set up weirs forthwith for us. Both which he at that present [time] went in hand withal and did so labor the expedition of it that in the end of April he had sowed a good quantity of ground, so much as had been sufficient to have fed our whole company (God blessing the growth) and that by the belly for a whole year. Besides that he gave us a certain plot of ground for ourselves to sow. All which put us in marvelous comfort, if we could pass from April until the beginning of July (which was to have been the beginning of their harvest) that then a new supply out of England or else our own store would well enough maintain us. All our fear was of the two months betwixt in which mean space if the savages should not help us with cassava and china [a thick, fleshy root] and that our weirs should fail us (as often they did) we might very well starve, notwithstanding the growing corn, like the starving horse in the stable with the growing grass, as the proverb is. Which we very hardly had escaped but only by the hand of God, as it pleased Him to try us. For within a few days after, as before is said, Ensenore our friend died, who was no sooner dead but certain of our great enemies about Pemisapan, as Osacan, a werowance, Tanaquiny and Wanchese most principally, were in hand again to put their old practices in use against us, which were readily embraced and all their former devices against us renewed and new brought in question. But that of starving us by their forbearing to sow was broken by Ensenore in his life by having made the king all at one instant to sow his ground not only in the island but also at Dasamonquepeio in the main [opposite Roanoke Island], within two leagues over against us. Nevertheless, there wanted no store of mischievous practices among them and of all they resolved principally of this following:

First, that Okisko, king of Weapomeiok, with the Mandoages should be moved and with great quantity of copper entertained to the number of seven or eight hundred bows, to enterprise the matter thus to be ordered. They of Weapomeiok should be invited to a certain kind of month's mind [memorial service] which they do use to solemnize in their savage manner for any great personage dead, and should have been for Ensenore. At this instant also should the Mangoaks, who were a great people, with the Chesepians and their friends to the number of seven hundred of them be armed at a day appointed to the main of Dasamonquepeio, and there lying close at the sign of fires, which should interchangeably be made on both sides, when Pemisapan with his troops above named should have executed me and some of our werowances (as they called all our principal officers) the main forces of the rest should have come over into the island, where they meant to have dispatched the rest of the company, whom they did imagine to find both dismayed and dispersed abroad in the island seeking of crabs and fish to live withal. The manner of their enterprise was this:

Tarraquine and Andacon, two principal men about Pemisapan and very lusty fellows, with twenty more appointed to them, had the charge of my person to see an order taken for the same, which they meant should in this sort have been executed. In the dead time of the night they would have beset my house and put fire in the reeds that the same was covered with, meaning (as it was likely) that myself would have come running out of a sudden amazed in my shirt without arms upon the instant whereof they would have knocked out my brains.

The same order was given to certain of his fellows, for Master Hariot, [and] so for all the rest of our better sort, all our houses at one instant being set on fire as afore is said, and that as well for them of the fort as for us at the town. Now to the end that we might be the fewer in number together and so be the more easily dealt withal (for indeed ten of us with our arms prepared were a terror to a hundred of the best sort of them), they agreed and did immediately put it in practice that they should not for any copper sell us any victuals whatsoever. Besides that in the night they should send to have our weirs robbed and also to cause them to be broken, and once being broken never to be repaired again by them. By this means the king stood assured that I must be enforced for lack of sustenance there to disband my company into sundry places to live upon shellfish, for so the savages themselves do, going to Hatteras [Island], Croatoan [Ocracoke Island], and other places, fishing and hunting while their grounds be in sowing and their corn growing; which failed not his expectation. For the famine grew so extreme among us, our weirs failing us of fish, that I was enforced to send Captain Stafford with twenty with him to Croatoan, my lord admiral's island, to serve two turns in one; that is to say, to feed himself and his company and also to keep watch if any shipping came upon the coast to warn us of the same. I sent Master Pridiox with the pinnace to Hatteras and ten with him with the provost marshal to live there, and also to wait for shipping. Also I sent every week sixteen or twenty of the rest of the company to the main over against us to live off casada [cassava?] and oysters.

In the meanwhile Pemisapan went of purpose to Dasamonquepeio for three causes. The one to see his grounds there broken up and sowed for a second crop; the other to withdraw himself from my daily sending to him for supply of victual for my company, for he was afraid to deny me anything, neither durst he in my presence but by color and with excuses, which I was content to accept for the time, meaning in the end as I had reason to give him the jump once for all. But in the meanwhile, as I had ever done before, I and mine bare all wrongs and accepted of all excuses.

My purpose was to have relied myself with Menatonon and the Choanists, who in truth as they are more valiant people and in greater number than the rest, so are they more faithful in their promises, and since my late being there had given many tokens of earnest desire they had to join in perfect league with us and therefore were greatly offended with Pemisapan and Weapomeiok for making him believe such tales of us.

The third cause of this going to Dasamonquepeio was to dispatch his messengers to Weapomeiok and to the Mandoages as aforesaid. All which he did with great imprest [advance payment] of copper in hand, making large promises to them of greater spoil.

The answer within few days after came from Weapomeiok, which was divided into two parts. First, for the King Okisko, who denied to be of the party for himself or any of his especial followers and therefore did immediately retire himself with his force into the main. The other was concerning the rest of the said province who accepted it. And in like sort the Mandoages received the imprest.

The day of their assembly aforesaid at Roanoke was appointed the tenth of June, all which the premises [aforesaid matters] were discovered by Skiko, the King Menatonon's son, my prisoner, who having once attempted to run away I laid him in the bilboes [ankle shackles], threatening to cut off his head, whom I remitted at Pemisapan's request. Whereupon he [Pemisapan] being persuaded that he [Skiko] was our enemy to the death, he did not only feed him with himself but also made him acquainted with all his practices. On the other side, the young man finding himself as well used at my hand as I had means to show and that all my company made much of him, he flatly discovered all unto me, which also afterwards was revealed unto me by one of Pemisapan's own men that night before he was slain.

These mischiefs being all instantly upon me and my company to be put in execution, it stood me in hand to study how to prevent them and also to save all others which were at that time as aforesaid so far from me. Whereupon I sent to Pemisapan to put suspicion out of his head that I meant presently to go to Croatoan for that I had heard of the arrival of our fleet (though I in truth had neither heard nor hoped for so good adventure) and that I meant to come by him to borrow of his men to fish for my company and to hunt for me at Croatoan as also to buy some four days' provision to serve for my voyage.

He sent me word that he would himself come over to Roanoke, but from day to day he deferred, only to bring the Weapomeioks with him and the Mandoages, whose time appointed was within eight days after. It was the last of May, 1586 when all his own savages began to make their assembly at Roanoke at his commandment sent abroad unto them, and I resolved not to stay longer upon his coming over, since he meant to come with so good company, but thought good to go the next day. But that night I meant by the way to give them in the island a camisado [night attack], and at the instant to seize upon all the cannons about the island to keep him from advertisements [warnings].

But the town took the alarm before I meant it to them. The occasion was this. I had sent the master of the light horsemen with a few with him to gather up many as were going from us to Dasamonquepeio, but to suffer any that came from thence to land. He met with a canoe going from the shore and overthrew the canoe and cut off two savages' heads. This was not done so secretly but he was discovered from the shore; whereupon the cry arose, for in truth they saw [us] privy to their own villainous purposes against us, held as good espial upon us both day and night as we did upon them.

The alarm given, they took themselves to their bows and we to our arms. Some three or four of them at the first were slain with our shot. The rest fled into the woods. The next morning, with the light horseman and one canoe taking twenty-five with the colonel of the Chesepians and the sergeant major, I went to Dasamonquepeio; and being landed sent Pemisapan word by one of his own savages that met me at the shore that I was going to Croatoan and meant to take him in the way to complain unto him of Osacan, who the night past was conveying away my prisoner, whom I had there present tied in an handlock. Hereupon the king did abide my coming to him, and finding myself amidst seven or eight of his principal werowances and followers (not regarding any of the common sort) I gave the watchword agreed upon (which was "Christ our victory") and immediately those his chief men and himself had by the mercy of God for our deliverance that which they had purposed for us. The king himself being shot through by the colonel with a pistol, lying on the ground for dead, and I looking as watchfully for the saving of Manteo's friends, as others were busy that none of the rest should escape, suddenly started up and ran away as though he had not been touched, insomuch as he overran all the company, being by the way shot thwart the buttocks by mine Irish boy with my petronel [large pistol]. In the end an Irishman serving me, one [Edward] Nugent, and the deputy provost undertook him, and following him in the woods overtook him; and I in some doubt least we had lost both the king and my man by our own negligence to have been intercepted by the savages, we met him returning out of the woods with Pemisapan's head in his hand.

This fell out the first of June, 1586, and the eighth of the same came advertisement to me from Captain Stafford, lying at my lord admiral's island, that he had discovered a great fleet of three and twenty sails, but whether they were friends or foes he could not yet discern. He advised me to stand upon as good guard as I could.

The ninth of the said month he himself came unto me, having that night before and that same day traveled by land twenty miles. And I must truly report of him from the first to the last he was the gentleman that never spared labor or peril either by land or water, fair weather or foul, to perform any service committed unto him.

He brought me a letter from the general, Sir Francis Drake, with a most bountiful and honorable offer for the supply of our necessities to the performance of the action we were entered into; and that not only of victuals, munition, and clothing, but also of barks, pinnaces, and boats. They also by him to be victualed, manned, and furnished to my contentation.

The tenth day he arrived in the road of our bad harbor. And coming there to an anchor the eleventh day, I came to him whom I found in deeds most honorable to perform that which in writing and message he had most courteously offered, he having aforehand propounded the matter to all the captains of his fleet and got their liking and consent thereto.

With such thanks unto him and his captains for his care both of us and of our action, not as the matter deserved but as I could both for my company and myself, I (being aforehand prepared what I would desire) craved at his hands that it would please him to take with him into England a number of weak and unfit men for my good action, which I would deliver to him; and in place of them to supply me of his company with oarsmen, artificers, and others.

That he would leave us so much shipping and victual as about August then next following would carry me and all my company into England, when we had discovered somewhat that for lack of needful provision in time left with us as yet remained undone.

That it would please him withal to leave some sufficient masters not only to carry us into England when time should be but also to search the coast for some better harbor if there were any and especially to help us to some small boats and oarsmen.

Also for a supply of calivers, hand weapons, match and lead, tools, apparel, and such like.

He having received these my requests, according to his usual commendable manner of government (as it was told me) calling his captains to council; the resolution was that I should send such of my officers of my company as I used in such matters, with their notes, to go aboard with him; which were the master of the victuals, the keeper of the store, and the vice-treasurer; to whom he appointed forthwith for me the *Francis,* being a very proper bark of seventy ton, and took present order for bringing of victual aboard her for one hundred men for four months, with all my other demands whatsoever to the uttermost.

And further, he appointed for me two pinnaces and four small boats. And that which was to perform all his former liberality towards us was that he had gotten the full assents of two of as sufficient experimented masters as were any in his fleet, by judgment of them that knew them, with very sufficient gings [ship's crews] to tarry with me and to employ themselves most earnestly in the action as I should appoint them until the term which I promised of our return into England again. The names of one of those masters was Abraham Kendall, the other Griffith Herne.

While these things were in hand, the provision aforesaid being brought and in bringing aboard my said masters being also gone aboard my said barks having accepted of their charge, and mine own officers with others in like sort of my company with them (all which was dispatched by the said general the twelfth of the said month), the thirteenth of the same there arose such an unwonted storm and continued four days that had like to have driven all on shore if the Lord had not held His holy hand over them and the general very providently forseen the worst himself, then about my dispatch putting himself aboard. But in the end having driven sundry of the fleet to put to sea, the *Francis* also with all my provisions, my two masters, and my company aboard, she was seen to be free from the same and to put clear to sea.

This storm having continued from the thirteenth to the sixteenth of the month, and thus my bark put away as aforesaid, the general coming ashore made a new proffer unto me; which was a ship of 170 ton, called the bark *Bonner*, with a sufficient master and guide to tarry with me the time appointed and victualed sufficiently to carry me and my company into England, with all provisions as before. But he told me that he would not for anything undertake to have her brought into our harbor, and therefore he was to leave her in the road and to leave the care of the rest unto myself, and advised me to consider with my company of our case, and to deliver presently unto him in writing what I would require him to do for us, which being within his power, he did assure me (as well for his captains as for himself) should be most willingly performed.

Hereupon calling such captains and gentlemen of my company as then were at hand who were all as privy as myself to the general's offer, their whole request was to me that, considering the case that we stood in, the weakness of our company, the small number of the same, the carrying away of our first appointed bark with those two especial masters, with our principal provisions in the same, by the very hand of God as it seemed, stretched out to take us from thence; considering also that his second offer though most honorable of his part yet of ours not to be taken, insomuch as there was no possibility for her with any safety to be brought into the harbor; seeing furthermore our hope for supply with Sir Richard Grenville so undoubtedly promised us before Easter not yet come, neither then likely to come this year considering the doings in England for Flanders and also for America, that therefore I would resolve myself with my company to go into England in that fleet, and accordingly to make request to the general in all our names that he would be pleased to give us present passage with him. Which request of ours by myself delivered unto him, he most readily assented unto. And so he sending immediately his pinnaces unto our island for the fetching away of a few that there were left with our baggage, the weather was so boisterous and the pinnaces so often on ground that the most of all we had with all our cards, books, and writings were by the sailors cast overboard, the greater number of the fleet being much aggrieved with their long and dangerous abode in that miserable road.

From whence the general in the name of the Almighty weighing his anchors (having bestowed us among his fleet) for the relief of whom he had in that storm sustained more peril of wrack than in all his former most honorable actions against the Spaniards, with praises unto God for all, set sail the nineteenth of June, 1586, and arrived in Portsmouth the seven and twentieth of July the same year.

5.
The Third Voyage Made by a Ship
Sent in the Year 1586
to the Relief of the Colony Planted in Virginia
at the Sole Charge of Sir Walter Raleigh.
[Written by Hakluyt.]

In the year of our Lord 1586 Sir Walter Raleigh at his own charge prepared a ship of a hundred ton, freighted with all manner of things in most plentiful manner for the supply and relief of his colony then remaining in Virginia. But before they set sail from England it was after Easter, so that our colony half despaired of the coming of any supply; wherefore every man prepared for himself, determining resolutely to spend the residue of their lifetime in that country. And for the better performance of this their determination, they sowed, planted, and set such things as were necessary for their relief in so plentiful a manner as might have sufficed them two years without any further labor. Thus trusting to their own harvest,

they passed the summer till the tenth of June, at which time
their corn which they had sowed was within one fortnight of
reaping. But then it happened that Sir Francis Drake in his
prosperous return from the sacking of Santo Domingo, Cartagena, and Saint Augustine determined in his way homeward to
visit his countrymen, the English colony then remaining in
Virginia. So passing along the coasts of Florida, he fell with the
parts where our English colony inhabited, and having espied
some of that company, there he anchored and went aland,
where he conferred with them of their state and welfare and
how things had passed with them. They answered him that
they lived all, but hitherto in some scarcity, and as yet could
hear of no supply out of England. Therefore they requested
him that he would leave with them some two or three ships,
that if in some reasonable time they heard not out of England
they might then return themselves. Which he agreed to. Whilst
some were then writing their letters to send into England and
some others making reports of the accidents of their travels
each to other, some on land, some on board, a great storm arose
and drove the most of their fleet from their anchors to sea, in
which ships at that instant were the chiefest of the English
colony. The rest on land perceiving this, hasted to those three
sails which were appointed to be left there; and for fear they
should be left behind they left all things confusedly, as if they
had been chased from thence by a mighty army. And no doubt
so they were, for the hand of God came upon them for the
cruelty and outrages committed by some of them against the
native inhabitants of that country.

Immediately after the departing of our English colony out of
this paradise of the world, the ship above mentioned sent and
set forth at the charge of Sir Walter Raleigh and his direction
arrived at Hatteras; who after some time spent in seeking our
colony up in the country and not finding them returned with
all the aforesaid provision into England.

About fourteen or fifteen days after the departure of the
aforesaid ship, Sir Richard Grenville, general of Virginia, accompanied with three ships well appointed for the same
voyage, arrived there; who, not finding the aforesaid ship
according to his expectation nor hearing any news of our

English colony there seated and left by him Anno [Domini] 1585, himself traveling up into divers places of the country as well to see if he could hear any news of the colony left there by him the year before under the charge of Master Lane, his deputy, as also to discover some places of the country, but after some time spent therein, not hearing any news of them and finding the places which they inhabited desolate, yet unwilling to lose the possession of the country which Englishmen had so long held, after good deliberation he determined to leave some men behind to retain possession of the country. Whereupon he landed fifteen men in the isle of Roanoke, furnished plentifully with all manner of provision for two years, and so departed for England.

Not long after he fell with the islands of Azores on some of which islands he landed and spoiled the towns of all such things as were worth carriage, where also he took divers Spaniards. With these and many other exploits done by him in this voyage, as well outward as homeward, he returned into England.

6.

The Fourth Voyage Made to Virginia with Three Ships in the Year 1587, Wherein Was Transported the Second Colony. [Written by John White.]

In the year of our Lord 1587 Sir Walter Raleigh, intending to persevere in the planting of his country of Virginia, prepared a new colony of 150 men to be sent thither, under the charge of John White, whom he appointed governor, and also appointed unto him twelve assistants, unto whom he gave a charter, and incorporated them by the name of governor and assistants of the City of Raleigh in Virginia.

Our fleet being in number three sails, viz., the admiral, a ship of 120 tons, a flyboat, and a pinnace, departed the six and twentieth of April from Portsmouth. . . .

The fifth of May, at nine of the clock at night we came to Plymouth, where we remained the space of two days.

The eighth we anchored at Plymouth, and departed thence for Virginia.

The sixteenth Simon Ferdinando, master of our admiral, lewdly forsook our flyboat, leaving her distressed in the bay of Portugal.

The nineteenth [of June] we fell with Dominica, and the same evening we sailed between it and Guadaloupe. . . .

About the sixteenth of July we fell with the main of Virginia, which Simon Ferdinando took to be the island of Croatoan, where we came to anchor, and rode there two or three days. But finding himself deceived, he weighed and bare along the coast, where in the night, had not Captain Stafford been more careful in looking out than our Simon Ferdinando, we had been all cast away upon the breach [surf made by the breaking of waves], called the Cape of Fear, for we were come within two cables' length upon it. Such was the carelessness and ignorance of our master.

The two and twentieth of July we arrived safe at Hatteras, where our ship and pinnace anchored. The governor went aboard the pinnace, accompanied with forty of his best men, intending to pass up to Roanoke forthwith, hoping there to find those fifteen Englishmen, which Sir Richard Grenville had left there the year before, with whom he meant to have conference concerning the state of the country and savages, meaning after he had so done to return again to the fleet and pass along the coast to the bay of Chesapeake, where we intended to make our seat and fort, according to the charge given us, among other directions, in writing under the hand of Sir Walter Raleigh. But as soon as we were put with our pinnace from the ship, a gentleman by the means [agency] of Ferdinando, who was appointed to return for England, called to the sailors in the pinnace, charging them not to bring any of the planters back again but to leave them in the island, except the governor and two or three such as he approved, saying that the summer was far spent, wherefore he would land all the planters in no other place. Unto this were all the sailors, both in the pinnace and ship, persuaded by the master, wherefore it booted not the governor to contend with them, but passed to Roanoke, and the same night at sunset went aland on the island, in the place where our fifteen men were left. But we found none of them, nor any sign that they had been there, saving only we found the bones of one of those fifteen, which the savages had slain long before.

The three and twentieth of July the governor with divers of his company walked to the north end of the island where Master Ralph Lane had his fort with sundry necessary and decent dwelling houses, made by his men about it the year before, where we hoped to find some signs or certain knowledge of our fifteen men. When we came thither, we found the fort razed down, but all the houses standing unhurt, saving that the nether rooms of them, and also of the fort, were overgrown with melons of divers sorts and deer within them feeding on those melons. So we returned to our company without hope of ever seeing any of the fifteen men living.

The same day order was given that every man should be employed for the repairing of those houses which we found standing and also to make other new cottages for such as should need.

The twenty-fifth [of July] our flyboat and the rest of our planters arrived all safe at Hatteras to the great joy and comfort of the whole company. But the master of our admiral, Ferdinando, grieved greatly at their safe coming; for he purposely left them in the bay of Portugal and stole away from them in the night, hoping that the master thereof, whose name was Edward Spicer, for that he never had been in Virginia, would hardly find the place, or else being left in so dangerous a place as that was, by means of so many men-of-war as at that time were abroad, they would surely be taken or slain. But God disappointed his wicked pretenses [purposes].

The eight and twentieth, George Howe, one of our twelve assistants, was slain by divers savages, which were come over to Roanoke, either of purpose to espy our company and what number we were or else to hunt deer, whereof were many in the island. These savages being secretly hidden among high reeds, where oftentimes they find the deer asleep and so kill them, espied our man wading in the water alone, almost naked, without any weapon, save only a small forked stick, catching crabs therewithal, and also being strayed two miles from his company, and shot at him in the water, where they gave him sixteen wounds with their arrows. And after they had slain him with their wooden swords, they beat his head in pieces, and fled over the water to the main.

On the thirtieth of July Master Stafford and twenty of our men passed by water to the island of Croatoan, with Manteo, who had his mother and many of his kindred dwelling in that island, of whom we hoped to understand some news of our fifteen men, but especially to learn the disposition of the people of the country towards us and to renew our old friendship with them. At our first landing they seemed as though they would fight with us; but perceiving us begin to march with our shot towards them, they turned their backs and fled. Then Manteo, their countryman, called to them in their own language, whom as soon as they heard, they returned and threw away their bows and arrows, and some of them came unto us, embracing and entertaining us friendly, desiring us not to gather or spill any of their corn, for that they had but little. We answered them, that neither their corn nor any other thing of theirs, should be diminished by any of us, and that our coming was only to renew the old love that was between us and them at the first, and to live with them as brethren and friends. Which answer seemed to please them well, wherefore they requested us to walk up to their town, who there feasted us after their manner and desired us earnestly that there might be some token or badge given them of us, whereby we might know them to be our friends, when we met them anywhere out of the town or island. They told us further that for want of some such badge divers of them were hurt the year before, being found out of the island by Master Lane's company, whereof they showed us one, which at that very instant lay lame and had lain of that hurt ever since. But they said they knew our men mistook them and hurt them instead of Wingina's men, wherefore they held us excused.

The next day we had conference further with them, concerning the people of Secotan, Aquascogoc [near the town of Scranton], and Pomeiock, willing them of Croatoan to certify the people of those towns that if they would accept our friendship we would willingly receive them again and that all

unfriendly dealings past on both parts should be utterly
forgiven and forgotten. To this the chief men of Croatoan
answered that they would gladly do the best they could, and
within seven days bring the werowances and chief governors
of those towns with them to our governor at Roanoke, or their
answer. We also understood of the men of Croatoan that our
man Master Howe was slain by the remnant of Wingina's men
dwelling then at Dasamonquepeio, with whom Wanchese kept
company. And also we understood by them of Croatoan how
that the fifteen Englishmen left at Roanoke the year before by
Sir Richard Grenville were suddenly set upon by thirty of the
men of Secotan, Aquascogoc, and Dasamonquepeio in manner
following. They conveyed themselves secretly behind the trees
near the houses where our men carelessly lived; and having
perceived that of those fifteen they could see but eleven only,
two of those savages appeared to the eleven Englishmen, calling to them by friendly signs that but two of their chiefest
men should come unarmed to speak with those two savages,
who seemed also to be unarmed. Wherefore two of the chiefest
Englishmen went gladly to them. But whilst one of those
savages traitorously embraced one of our men, the other with
his sword of wood, which he had secretly hidden under his
mantle, struck him on the head and slew him, and presently
the other eight and twenty savages showed themselves. The
other Englishman perceiving this fled to his company, whom
the savages pursued with their bows and arrows, so fast that
the Englishmen were forced to take the house, wherein all
their victual and weapons were. But the savages forthwith set
the same on fire; by means whereof our men were forced to
take up such weapons as came first to hand and without order
to run forth among the savages, with whom they skirmished
above an hour. In this skirmish another of our men was shot
into the mouth with an arrow, where he died. And also one of
the savages was shot into the side by one of our men, with a
wild fire arrow, whereof he died presently. The place where
they fought was of great advantage which the savages through
their nimbleness defended themselves and so offended our men
with their arrows that our men being some of them hurt retired
fighting to the waterside, where their boat lay, with which

they fled towards Hatteras. By that time they had rowed but a quarter of a mile they espied their four fellows coming from a creek thereby, where they had been to fetch oysters. These four they received into their boat, leaving Roanoke, and landed on a little island on the right hand of our entrance into the harbor of Hatteras, where they remained a while, but afterward departed whither as yet we know not.

Having now sufficiently dispatched our business at Croatoan, the same day we departed friendly, taking our leave and came aboard the fleet at Hatteras.

The eighth of August the governor, having long expected the coming of the werowances of Pomeiock, Aquascogoc, Secotan, and Dasamonquepeio, seeing that the seven days were past, within which they promised to come in, or to send their answers by the men of Croatoan, and no tidings of them heard, being certainly also informed by those men of Croatoan that the remnant of Wingina's men, which were left alive, who dwelt at Dasamonquespeio, were they which had slain George Howe and were also at the driving of our eleven Englishmen from Roanoke, he thought to defer the revenge thereof no longer. Wheretofore the same night about midnight he passed over the water, accompanied with Captain Stafford and twenty-four men, whereof Manteo was one, whom we took with us to be our guide to the place where those savages dwelt, where he behaved himself toward us as a most faithful Englishman.

The next day, being the ninth of August, in the morning so early that it was yet dark, we landed near the dwelling place of our enemies and very secretly conveyed ourselves through the woods to that side where we had their houses between us and the water. And having espied their fire and some sitting about it, we presently set on them. The miserable souls herewith amazed, fled into a place of thick reeds, growing fast by, where our men perceiving them, shot one of them through the body with a bullet, and therewith we entered the reeds, among which we hoped to acquit their evil doing towards us, but we were deceived, for those savages were our friends, and were come from Croatoan to gather the corn and fruit of that place, because they understood our enemies were fled immediately after they had slain George Howe, and for haste had left all their corn, tobacco, and pumpkins standing in such sort that all had been devoured of the birds and deer if it had not been gathered in time. But they had like to have paid dearly for it, for it was so dark that they being naked and their men and women appareled all so like others, we knew not but that they were all men. And if that one of them which was a werowance's wife had not had a child at her back, she had been slain instead of a man, and as hap was, another savage knew Master Stafford and ran to him, calling him by his name, whereby he was saved. Finding ourselves thus disappointed of our purpose, we gathered all the corn, peas, pumpkins, and tobacco that we found ripe, leaving the rest unspoiled, and took Menatonon, his wife, with the young child, and the other savages with us over the water to Roanoke. Although the mistaking of these savages somewhat grieved Manteo, yet he imputed their harm to their own folly, saying to them that if their werowances had kept their promise in coming to the governor at the day appointed, they had not known that mischance.

The thirteenth of August our savage Manteo, by the commandment of Sir Walter Raleigh, was christened in Roanoke and called lord thereof and of Dasamonquepeio, in reward of his faithful service.

The eighteenth Eleanor, daughter of the governor and wife of Ananias Dare, one of the assistants, was delivered of a daughter in Roanoke, and the same was christened there the Sunday following, and because this child was the first Christian born in Virginia she was named Virginia. By this time our ships had unladen the goods and victuals of the planters and begun to take in wood and fresh water and to new caulk and trim them for England. The planters also prepared their letters and tokens to send back into England.

Our two ships, the *Lion* and the flyboat, almost ready to depart, the twenty-first of August there arose such a tempest at northeast that our admiral then riding out of the harbor, was forced to cut his cables and put to sea, where he lay beating off and on six days before he could come to us again, so that we feared he had been cast away and the rather for that at the time that the storm took them, the most and best of their sailors were left aland.

At this time some controversies arose between the governor and assistants about choosing two out of the twelve assistants which should go back as factors for the company into England. For every one of them refused, save only one, which all other thought not sufficient. But at length by much persuading of the governor, Christopher Cooper only agreed to go for England. But the next day, through the persuasion of divers of his familiar friends, he changed his mind, so that now the matter stood as at the first.

The next day, the twenty-second of August, the whole company both of the assistants and planters came to the governor, and with one voice requested him to return himself into England, for the better and sooner obtaining supplies and other necessaries for them. But he refused it, and alleged many sufficient causes why he would not. The one was that he could not so suddenly return back again without his great discredit, leaving the action and so many whom he partly had procured through his persuasions to leave their native country and undertake that voyage, and that some enemies to him and the action at his return into England would not spare to slander falsely both him and the action by saying he went to Virginia but politicly and to no other end but to lead so many into a country in which he never meant to stay himself and there to leave them behind him. Also he alleged that seeing they intended to remove fifty miles further up into the main presently, he being then absent his stuff and goods might be both spoiled and most of them pilfered away in the carriage, so that at his return he should be either forced to provide himself of all such things again or else at his coming again to Virginia find himself utterly unfurnished, whereof already he had found some proof, being but once from them but three days. Wherefore he concluded that he would not go himself.

The next day not only the assistants but divers others, as well women as men, began to renew their requests to the governor again to take upon him to return into England for the supply and dispatch of all such things as there were to be done, promising to make him their bond under all their hands and seals for the safe preserving of all his goods for him at his return to Virginia, so that if any part thereof were spoiled or lost they would see it restored to him or his assigns whensoever the same should be missed and demanded. Which bond, with a testimony under their hands and seals, they forthwith made and delivered into his hands. The copy of the testimony I thought good to set down:

May it please you, her Majesty's subjects of England, we your friends and countrymen, the planters in Virginia, do by these presents let you and every of you to understand that for the present and speedy supply of certain our known and apparent lacks and needs, most requisite and necessary for the good and happy planting of us, or any other in this land of Virginia, we all of one mind and consent, have most earnestly entreated and uncessantly requested John White, governor of the planters in Virginia, to pass into England, for the better and more assured help, and setting forward of foresaid supplies. And knowing assuredly that he both can best and will labor and take pains in that behalf for us all, and he not once but often refusing it for our sakes and for the honor and maintenance of the action, hath at last, though much against his will, through our importunacy, yielded to leave his government and all his goods among us, and himself in all our behalves to pass into England, of whose knowledge and fidelity in handling this matter, as all others, we do assure ourselves by these presents, and will you give all credit thereunto, the twenty-fifth of August, 1587.

The governor being at the last through their extreme entreating constrained to return into England, having then but half a day's respite to prepare himself for the same, departed from Roanoke the seven and twentieth of August in the morning, and the same day about midnight came aboard the flyboat, who already had weighed anchor and rode without the bar, the admiral riding by them, who but the same morning was newly come thither again. The same day both the ships weighed anchor and set sail for England. . . .

7.

[A Letter from John White] to the Worshipful and My Very Friend Master Richard Hakluyt, Much Happiness in the Lord.

Sir, as well for the satisfying of your earnest request as the performance of my promise made unto you at my last being with you in England, I have sent you (although in a homely style, especially for the contentation of a delicate ear) the true discourse of my last voyage into the West Indies and parts of America called Virginia, taken in hand about the end of February in the year of our redemption 1590. And what events happened unto us in this our journey you shall plainly perceive by the sequel of my discourse. There were at the time aforesaid three ships absolutely determined to go for the West Indies, at the special charges of Master John Watts of London, merchant. But when they were fully furnished and in readiness to make their departure, a general stay was commanded of all ships throughout England. Which so soon as I heard, I presently (as I thought it most requisite) acquainted Sir Walter Raleigh therewith, desiring him that as I had sundry times afore been chargeable and troublesome unto him for the supplies and reliefs of the planters in Virginia; so likewise that by his endeavor it would please him at that instant to procure license for those three ships to proceed on with their determined voyage that thereby the people in Virginia (if it were God's pleasure) might speedily be comforted and relieved without further charges unto him. Whereupon he by his good means obtained license of the Queen's Majesty and order to be taken that the owner of the three ships should be bound unto Sir Walter Raleigh or his assigns in three thousand pounds, that those three ships in consideration of their releasement should take in and transport a convenient number of passengers with their furnitures and necessaries to be landed in Virginia. Nevertheless, that order was not observed, neither was the bond taken according to the intention aforesaid. But rather in contempt of the aforesaid order I was by the owner and commanders of the ships denied to have any passengers or anything else transported in any of the said ships, saving only myself and my chest. No, not so much as a boy to attend upon me, although I made great suit and earnest entreaty as well to the chief commanders, as to the owner of the said ships. Which cross and unkind dealing, although it very much discontented me, notwithstanding the scarcity of time was such that I could have no opportunity to go unto Sir Walter Raleigh with complaint; for the ships being then all in readiness to go to the sea would have been departed before I could have made my return. Thus both governors, masters, and sailors, regarding very smally the good of their countrymen in Virginia, determined nothing less than to touch at those places but wholly disposed themselves to seek after purchase and spoils, spending so much time there in that summer was spent before we arrived at Virginia. And when we were come thither the season was so unfit and weather so foul that we were constrained of force to forsake that coast, having not seen any of our planters, with loss of one of our ship boats and seven of our chiefest men; and also with loss of three of our anchors and cables and most of our casks with fresh water left on shore, not possible to be had aboard. Which evils and unfortunate events (as well to their own loss as to the hindrance of the planters in Virginia) had not chanced if the order set down by Sir Walter Raleigh had been observed or if my daily and continual petitions for the performance of the same might have taken any place. Thus may you plainly perceive the success of my fifth and last voyage to Virginia, which was no less unfortunately ended than forwardly begun, and as luckless to many as sinister to myself. But I would to God it had been as prosperous to all as noisome to the planters, and as joyful to me as discomfortable to them. Yet seeing it is not my first crossed voyage, I remain contented. And wanting my wishes, I leave off from prosecuting that whereunto I would to God my wealth were answerable to my will. Thus committing the relief to my discomfortable company, the planters in Virginia, to the merciful help of the Almighty, whom I most humbly beseech to help and comfort them, according to His most holy will and their good desire, I take my leave.

From my house at Newtown in Klymore the fourth of February, 1593.

Your most well-wishing friend,
JOHN WHITE

8.

The Fifth Voyage of M[aster] John White into the West Indies and Parts of America Called Virginia, in the Year 1590. [Written by White.]

The twentieth of March the three ships, the *Hopewell*, the *John Evangelist*, and the *Little John*, put to sea from Plymouth with two small shallops.

The twenty-fifth at midnight both our shallops were sunk [while] being towed at the ships' sterns, by the boatswains' negligence.

On the thirtieth we saw ahead of us that part of the coast of Barbary lying east of Cape Cantin and the bay of Safi [both on Moroccan coast].

The next day we came to the isle of Mogador [Morocco], where rode at our passing by a pinnace of London called the *Moonshine*.

APRIL

On the first of April we anchored in Santa Cruz [de Tenerife] road, where we found two great ships of London lading in sugar, of whom we had two ship boats to supply the loss of our shallops.

On the second we set sail from the road of Santa Cruz for the Canaries.

On Saturday, the fourth, we saw Alegranza, the east isle of the Canaries.

On Sunday, the fifth of April, we gave chase to a double flyboat, the which we also the same day fought with and took her, with loss of three of their men slain and one hurt.

On Monday, the sixth, we saw Grand Canary and the next day we landed and took in fresh water on the southside thereof.

On the ninth we departed from Grand Canary and framed our course for Dominica.

The last of April we saw Dominica and the same night we came to an anchor on the southside thereof . . . .

AUGUST

On the first of August the wind scanted and from thence forward we had very foul weather with much rain, thundering, and great spouts, which fell round about us nigh unto our ships.

The third we stood again in for the shore and at midday we took the height of the same. The height of that place we found to be thirty-four degrees of latitude. Towards night we were within three leagues of the low sandy islands west of Wocokon.

But the weather continued so exceeding foul that we could not come to an anchor nigh the coast, wherefore we stood off again to sea until Monday, the ninth of August.

On Monday the storm ceased and we had very great likelihood of fair weather. Therefore we stood in again for the shore and came to an anchor at eleven fathom in thirty-five degrees of latitude, within a mile of the shore, where we went on land on the narrow sandy island, being one of the islands west of Wocokon. In this island we took in some fresh water and caught great store of fish in the shallow water. Between the main (as we supposed) and that island it was but a mile over and three or four foot deep in most places.

On the twelfth in the morning we departed from thence and toward night we came to an anchor at the northeast end of the island of Croatoan, by reason of a breach which we perceived to lie out two or three leagues into the sea. Here we rode all that night.

The thirteenth in the morning before we weighed our anchors our boats were sent to sound over this breach. Our ships riding on the side thereof at five fathom; and a ship's length from us we found but four and a quarter, and then deepening and shallowing for the space of two miles, so that sometimes we found five fathom and by and by seven and within two casts with the lead nine and then eight, next cast five, and then six and then four and then nine again, and deeper; but three fathom was the last, two leagues off from the shore. This breach is in thirty-five degrees and a half and lieth at the very northeast point of Croatoan, whereas goeth a fret [strait] out of the main sea into the inner waters, which part the islands and the mainland.

The fifteenth of August towards evening we came to an anchor at Hatteras in thirty-six degrees and one third in five fathom of water, three leagues from shore. At our first coming to anchor on this shore we saw a great smoke rise in the isle of Roanoke near the place where I left our colony in the year 1587, which smoke put us in good hope that some of the colony were there expecting my return out of England.

The sixteenth and next morning our two boats went ashore and Captain [Abraham] Cocke and Captain Spicer and their company with me, with intent to pass to the place at Roanoke where our countrymen were left. At our putting from the ship we commanded our master gunner to make ready two minions and a falcon well loaden and to shoot them off with reasonable space between every shot, to the end that their reports might be heard to the place where we hoped to find some of our people. This was accordingly performed and our two boats put off unto the shore. In the admiral's boat we sounded all the way and found from our ship until we came within a mile of the shore nine, eight, and seven fathom. But before we were halfway between our ships and the shore we saw another great smoke to the southwest of Kenrick's mounts. We therefore thought good to go to that second smoke first, but it was much further from the harbor where we landed than we supposed it to be, so that we were very sore tired before we came to the smoke. But that which grieved us more was that when we came to the smoke we found no man nor sign that any had been there lately, nor yet any fresh water in all this way to drink. Being thus wearied with this journey, we returned to the harbor where we left our boats, who in our absence had brought their cask ashore for fresh water, so we deferred our going to Roanoke until the next morning and caused some of those sailors to dig in those sandy hills for fresh water whereof we found very sufficient. That night we returned aboard with our boats and our whole company in safety.

The next morning being the seventeenth of August, our boats and company were prepared again to go up to Roanoke, but Captain Spicer had then sent his boat ashore for fresh water, by means whereof it was ten of the clock aforenoon before we put from our ships which were then come to an anchor within two miles of the shore. The admiral's boat was halfway toward the shore when Captain Spicer put off from his ship. The admiral's boat first passed the breach, but not without some danger of sinking, for we had a sea break into our boat which filled us half full of water. But by the will of God and careful steerage of Captain Cocke, we came safe ashore, saving only that our furniture, victuals, match, and powder were much wet and spoiled. For at this time the wind blew at northeast and direct into the harbor so great a gale, that the sea broke extremely on the bar, and the tide went very forcibly at the entrance.

By that time our admiral's boat was hauled ashore and most of our things taken out to dry, Captain Spicer came to the entrance of the breach with his mast standing up, and was half passed over, but by the rash and undiscreet steerage of Ralph Skinner, his master's mate, a very dangerous sea broke into their boat and overset them quite. The men kept [with] the boat—some in it and some hanging on it—but the next sea set the boat on ground, where it beat so that some of them were forced to let go their hold, hoping to wade ashore. But the sea still beat them down, so that they could neither stand nor swim, and the boat twice or thrice was turned the keel upward, whereon Captain Spicer and Skinner hung until they sunk, and were seen no more. But four that could swim a little kept themselves in deeper water and were saved by Captain Cocke's means, who so soon as he saw their oversetting, stripped himself, and four other that could swim very well, and with all haste possible rowed unto them and saved four. They were eleven in all, and seven of the chiefest were drowned . . . .

This mischance did so much discomfort the sailors that they were all of one mind not to go any further to seek the planters. But in the end by the commandment and persuasion of me and Captain Cocke, they prepared the boats; and seeing the captain and me so resolute, they seemed much more willing. Our boats and all things fitted again, we put off from Hatteras, being the number of nineteen persons in both boats. But before we could get to the place, where our planters were left, it was so exceeding dark that we overshot the place a quarter of a mile. There we espied towards the north end of the island the light of a great fire through the woods, to the which we presently rowed. When we came right over against it, we let fall our grapnel near the shore, and sounded with a trumpet a call, and afterwards many familiar English tunes of songs, and called to them friendly; but we had no answer.

We therefore landed at daybreak, and coming to the fire we found the grass and sundry rotten trees burning about the place. From hence we went through the woods to that part of the island directly over against Dasamonquepeio and from thence we returned by the waterside, round about the north point of the island, until we came to the place where I left our colony in the year 1587. In all this way we saw in the sand the print of the savages' feet of two or three sorts trodden the night. And as we entered up the sandy bank, upon a tree, in the very brow thereof, were curiously carved these fair Roman letters C R O. Which letters presently we knew to signify the place, where I should find the planters seated, according to a secret token agreed upon between them and me at my last departure from them, which was, that in any ways they should not fail to write or carve on the trees or posts of the doors the name of the place where they should be seated; for at my coming away they were prepared to remove from Roanoke fifty miles into the main. Therefore, at my departure from them in Anno [Domini] 1587 I willed them that if they should happen to be distressed in any of those places, that then they should carve over the letters or name, a cross ✠ in this form. But we found no such sign of distress.

And having well considered of this, we passed toward the place where they were left in sundry houses, but we found the houses taken down, and the place very strongly enclosed with a high palisado of great trees, with cortines and flankers [entrenchments] very fortlike, and one of the chief trees or posts at the right side of the entrance had the bark taken off, and five foot from the ground in fair capital letters was graven CROATOAN, without any cross or sign of distress. This done, we entered into the palisado, where we found many bars of iron, two pigs of lead, four iron fowlers, iron sakershot, and such like heavy things, thrown here and there, almost overgrown with grass and weeds. From thence we went along by the waterside, towards the point of the creek to see if we could find any of their boats or pinnace, but we could perceive no sign of them, nor any of the last falcons and small ordnance which were left with them, at my departure from them.

At our return from the creek, some of our sailors meeting us, told us that they had found where divers chests had been hidden, and long since digged up again and broken up, and much of the goods in them spoiled and scattered about, but nothing left, of such things as the savages knew any use of, undefaced. Presently Captain Cocke and I went to the place, which was in the end of an old trench, made two years past by

Captain Amadas; where we found five chests that had been carefully hidden of the planters, and of the same chests three were my own, and about the place many of my things spoiled and broken, and my books torn from the covers, the frames of some of my pictures and maps rotten and spoiled with rain, and my armor almost eaten through with rust. This could be no other but the deed of the savages, our enemies at Dasamonquepeio, who had watched the departure of our men to Croatoan; and as soon as they were departed, digged up every place where they suspected anything to be buried. But although it much grieved me to see such spoil of my goods, yet on the other side I greatly joyed that I had safely found a certain token of their safe being at Croatoan, which is the place where Manteo was born, and the savages of the island our friends.

When we had seen in this place so much as we could, we returned to our boats, and departed from the shore towards our ships with as much speed as we could. For the weather began to overcast, and very likely that a foul and stormy night would ensue. Therefore, the same evening with much danger and labor we got ourselves aboard, by which time the wind and seas were so greatly risen that we doubted our cables and anchors would scarcely hold until morning. Wherefore the captain caused the boats to be manned with five lusty men, who could swim all well, and sent them to the little island on the right hand of the harbor, to bring aboard six of our men, who had filled our cask with fresh water. The boat the same night returned aboard with our men, but all our cask ready filled they left behind, unpossible to be had aboard without danger of casting away both men and boats; for this night proved very stormy and foul.

The next morning it was agreed by the captain and myself, with the master and others, to weigh anchor and go for the place at Croatoan where our planters were. For that then the wind was good for that place, and also to leave that cask with fresh water on shore in the island until our return. So then they brought the cable to the capstan, but when the anchor was almost apeak, the cable broke, by means whereof we lost another anchor, wherewith we drove so fast into the shore that we were forced to let fall a third anchor, which came so fast home that the ship was almost aground by Kenrick's mounts. So that we were forced to let slip the cable end for end. And if it had not chanced that we had fallen into a channel of deeper water, closer by the shore than we accounted of, we could never have gone clear of the point that lieth to the southwards of Kenrick's mounts. Being thus clear of some dangers, and gotten into deeper waters, but not without some loss; for we had but one cable and anchor left us of four, and the weather grew to be fouler and fouler; our victuals scarce, and our cask and fresh water lost. It was therefore determined that we should go for Saint John [Puerto Rico] or some other island to the southward for fresh water. And it was further proposed that if we could anyways supply our wants of victuals and other necessaries, either at Hispaniola, Saint John, or Trinidad, that then we should continue in the Indies all the winter following, with hope to make two rich voyages of one, and at our return to visit our countrymen at Virginia. The captain and the whole company in the admiral (with my earnest petitions) thereunto agreed, so that it rested only to know what the master of the *Moonlight,* our consort, would do herein. But when we demanded them if they would accompany us in that new determination, they alleged that their weak and leaky ship was not able to continue it. Wheretofore the same night we parted, leaving the *Moonlight* to go directly for England, and the admiral set his course for Trinidad, which course we kept two days. . . .

PART THREE

The Caribbean

1.
The First Voyage of the Right Worshipful and Valiant Knight, Sir John Hawkins, Sometimes Treasurer of Her Majesty's Navy Royal, Made to the West Indies 1562.

Master John Hawkins having made divers voyages to the isles of the Canaries and there by his good and upright dealing being grown in love and favor with the people, informed himself amongst them by diligent inquisition of the state of the West Indies, whereof he had received some knowledge by the instructions of his father but increased the same by the advertisements and reports of that people. And being amongst other particulars assured that Negroes were very good merchandise in Hispaniola, and that store of Negroes might easily be had upon the coast of Guinea, resolved with himself to make trial thereof, and communicated that devise with his worshipful friends of London—namely, with Sir Lionel Ducket; Sir Thomas Lodge; Master [Mathew] Gunson, his father-in-law; Sir William Winter; Master Bromfield; and others. All which persons liked so well of his intention that they became liberal contributors and adventurers in the action. For which purpose there were three good ships immediately provided—the one called the *Salomon*, of the burden of 120 ton, wherein Master Hawkins himself went as general; the second the *Swallow*, of 100 tons, wherein went for captain Master Thomas Hampton; and the third the *Jonas*, a bark of 40 tons, wherein the master supplied the captain's room. In which small fleet Master Hawkins took with him not above one hundred men for fear of sickness and other inconveniences, whereunto men in long voyages are commonly subject.

With this company he put off and departed from the coast of England in the month of October, 1562, and in his course touched first at Tenerife, where he received friendly entertainment. From thence he passed to Sierra Leone, upon the coast of Guinea, which place by the people of the country is called Tagarin, where he stayed some good time and got into his possession, partly by the sword and partly by other means, to the number of three hundred Negroes at the least, besides other merchandises which that country yieldeth. With this prey he sailed over the ocean sea unto the island of Hispaniola, and arrived first at the port of Isabela. And there he had reasonable utterance of his English commodities, as also of some part of his Negroes, trusting the Spaniards no further than that by his own strength he was able still to master them. From the port of Isabela he went to Puerto Plata, where he made like sales, standing always upon his guard. From thence also he sailed to Montecristi, another port on the north side of Hispaniola and the last place of his touching, where he had peaceable traffic and made vent of the whole number of his Negroes. For which he received in those three places by way of exchange such quantity of merchandise that he did not only lade his own three ships with hides, ginger, sugars, and some quantity of pearls, but he freighted also two other hulks with hides and other like commodities, which he sent into Spain. And thus leaving the island he returned and disemboqued [sailed out], passing out by the islands of the Caicos without further entering into the Bay of Mexico, in this his first voyage to the West Indies. And so with prosperous success and much gain to himself and the aforesaid adventurers, he came home and arrived in the month of September, 1563.

2.

The Third Troublesome Voyage Made with the *Jesus of Lübeck,* the *Minion,* and Four Other Ships to the Parts of Guinea and the West Indies in the Years 1567 and 1568 by Master John Hawkins. [Written by Hawkins.]

The ships departed from Plymouth the second day of

October, anno 1567, and had reasonable weather until the seventh day, at which time, forty leagues north from Cape Finisterre, there arose an extreme storm, which continued four days in such sort that the fleet was dispersed and all our great boats lost and the *Jesus*, our chief ship, in such case as not thought able to serve the voyage. Whereupon, in the same storm we set our course homeward, determining to give over the voyage; but the eleventh day of the same month the wind changed with fair weather, whereby we were animated to follow our enterprise and so did, directing our course with the islands of the Canaries, where, according to an order before prescribed, all our ships, before dispersed, met at one of those islands called Gomera, where we took water, and departed from thence the fourth day of November towards the coast of Guinea and arrived at Cape Verde the eighteenth of November, where we landed 150 men, hoping to obtain some Negroes; where we got but few and those with great hurt and damage to our men, which chiefly proceeded of their envenomed arrows, and although in the beginning they seemed to be but small hurts, yet there hardly escaped any that had blood drawn of them but died in strange sort, with their mouths shut some ten days before they died and after their wounds were whole; where I myself had one of the greatest wounds yet, thanks be to God, escaped.

From thence we passed the time upon the coast of Guinea, searching with all diligence the rivers from Rio Grande unto Sierra Leone till the twelfth of January, in which time we had not gotten together 150 Negroes; yet, notwithstanding, the sickness of our men and the late time of the year commanded us away. And thus, having nothing wherewith to seek the coast of the West Indies, I was with the rest of our company in consultation to go to the coast of the Mine [Gold Coast], hoping there to have obtained some gold for our wares and thereby to have defrayed our charge. But even in that present instant there came to us a Negro, sent from a king oppressed by other kings, his neighbors, desiring our aid, with promise that as many Negroes as by these wars might be obtained, as well of his part as of ours, should be at our pleasure; whereupon we concluded [agreed] to give aid and sent 120 of our men, which the fifteenth of January assaulted a town of the Negroes of our

ally's adversaries, which had in it 8,000 inhabitants, being very
strongly impaled and fenced after their manner; but it was so
well defended that our men prevailed not but lost six men and
forty hurt, so that our men sent forthwith to me for more help.
Whereupon, considering that the good success of this enterprise might highly further the commodity of our voyage, I
went myself and with the help of the king of our side assaulted
the town, both by land and sea, and very hardly with fire (their
houses being covered with dry palm leaves) obtained the town
and put the inhabitants to flight, where we took 250 persons,
men, women, and children, and by our friend the king of our
side there were taken six hundred prisoners, whereof we hoped
to have had our choice; but the Negro (in which nation is seldom or never found truth) meant nothing less [had other
plans], for that night he removed his camp and prisoners so
that we were fain to content us with those few which we had
gotten ourselves.

Now had we obtained between four and five hundred
Negroes, wherewith we thought it somewhat reasonable to
seek the coast of the West Indies, and there for our Negroes
and other our merchandise we hoped to obtain whereof to
countervail our charges with some gains, whereunto we proceeded with all diligence, furnished our watering, took fuel,
and departed the coast of Guinea the third of February, continuing at the sea with a passage more hard than before hath
been accustomed till the twenty-seventh day of March, which
day we had sight of an island called Dominica upon the coast
of the West Indies, in fourteen degrees; from thence we coasted
from place to place, making our traffic with the Spaniards as
we might, somewhat hardly, because the king had straitly
commanded all his governors in those parts by no means to
suffer any trade to be made with us. Notwithstanding, we had
reasonable trade and courteous entertainment from the isle of
Margarita unto Cartagena, without anything greatly worth the
noting saving at Capo de la Vela, in a town called Rio de la
Hacha, from whence come all the pearls, the treasurer who had
the charge there would by no means agree to any trade or suffer
us to take water. He had fortified his town with divers bulwarks

in all places where it might be entered and furnished himself
with a hundred harquebusiers, so that he thought by famine to
have enforced us to have put aland our Negroes; of which purpose he had not greatly failed unless we had by force entered
the town, which (after we could by no means obtain his favor)
we were enforced to do and so with two hundred men broke in
upon their bulwarks and entered the town with the loss only
of two men of our parts and no hurt done to the Spaniards,
because after their volley of shot discharged they all fled.

Thus, having the town with some circumstance [advantage],
as partly by the Spaniards' desire of Negroes and partly by
friendship of the treasurer, we obtained a secret trade whereupon the Spaniards resorted to us by night and bought of us
to the number of two hundred Negroes; in all other places
where we traded the Spaniard inhabitants were glad of us and
traded willingly.

At Cartagena, the last town we thought to have seen on the
coast, we could by no means obtain to deal with any Spaniard,
the governor was so strait; and because our trade was so near
finished we thought not good either to adventure any landing
or to detract [delay] further time but in peace departed from
thence the twenty-fourth of July, hoping to have escaped the
time of their storms, which then soon after began to rain, the
which they called furicanos [hurricanes]; but, passing by the
west end of Cuba towards the coast of Florida, there happened
to us the twelfth day of August an extreme storm which continued by the space of four days, which so beat the *Jesus* that
we cut down all her higher buildings; her rudder also was
sore shaken and withal was in so extreme a leak that we were
rather upon the point to leave her than to keep her any longer;
yet, hoping to bring all to good pass, we sought the coast of
Florida, where we found no place nor haven for our ships
because of the shallowness of the coast. Thus, being in greater
despair and taken with a new storm which continued other
three days, we were enforced to take for our succor the port
which serves the city of Mexico, called San Juan de Ulúa
[an island off Veracruz], which stands in nineteen degrees; in
seeking of which port we took in our way three ships which

carried passengers to the number of a hundred, which passengers we hoped should be a mean to us the better to obtain victuals for our money and a quiet place for the repairing of our fleet.

Shortly after this, the sixteenth of September, we entered the port of San Juan de Ulúa and, in our entry, the Spaniards thinking us to be the fleet of Spain, the chief officers of the country came aboard us, which, being deceived of their expectation, were greatly dismayed, but immediately when they saw our demand was nothing but victuals were recomforted. I found also in the same port twelve ships which had in them, by report, £200,000 in gold and silver, all which (being in my possession, with the king's island, as also the passengers before in my way thitherward stayed) I set at liberty, without the taking from them the weight of a groat; only, because I would not be delayed of my dispatch, I stayed two men of estimation and sent post immediately to Mexico, which was two hundred miles from us, to the presidents and council there, showing them of our arrival there by the force of weather and the necessity of the repair of our ships and victuals, which wants we required as friends to King Philip to be furnished of for our money, and that the presidents and council there should with all convenient speed take order that at the arrival of the Spanish fleet, which was daily looked for, there might no cause of quarrel rise between us and them, but for the better maintenance of amity their commandment might be had in that behalf.

This message, being sent away the sixteenth day of September at night, being the very day of our arrival, in the next morning, which was the seventeenth day of the same month, we saw open of the haven thirteen great ships, and, understanding them to be the fleet of Spain, I sent immediately to advertise the general of the fleet of my being there, doing him to understand that before I would suffer them to enter the port there should some order of conditions pass between us for our safe being there and maintenance of peace.

Now it is to be understood that this port is made by a little island of stones not three foot above the water in the highest place and but a bowshot of length any way; this island standeth from the mainland two bowshots or more; also it is to be understood that there is not in all this coast any other place for ships to arrive in safety, because the north wind hath there such violence that unless the ships be very safely moored with their anchors fastened upon this island there is no remedy for these north winds but death; also the place of the haven was so little that of necessity the ships must ride one aboard the other, so that we could not give place to them nor they to us; and here I began to bewail that which after followed. For now, said I, I am in two dangers and forced to receive the one of them. That was, either I must have kept out the fleet from entering the port, the which with God's help I was very well able to do, or else suffer them to enter in with their accustomed treason, which they never fail to execute where they may have opportunity to compass it by any means. If I had kept them out, then had there been present shipwreck of all the fleet, which amounted in value to six millions, which was in value of our money £1.8 million, which I considered I was not able to answer, fearing the Queen Majesty's indignation in so weighty a matter. Thus with myself revolving the doubts, I thought rather better to abide the jut [jolt] of the uncertainty than the certainty. The uncertain doubt I account was their treason, which by good policy I hoped might be prevented, and therefore, as choosing the least mischief, I proceeded to conditions.

Now was our first messenger come and returned from the fleet with report of the arrival of a viceroy, so that he had authority, both in all this province of Mexico (otherwise called *Nueva España*) and in the sea, who sent us word that we should send our conditions, which of his part should (for the better maintenance of amity between the princes) be both favorably granted and faithfully performed, with many fair words how, passing the coast of the Indies, he had understood of our honest behavior towards the inhabitants where we had to do, as well elsewhere as in the same port, the which I let pass. Thus following our demand, we required victuals for our money and license to sell as much ware as might furnish our wants, and that there might be of either part twelve gentlemen as hostages for the maintenance of peace; and that the island for our better safety might be in our own possession during our abode there, and such ordnance as was planted in the same island, which were eleven pieces of brass; and that no Spaniard might land in the island with any kind of weapon.

These conditions at the first he somewhat misliked, chiefly the guard of the island to be in our own keeping, which if they had had, we had soon known our fare, for with the first north wind they had cut our cables and our ships had gone ashore; but in the end he concluded to our request, bringing the twelve hostages to ten, which with all speed of either part were received, with a writing from the viceroy signed with his hand and sealed with his seal of all the conditions concluded, and forthwith a trumpet blown with commandment that none of either part should bemean to violate the peace upon pain of death; and further it was concluded that the two generals of the fleets should meet and give faith each to other for the performance of the premises, which was so done.

Thus, at the end of three days all was concluded and the fleet entered the port, saluting one another as the manner of the sea doth require. Thus, as I said before, Thursday we entered the port, Friday we saw the fleet, and on Monday at night they entered the port; then we labored two days placing the English ships by themselves and the Spanish ships by themselves, the captains of each part and inferior men of their parts promising great amity of all sides; which even as with all fidelity it was meant on our part, so the Spaniards meant nothing less on their parts, but from the mainland had furnished themselves with a supply of men to the number of one thousand and meant the next Thursday, being the twenty-third of September, at dinner-time, to set upon us on all sides.

The same Thursday in the morning, the treason being at hand, some appearance showed, as shifting of weapon from ship to ship, planting and bending of ordnance from the ship to the island where our men warded [kept guard], passing to and fro of companies of men more than required for their necessary business, and many other ill likelihoods, which caused us to have a vehement suspicion and therewithal sent to the viceroy to inquire what was meant by it, which sent immediately strait commandment to unplant all things suspicious, and also sent word that he in the faith of a viceroy would be our defense from all villainies. Yet we, being not satisfied with this answer, because we suspected a great number of men to be hid in a great ship of nine hundred tons, which was moored next unto the *Minion,* sent again to the viceroy the master of the *Jesus,* which had the Spanish tongue, and required to be satisfied if any such thing were or not. The viceroy, now seeing that the treason must be discovered, forthwith stayed our master, blew the trumpet, and of all sides set upon us. Our men which warded ashore, being stricken with sudden fear, gave place, fled, and sought to recover succor of the ships. The Spaniards, being before provided for the purpose, landed in all places in multitudes from their ships, which they might easily do without boats, and slew all our men ashore without mercy; a few of them escaped aboard the *Jesus.* The great ship, which had by the estimation three hundred men placed in her secretly, immediately fell aboard the *Minion,* but by God's appointment in the time of suspicion we had, which was only one-half hour, the *Minion* was made ready to avoid; and so leesing [loosening] her head fasts and hauling away by the stern fasts, she was gotten out: thus with God's help she defended the violence of the first brunt of these three hundred men.

The *Minion* being passed, they came aboard the *Jesus,* which also, with very much ado and the loss of many of our men, was defended and kept out. Then there were also two other ships that assaulted the *Jesus* at the same instant, so that she had hard getting loose, but yet with some time we had cut our head fasts and gotten out by the stern fasts. Now when the *Jesus* and the *Minion* were gotten about two ships' length from the Spanish fleet, the fight began so hot on all sides that within one hour the admiral of the Spaniards was supposed to be sunk, their vice admiral burned, and one other of their principal ships supposed to be sunk, so that the ships were little able to annoy us.

Then it is to be understood that all the ordnance upon the island was in the Spaniards' hands, which did us so great annoyance that it cut all the masts and yards of the *Jesus,* in such sort that there was no hope to carry her away; also it sunk our small ships, whereupon we determined to place the *Jesus* on that side of the *Minion* that she might abide all the battery from the land and so be a defense for the *Minion* till night, and then to take such relief of victual and other necessaries from the *Jesus* as the time would suffer us and to leave her. As we were thus determining and had placed the *Minion* from the shot of the land, suddenly the Spaniards had fired two great ships, which were coming directly with us, and having no means to avoid the fire, it bred among our men a marvelous fear, so that some said, "Let us depart with the *Minion*"; others said, "Let us see whether the wind will carry the fire from us." But, to be short, the *Minion's* men, which had always their sails in a readiness, thought to make sure work, and so, without either consent of the captain or master, cut their sail, so that very hardly I was received into the *Minion*.

The most part of the men that were left alive in the *Jesus* made shift and followed the *Minion* in a small boat; the rest, which the little boat was not able to receive, were enforced to abide the mercy of the Spaniards (which I doubt was very little). So with the *Minion* only and the *Judith* (a small bark of fifty ton) we escaped, which bark the same night forsook us in our great misery. We were now removed with the *Minion* from the Spanish ships two bowshots and there rode all that night. The next morning we recovered an island a mile from the Spaniards, where there took us a north wind and, being left only with two anchors and two cables (for in this conflict we lost three cables and two anchors), we thought always upon death, which ever was present, but God preserved us to a longer time.

The weather waxed reasonable, and the Saturday we set sail and, having a great number of men and little victuals, our hope of life waxed less and less. Some desired to yield to the Spaniards, some rather desired to obtain a place where they might give themselves to the infidels, and some had rather abide with a little pittance the mercy of God at sea. So thus, with many sorrowful hearts, we wandered in an unknown sea by the space of fourteen days, till hunger enforced us to seek the land, for hides were thought very good meat: rats, cats, mice, and dogs, none escaped that might be gotten. Parrots and monkeys, that were had in great price, were thought there very profitable if they served the turn one dinner. Thus in the end the eighth day of October we came to the land in the bottom of the same Bay of Mexico in 23½ degrees, where we hoped to have found inhabitants of the Spaniards, relief of victuals, and place for the repair of our ship, which was so sore beaten with shot from our enemies and bruised with shooting off our own ordnance that our weary and weak arms were scarce able to defend and keep out water. But all things happened to the contrary, for we found neither people, victual, nor haven of relief, but a place where, having fair weather, with some peril we might land a boat. Our people, being forced with hunger, desired to be set on land, whereunto I consented.

And such as were willing to land I put them apart, and such as were desirous to go homewards I put apart, so that they were indifferently parted a hundred of one side and a hundred of the other side. These hundred men we set aland with all diligence in this little place before said, which, being landed, we determined there to take in fresh water and so with our little remain of victuals to take the sea.

The next day, having aland with me fifty of our hundred men that remained, for the speedier preparing of our water aboard, there arose an extreme storm, so that in three days we could by no means repair aboard our ship; the ship also was in such peril that every hour we looked for shipwreck.

But yet God again had mercy on us and sent fair weather. We had aboard our water and departed the sixteenth day of October, after which day we had fair and prosperous weather till the sixteenth day of November, which day, God be praised, we were clear from the coast of the Indies and out of the channel and gulf of Bahama, which is between the cape of Florida and the islands of Lucayo [Bahamas]. After this, growing near to the cold country, our men, being oppressed with famine, died continually, and they that were left grew into such weakness that we were scantly able to manage our ship, and, the wind being always ill for us to recover England, we determined to go with Galicia in Spain with intent there to relieve our company and other extreme wants. And being arrived the last day of December in a place near unto Vigo called Pontevedra, our men with excess of fresh meat grew into miserable diseases and died, a great part of them.

This matter was borne out as long as it might be, but in the end, although there were none of our men suffered to go aland, yet, by access of the Spaniards, our feebleness was known to them. Whereupon they ceased not to seek by all means to betray us, but with all speed possible we departed to Vigo, where we had some help of certain English ships and twelve fresh men, wherewith we repaired our wants as we might and, departing the twentieth day of January, 1568 [1569 new style], arrived in Mounts Bay in Cornwall the twenty-fifth of the same month, praised be God therefor.

If all the miseries and troublesome affairs of this sorrowful voyage should be perfectly and thoroughly written, there should need a painful [painstaking] man with his pen and as great a time as he had that wrote the lives and deaths of the martyrs.

3.

A Relation of the Commodities of Nova Hispania, and the Manners of the Inhabitants, Written by Henry Hawks, Merchant, Which Lived Five Years in the Said Country, and Drew the Same at the Request of M[aster] Richard Hakluyt, Esquire, of Eyton in the County of Hereford, 1572.

San Juan de Ulúa is an island not high above the water, whereas now the Spaniards, upon Master John Hawkins' being there, are in making a strong fort. In this place all the ships that come out of Spain with good for these parts do unlade . . . .

Five leagues from San Juan de Ulúa is a fair river; it lieth northwest from the port and goeth to a little town of the Spaniards called Veracruz, and with small vessels or barks, which they call frigates, they carry all their merchandise which cometh out of Spain to the said town and in like manner bring all the gold, silver, cochineal, hides, and all other things that the ships carry into Spain unto them. And the goods being in Veracruz, they carry it to Mexico and to Pueblo de los Angelos, Zacatecas, and San Martín [all three in Mexico], and divers other places so far within the country that some of them are seven hundred miles off, and some more and some less, all upon horses, mules, and in wains drawn with oxen, and in cars drawn with mules.

In this town of Veracruz within these twenty years, when women were brought to bed, the children newborn incontinently died, which is not so now in these days, God be thanked.

This town is inclined to many kinds of diseases, by reason of the great heat and a certain gnat or fly which they call a mosquito, which biteth both men and women in their sleep, and as soon as they are bitten, incontinently the flesh swelleth as though they had been bitten with some venomous worm. And this mosquito or gnat doth most follow such as are newly come into the country. Many there are that die of this annoyance.

This town is situated upon the river aforesaid and compassed with woods of divers manners and sorts and many fruits, as oranges and lemons, guavas, and divers others, and birds in them, popinjays both small and great, and some of them as big as a raven and their tails as long as the tail of a pheasant. There are also many other kinds of birds of purple color and small monkeys marvelous proper.

This hot or sick country continueth forty-five miles towards the city of Mexico, and the forty-five miles being passed, then there is a temperate country and full of tillage; but they water all their corn with rivers which they turn in upon it. And they gather their wheat twice a year. And if they should not water the ground whereas their corn is sown, the country is so hot it would burn all.

Before you come to Mexico there is a great town called Tlaxcala, which hath in it above sixteen thousand households. All the inhabitants thereof are free by the kings of Spain; for these were the occasion that Mexico was won in so short time and with so little loss of men. Wherefore they are all gentlemen and pay no tribute to the king. In this town is all the cochineal growing.

Mexico is a great city. It hath more than fifty thousand households, whereof there are not past five or six thousand houses of Spaniards; all the other are the people of the country, which live under the Spaniards' laws. There are in this city stately buildings and many monasteries of friars and nuns which the Spaniards have made. And the building of the Indians is somewhat beautiful outwardly, and within full of small chambers, with very small windows, which is not so comely as the building of the Spaniards. This city standeth in the midst of a great lake, and the water goeth through all or the most part of the streets, and there come small boats, which they call "canoas," and in them they bring all things necessary, as wood and coals, and grass for their horses, stones and lime to build, and corn.

This city is subject to many earthquakes, which oftentimes cast down houses and kill people. This city is very well provided of water to drink and with all manner of victuals, as fruits, flesh and fish, bread, hens and capons, guinea-cocks and hens, and all other fowl. There are in this city every week three fairs or markets, which are frequented with many people, as well Spaniards as the people of the country. There are in these fairs or markets all manner of things that may be invented to sell, and in especial things of the country. . . .

Many rivers fall into this lake which the city standeth in; but there was never any place found whither it goeth out. The Indians know a way to drown the city, and within these three years they would have practiced the same, but they which should have been the doers of it were hanged, and ever since the city hath been well watched both day and night for fear lest at some time they might be deceived; for the Indians love not the Spaniards. Round about the town there are very many gardens and orchards of the fruits of the country, marvelous fair, where the people have great recreation. The men of this city are marvelous vicious, and in like manner the women are dishonest of their bodies, more than they are in other cities or towns in this country.

There are near about this city of Mexico many rivers and standing waters, which have in them a monstrous kind of fish [crocodiles], which is marvelous ravening and a great devourer of men and cattle. He is wont to sleep upon the dry land many times, and if there come in the meantime any man or beast and wake or disquiet him, he speedeth well if he get from him. He is like unto a serpent saving that he doth not fly, neither hath he wings.

There is west out of Mexico a port town which is on the South Sea, called Puerto de Navidad [Acapulco], whereas there are ships which they have ordinarily for the navigation of China, which they have newly found. This port is threescore leagues from Mexico.

There is another port town, which is called Culiacán, on the South Sea, which lieth west and by north out of Mexico and is 150 leagues from the same. And there the Spaniards made two ships to go seek the strait or gulf which as they say is between the Newfoundland and Greenland; and they call it the Englishmen's Strait, which as yet was never fully found. They say that strait lieth not far from the mainland of China, which the Spaniards account to be marvelous rich.

Toward the north from Mexico there are great store of silver mines. There is greater quantity of silver found in these mines toward the north than there is in any other parts, and as the most men of experience said always, they find the richer mines the more northerly. These mines are commonly upon great hills and stony ground, marvelous hard to be labored and wrought.

Out of some of the mines the Indians find a certain kind of earth of divers colors, wherewith they paint themselves in times of their dances and other pastimes which they use.

In this country of Nova Hispania there are also mines of gold, although the gold be commonly found in rivers or very near unto rivers. And now in these days there is not so much gold found as there hath been heretofore.

There are many great rivers and great store of fish in them, not like unto our kinds of fish. And there are marvelous great woods and as fair trees as may be seen of divers sorts, and especially fir trees, that may mast any ship that goeth upon the sea, oaks and pineapples [pine trees], and another tree which they call mesquite; it beareth a fruit like unto a peasecod marvelous sweet, which the wild people gather and keep it all the year and eat it instead of bread.

The Spaniards have notice of seven cities which old men of the Indians show them should lie towards the northwest from Mexico. They have used and use daily much diligence in the seeking of them, but they cannot find any one of them. They say that the witchcraft of the Indians is such that when they come by these towns they cast a mist upon them so that they cannot see them.

They have understanding of another city which they call Copalla, and in like manner, at my being in the country, they have used much labor and diligence in the seeking of it. They have found the lake on which it should stand, and a canoa, the head whereof was wrought with copper curiously, and could not find nor see any man nor the town, which to their understanding should stand on the same water or very near the same.

There is a great number of beasts or kine [ordinarily cattle, here probably bison] in the country of Cibola, which were never brought thither by the Spaniards but breed naturally in the country. They are like unto our oxen, saving that they have long hair like a lion and short horns, and they have upon their shoulders a bunch like a camel, which is higher than the rest of their body. They are marvelous wild and swift in running. They call them the beasts or kine of Cibola.

This Cibola is a city which the Spaniards found now of late, without any people in the same, goodly buildings, fair chimneys, windows made of stone and timber excellently wrought, fair wells with wheels to draw their water, and a place where they had buried their dead people, with many fair stones upon the graves. And the captain would not suffer his soldiers to break up any part of these graves, saying he would come another time to do it.

They asked certain people which they met whither the people of this city were gone; and they made answer they were gone down a river which was thereby very great and there had builded a city which was more for their commodity.

This captain, lacking things necessary for himself and his men, was fain to return back again without finding any treasure according to his expectation; neither found they but few people, although they found beaten ways which had been much haunted and frequented. The captain at his coming back again had a great check of the governor because he had not gone forwards and seen the end of that river.

They have in the country far from the seaside standing waters which are salt; and in the months of April and May the water of them congealeth into salt, which salt is all taken for the king's use and profit.

Their dogs are all crooked-backed, as many as are of the country breed, and cannot run fast; their faces are like the face of a pig or a hog, with sharp noses.

In a certain province which is called Guatemala and Sacanusco [province of Guatemala] there is growing great store of cacao, which is a berry like unto an almond. It is the best merchandise that is in all the Indies. The Indians make a drink of it and in like manner meat to eat. It goeth currently for money in any market or fair and may buy any flesh, fish, bread, or cheese or other things.

There are many kinds of fruits of the country, which are very good, as plantains, sapotes, guavas, pinas, aluacatas [avocados], tunas [prickly pears], mammees, lemons, oranges, walnuts very small and hard with little meat on them, grapes which the Spaniards brought into the country, and also wild grapes, which are of the country and are very small, quinces, peaches, figs, and but few apples and very small, and no pears, but there are melons and calabashes.

There is much honey, both of bees and also of a kind of tree which they call maguey. This honey of maguey is not so sweet as the other honey is, but it is better to be eaten only with bread than the other is; and the tree serveth for many things, as the leaves make thread to sew any kind of bags and are good to cover or thatch houses, and for divers other things.

They have in divers places of the country many hot springs of water. As, above all other, I have seen one in the province of Michoacán. In a plain field without any mountain there is a spring which hath much water, and it is so hot that if a whole quarter of beef be cast into it, within a half hour it will be as well sodden as it will be over a fire in half a day. I have seen half a sheep cast in and immediately it hath been sodden, and I have eaten part of it.

There are many hares and some conies. There are no partridges, but abundance of quails.

They have great store of fish in the South Sea and many oysters and very great. The people do open the oysters and take out the meat of them and dry it, as they do any other kind of fish, and keep them all the year; and when the times serve they send them abroad into the country to sell, as all other fish. They have no salmon, nor trout, nor peal [young salmon], nor carp, tench, nor pike, in all the country.

There are in the country mighty high mountains and hills, and snow upon them. They commonly burn, and twice every day they cast out much smoke and ashes at certain open places which are in the tops of them.

There is among the wild people much manna. I have gathered

of the same and have eaten it, and it is good; for the apothe-
caries send their servants at certain times to gather of the same
for purgations and other uses.

There are in the mountains many wild hogs, which all men
may kill, and lions and tigers [pumas and cougars], which
tigers do much harm to men that travel in the wilderness.

In this country not long since there were two poor men that
found a marvelous rich mine, and when these men went to
make a register of the same, according to the law and custom,
before the king's officers, they thought this mine not meet for
such men as they were and violently took the said mine for
the king and gave no part thereof unto the two poor men. And
within certain days the king's officers resorted thither to labor
in the mine and they found two great mighty hills were come
together, so they found no place to work in. And in the time
while I was among them, which was five years, there was a
poor shepherd, who, keeping of his sheep, happened to find
a well of quicksilver, and he went in like manner to manifest
the same, as the custom and manner is. The king's officers dealt
in like order as they did with the two poor men that found the
rich mine, taking it quite from the shepherd; but when they
went to fetch home the quicksilver, or part thereof, they could
never find it again. So these things have been declared unto the
king, who hath given commandment that nothing being found
in the fields, as mines and such like, shall be taken away from
any man. And many other things have been done in this
country which men might count for great marvels.

There is great abundance of sugar here, and they make divers
conserves and very good and send them into Peru, whereas
they sell them marvelous well, because they make none in
those parts.

The people of the country are of a good stature, tawny
colored, broad faced, flat nosed, and given much to drink both
wine of Spain and also a certain kind of wine which they make
with honey of maguey and roots and other things which they
use to put into the same. They call the same wine "pulco."
They are soon drunk and given to much beastliness and void
of all goodness. In their drunkenness they use and commit
sodomy, and with their mothers and daughters they have their

pleasures and pastimes. Whereupon they are defended [forbidden] from the drinking of wines upon pains of money, as well he that selleth the wines as the Indian that drinketh the same. And if this commandment were not, all the wine in Spain and in France were not sufficient for the West Indies only.

They are of much simplicity and great cowards, void of all valor, and are great witches. They use divers times to talk with the Devil, to whom they do certain sacrifices and oblations; many times they have been taken with the same, and I have seen them most cruelly punished for that offense.

The people are given to learn all manner of occupations and sciences, which for the most part they learned since the coming of the Spaniards. I say all manner of arts: they are very artificial in making of images with feathers, or the proportion or figure of any man, in all kind of manner as he is. The fineness and excellency of this is wonderful, that a barbarous people as they are should give themselves to so fine an art as this is. They are goldsmiths, blacksmiths and coppersmiths, carpenters, masons, shoemakers, tailors, saddlers, embroiderers, and of all other kinds of sciences; and they will and do work so good cheap that poor young men that go out of Spain to get their living are not set on work. Which is the occasion there are many idle people in the country. For the Indian will live all the week with less than one groat, which the Spaniard cannot do, nor any man else.

They say that they came of the lineage of an old man which came thither in a boat of wood, which they call a canoa. But they cannot tell whether it were before the Flood or after, neither can they give any reason of the Flood nor from whence they came. And when the Spaniards came first among them, they did certain sacrifice to an image made in stone of their own invention. The stone was set upon a great hill, which they made of bricks of earth; they call it their "cowa." And certain days in the year they did sacrifice certain old men and young children, and only believed in the sun and the moon, saying that from them they had all things that were needful for them.

They have in these parts great store of cotton wool, with which they make a manner of linen cloth, which the Indians wear, both men and women, and it serveth for shirts and smocks and all other kind of garments which they wear upon their bodies; and the Spaniards use it to all such purposes, especially such as cannot buy other. And if it were not for this kind of cloth, all manner of cloth that goeth out of Spain, I say linen cloth, would be sold out of all measure.

The wild people go naked, without anything upon them. The women wear the skin of a deer before their privities and nothing else upon all their bodies. They have no care for anything but only from day to day for that which they have need to eat. They are big men and likewise the women. They shoot in bows, which they make of a cherry tree, and their arrows are of cane, with a sharp flintstone in the end of the same; they will pierce any coat of mail, and they kill deer, and cranes, and wild geese, ducks, and other fowl, and worms, and snakes, and divers other vermin, which they eat. They live very long, for I have seen men that have been one hundred years of age. They have but very little hair in their face, nor on their bodies.

The Indians have the friars in great reverence. The occasion is that by them and by their means they are free and out of bondage, which was so ordained by Charles the Emperor, which is the occasion that now there is not so much gold and silver coming into Europe as there was while the Indians were slaves. For when they were in bondage they could not choose but do their task every day and bring their masters so much metal out of their mines. But now they must be well paid and much entreated to have them work. So it hath been and is a great hindrance to the owners of the mines and to the king's *quinto*, or custom.

There are many mines of copper in great quantity, whereof they spend in the country as much as serveth their turns. There is some gold in it, but not so much as will pay the costs of the fining. The quantity of it is such, and the mines are so far from the sea, that it will not be worth the freight to carry it into Spain. On the other side, the king's officers will give no license to make ordnance thereof; whereupon the mines lie unlabored and of no valuation.

There is much lead in the country, so that with it they cover churches and other religious houses; wherefore they shall not need any of our lead, as they have had need thereof in times past.

The pomp and liberality of the owners of the mines is marvelous to behold. The apparel both of them and of their wives is more to be compared to the apparel of noble persons than otherwise. If their wives go out of their houses, as unto the church or any other place, they go out with great majesty and with as many men and maids as though she were the wife of some nobleman. I will assure you, I have seen a miner's wife go to the church with one hundred men and twenty gentlewomen and maids. They keep open house; who will may come to eat their meat. They call men with a bell to come to dinner and supper. They are princes in keeping of their houses and bountiful in all manner of things.

A good owner of mines must have at the least a hundred slaves to carry and to stamp his metals; he must have many mules and men to keep the mines; he must have mills to stamp his metals; he must have many wains and oxen to bring home wood to fine the ore; he must have much quicksilver and a marvelous quantity of salt brine for the metals; and he must be at many other charges. And as for this charge of quicksilver, it is a new invention, which they find more profitable than to fine their ore with lead. Howbeit, the same is very costly. For there is never a hundredth of quicksilver but costeth at the least £60 sterling. And the mines fall daily in decay and of less value, and the occasion is the few Indians that men have to labor their mines.

There is in New Spain a marvelous increase of cattle, which daily do increase, and they are of a greater growth than ours are. You may have a great steer that hath a hundredweight of tallow in his belly for sixteen shillings, and some one man hath twenty thousand head of cattle of his own. They sell the hides unto the merchants, who lade into Spain as many as may be well spared. They spend many in the country in shoes and boots and in the mines; and as the country is great, so is the increase of the cattle wonderful. In the island of Santo Domingo they commonly kill the beasts for their hides and tallow and the fowls eat the carcasses; and so they do in Cuba and Puerto Rico, whereas there is much sugar and canafistula, which daily they send into Spain. They have great increase of sheep in like manner, and daily do intend to increase them. They have much wool and as good as the wool of Spain. They make cloth as much as serveth the country for the common people and send much cloth into Peru. I have seen cloth made in the city of Mexico which hath been sold for ten pesos a vara, which is almost £4 English, and the vara is less than our yard. They have woad growing in the country, and alum and brazil and divers other things to dye withal, so that they make all colors. In Peru they make no cloth, but hereafter our cloth will be little set by in these parts, unless it be some fine cloth. The wools are commonly four shillings every row, which is five and twenty pounds; and in some places of the country, that are far from the places whereas they make cloth, it is worth nothing and doth serve but only to make beds for men to lie on.

They make hats, as many as do serve the country, as fine and good, and sell them better cheap, than they can be brought out of Spain, and in like manner send them into Peru.

Many people are set on work, both in the one and in the other. They spin their wool as we do, and instead of oil they have hogs' grease; they twist not their thread so much as we, neither work so fine a thread. They make no kerseys, but they make much cloth which is coarse and sell it for less than twelvepence the vara. It is called "sayal."

They have much silk and make all manner of sorts thereof, as taffetas, satins, velvets of all colors, and they are as good as the silks of Spain, saving that the colors are not so perfect; but the blacks are better than the blacks that come out of Spain.

They have many horses and mares and mules, which the Spaniards brought thither. They have as good jennets as any are in Spain, and better cheap than they be in Spain. And with their mules they carry all their goods from place to place.

There is rain usually in this country from the month of May to the midst of October every day, which time they call their winter, by reason of the said waters. And if it were not for the waters which fall in these hot seasons, their maize, which is the greatest part of their sustenance, would be destroyed. This maize is the greatest maintenance which the Indian hath, and also all the common people of the Spaniards. And their horses and mules which labor cannot be without the same. This grain is substantial and increaseth much blood. If the miners should be without it, they could not labor their mines; for all their servants eat none other bread but only of this maize, and it is made in cakes, as they make oaten cakes in some places of England.

The Indians pay tribute, being of the age of twenty years, four shillings of money and a fanega of maize, which is worth four shillings more, unto the king every year. This is paid in all Nova Hispania of as many as be of the age of twenty years, saving the city of Tlaxcala, which was made free because the citizens thereof were the occasion that Cortés took Mexico in so little a time. And although at the first they were freed from payment of tribute, yet the Spaniards now begin to usurp upon them and make them to till a great field of maize at their own costs every year for the king, which is as beneficial unto him and as great cost unto them as though they paid their tribute as the others do.

The ships which go out of Spain with goods for Peru go to Nombre de Dios and there discharge the said goods; and from thence they be carried over the neck of a land unto a port town in the South Sea called Panama, which is seventeen leagues distant from Nombre de Dios. And there they do ship their goods again and so from thence go to Peru. They are in going thither three months and they come back again in twenty days. They have seldom foul weather and few ships are lost in the South Sea. Four years past, to wit, 1568, there was a ship made out of Peru to seek Solomon Islands, and they came somewhat to the south of the equinoctial and found an island with many black people, in such number that the Spaniards durst not go on land among them. And because they had been long upon the voyage, their people were very weak and so went not on land to know what commodity was upon it. And for want of victuals they arrived in Nova Hispania in a port called Puerto de Navidad, and thence returned back again unto Peru, whereas they were evil entreated because they had not known more of the same island.

They have in this port of Navidad ordinarily their ships which go to the islands of China [the Philippines], which are certain islands which they have found within these seven years. They have brought from thence gold and much cinnamon, and dishes of earth, and cups of the same, so fine that every man that may have a piece of them will give the weight of silver for it. There was a mariner that brought a pearl as big as a dove's egg from thence, and a stone for which the viceroy would have given three thousand ducats. Many things they bring from thence most excellent. There are many of these islands, and the Spaniards have not many of them as yet; for the Portugals disturb them much and combat with them every day, saying it is part of their conquest, and to the mainland they cannot come at any hand. There are goodly people in them, and they are great mariners, richly appareled in cloth of gold and silver and silk of all sorts, and go appareled after the manner of the Turks.

This report make such as come from thence. The men of the mainland have certain traffic with some of these islanders and come thither in a kind of ship which they have with one sail, and bring of such merchandise as they have need of. And of these things there have been brought into New Spain both cloth of gold and silver and divers manners of silks and works of gold and silver, marvelous to be seen. So by their saying there is not such a country in the whole world.

The mainland is from the islands 150 leagues; and the islands are not far from the Moluccas northwards. And the people of those islands which the Spaniards have say that if they would bring their wives and children, that then they should have among them what they would have. So there go women daily, and the king payeth all the charges of the married men and their wives that go to those islands. And there is no doubt but the trade will be marvelous rich in time to come.

It was my fortune to be in company with one Diego Gutierrez, who was the first pilot that ever went to that country of the Philippines. He maketh report of many strange things in that country, as well riches as others, and saith if there be any paradise upon earth it is in that country; and addeth that, sitting under a tree, you shall have such sweet smells, with such great content and pleasure, that you shall remember nothing, neither wife nor children, nor have any kind of appetite to eat or drink, the odoriferous smells will be so sweet. This man hath good livings in Nova Hispania, notwithstanding he will return thither with his wife and children, and as for treasure, there is abundance, as he maketh mention.

In this country of Nova Hispania there are many bucks and does, but they have not so long horns as they have here in England. The Spaniards kill them with handguns and with greyhounds, and the Indians kill them with their bows and arrows, and with the skins they make chamois, such as we in England make doublets and hose of, as good as the skins that are dressed in Flanders, and likewise they make marvelous good Spanish leather of them. There is a bird which is like unto a raven, but he hath some of his feathers white; there is such abundance of them that they eat all the corrupt and dead flesh which is in the country. Otherwise the abundance of carrion is so much that it would make a marvelous corrupt air in all the country and be so noisome that no man could abide it. Therefore it is commanded there shall none of them be killed. These birds are always about cities and towns, where there is much flesh killed.

The Indians are much favored by the justices of the country, and they call them their orphans. And if any Spaniard should happen to do any of them harm or to wrong him in taking anything from him, as many times they do, or to strike any of them, being in any town whereas justice is, they are as well punished for the same as if they had done it one Spaniard to another. When a Spaniard is far from Mexico or any place of justice, thinking to do with the poor Indian what he list, considering he is so far from any place of remedy, he maketh the Indian do what he commandeth him, and if he will not do it he beateth and misuseth him, according to his own appetite. The Indian holdeth his peace until he find an opportunity and then taketh a neighbor with him and goeth to Mexico, although it be twenty leagues off, and maketh his complaint. This his complaint is immediately heard, and although it be a knight or a right good gentleman, he is forthwith sent for and punished, both by his goods and also his person is imprisoned, at the pleasure of the justice. This is the occasion that the Indians are so tame and civil as they are; and if they should not have this favor the Spaniards would soon dispatch all the Indians, or the Indians would kill them. But they may call them dogs and use other evil words as much as they will, and the Indian must needs put it up and go his way.

The poor Indians will go every day two or three leagues to a fair or market with a child upon their necks, with as much fruit or roots, or some kind of ware, as cotton wool or caddis [cotton tape] of all colors, as shall be not past worth a penny; and they will maintain themselves upon the same. For they live with a marvelous small matter.

They are in such poverty that if you need to ride into the country you shall have an Indian to go with you all the day with your bed upon his back for one rial of plate [coin about equal to a sixpence]; and this you shall have from one town to another. Here you are to understand that all men that travel by the way are always wont to carry their beds with them. They are great thieves and will steal all that they may, and you shall have no recompense at their hands.

The garments of the women are in this manner: the uppermost part is made almost like to a woman's smock, saving that it is as broad above as beneath and hath no sleeves but holes on each side to put out their arms. It is made of linen cloth, made of cotton wool, and filled full of flowers, of red caddis and blue, and other colors. This garment cometh down to the knees, and then they have another cloth made after the same manner and that goeth round about their waist and reacheth to their shoes, and over this a white fine sheet upon their heads, which goeth down half the leg. Their hair is made up round with a hair lace about their head. And the men have a small pair of breeches of the same cotton wool, and their shirts which hang over their breeches, and a broad girdle about their middles, and a sheet with flowers upon their backs and with a knot upon one shoulder, and a hat upon their heads, and a pair of shoes. And this is all their apparel, although it be a cacique [prince, chief], which they use in all the country.

The walls of the houses of the Indians are but plain, but the stones are laid so close that you shall not well perceive the joints between one stone and another, they are so finely cut; and by the means that the stones are so workmanly done and finely joined together there is some beauty in their walls. They are marvelous small and light, as pumice stones. They make their doors very little, so that there can go in but one man at a time. Their windows and rooms within their houses are small, and one room they have reserved for their friends when they come to talk one with another, and that is always fair matted and kept marvelous clean, and hanged full of images, and their chairs standing there to sit in. They eat their meat upon the ground and sleep on the ground upon a mat, without any bed, both the gentlemen and other.

The Indians strike their fire with one stick in another, as well the tame people as the wild; for they know not how to do it with an iron and a stone.

In Nova Hispania every ten or twelve leagues they have a contrary speech, saving only about Mexico; so there is a number of speeches in the country.

Montezuma, which was the last king of this country, was one of the richest princes which have been seen in our time, or long before. He had all kinds of beasts which were then in the country, and all manner of birds and fishes, and all manner of worms which creep upon the earth, and all trees and flowers and herbs, all fashioned in silver and gold, which was the greatest part of his treasure, and in these things had he great joy, as the old Indians report. And unto this day they say that the treasure of Montezuma is hidden and that the Spaniards have it not. This king would give none of his people freedom, nor forgive any of them that should [not] pay him tribute, though [they] were never so poor. For if it had been told him that one of his tributaries was poor and that he was not able to pay his tribute according to the custom, then he would have him bound to bring at such times as tributes should be paid a quill full of lice, saying he would have none free but himself.

He had as many wives or concubines as he would have and such as liked him. Always, whensoever he went out of his court to pass the time, he was borne upon four of his noblemen's shoulders, set upon a table, some say, of gold, and very richly dressed with feathers, of divers and many colors, and flowers. He washed all his body every day, were it never so cold. And unto this day so do all the Indians, and especially the women.

The Spaniards keep the Indians in great subjection. They

may have in their houses no sword nor dagger, nor knife with any point, nor may wear upon them any manner of arms; neither may they ride upon any horse nor mules in any saddle nor bridle; neither may they drink wine, which they take for the greatest pain of all. They have attempted divers times to make insurrections, but they have been overthrown immediately by their own great and beastly cowardliness.

There remain some among the wild people that unto this day eat one another. I have seen the bones of a Spaniard that have been as clean burnished as though it had been done by men that had no other occupation. And many times people are carried away by them, but they never come again, whether they be men or women.

They have in the sea islands of red salt in great abundance, whereas they lade it from place to place about the seacoast; and they spend very much salt with salting their hides and fish; and in their mines they occupy great quantity.

They have much alum and as good as any that is in all the Levant, so that they need none of that commodity.

They have also, of their own growing, much canafistula and much sarsaparilla, which is marvelous good for many kinds of diseases.

There are in Florida many gerfalcons and many other kinds of hawks, which the gentlemen of Nova Hispania send for every year. The Spaniards have two forts there, chiefly to keep out the Frenchmen from planting there.

4.

The First Voyage Attempted and Set Forth by the Expert and Valiant Captain M[aster] Francis Drake Himself, with a Ship Called the *Dragon* and Another Ship and a Pinnace, to Nombre de Dios and Darién, About the Year 1572. Written and Recorded by One Lopez Vaz, a Portugal Born in the City of Elvas, in Manner Follow: Which Portugal, with the Discourse About Him, Was Taken at the River of Plate by the Ships

Set Forth by the Right Honorable the
Earl of Cumberland in the Year 1586.

There was a certain Englishman named Francis Drake, who
having intelligence how the town of Nombre de Dios in Nueva
España had but small store of people remaining there, came
on a night and entered the port with four pinnaces and landed
about 150 men and leaving 70 men with a trumpet in a fort
which was there, with the other 80 he entered the town, without
doing any harm till he came to the marketplace, and there
discharged his calivers and sounded a trumpet very loud, and
the other which he had left in the fort answered him after the
same manner, with the discharging their calivers and sounding
their trumpets. The people hereupon not thinking of any such
matter were put in great fear, and waking out of their sleep
fled all into the mountains, inquiring one of another what
the matter should be, remaining as men amazed, not knowing
what that uproar was which happened so suddenly in the town.

But fourteen or fifteen of them joining together with their
harquebuses went to the marketplace to know what they were
that were in the town, and in a corner of the marketplace they
did discover the Englishmen, and seeing them to be but few,
discharged their calivers at those Englishmen. Their fortune
was such that they killed the trumpeter and shot one of the
principal men through the leg, who seeing himself hurt retired
to the fort, where the rest of their company was left. They which
were in the fort sounded their trumpet and seeing that they in
the town did not answer them and hearing the calivers thought
that all they in the town had been slain, and thereupon fled
to their pinnaces. The English captain coming to the fort and
not finding his men which he left there he and his were in so
great fear that leaving their furniture behind them and putting
off their hose [breeches] they swam and waded all to their
pinnaces, and so went with their ships again out of the port.

Thus this English captain called Francis Drake departed
from Nombre de Dios and slew only one man in the town which
was looking out of a window to see what the matter was, and
of his men had only his trumpeter slain.

But he being discontented with the repulse which he had

received there, came to the sound [Gulf] of Darién and having conference with certain Negroes which were fled from their masters of Panama and Nombre de Dios, the Negroes did tell him that certain mules came laden with gold and silver from Panama to Nombre de Dios. Who in company of these Negroes went thereupon on land and stayed in the way where the treasure should come, with a hundred shot, and so took two companies of mules, which came only with their drivers mistrusting nothing, and he carried away the gold only, for they were not able to carry the silver through the mountains. And two days after he came to the house of crosses, where he killed six or seven merchants but found no gold nor silver but much merchandise. So he fired the house, where was burnt above two hundred thousand ducats in merchandise and so went to his ship again. And within half an hour after he was ashipboard there came down to the sands three hundred shot of the Spaniards in the sight of his ships, of purpose to seek him, but he cared little for them, being out of their reach, and so departed with his treasure.

5.

A Summary and True Discourse of Sir Francis Drake's West Indian Voyage, Begun in the Year 1585. Wherein Were Taken the Cities of Saint Iago [Saint James or São Tiago, Cape Verde Islands], Santo Domingo, Cartagena, and the Town of Saint Augustine in Florida. Published by Master Thomas Cates. [Written by Walter Bigges.]

This worthy knight for the service of his Prince and country having prepared his whole fleet and gotten them down to Plymouth in Devonshire, to the number of five and twenty sail of ships and pinnaces, and having assembled of soldiers and mariners to the number of 2,300 in the whole, embarked them and himself at Plymouth aforesaid the twelfth day of September, 1585. . . .

After our going hence, which was the fourteenth of September, in the year of our Lord 1585, and taking our course toward Spain, we had the wind for a few days somewhat scant and sometimes calm. And being arrived near that part of Spain which is called the Moors, we happened to espy divers sails which kept their course close by the shore, the weather being fair and calm. The general caused the vice admiral to go with the pinnaces well manned to see what they were, who upon sight of the said pinnaces approaching near unto them, abandoned for the most part all their ships (being Frenchmen) laden all with salt and bound homewards into France, amongst which ships (being all of small burden) there was one so well liked which also had no man in her, as being brought unto the general he thought good to make stay of her for the service, meaning to pay for her, as also accordingly he performed at our return. Which bark was called the *Drake*. The rest of these ships (being eight or nine) were dismissed without anything at all taken from them. Who being afterwards put somewhat farther off from the shore by the contrary of the wind, we happened to meet with some other French ships, full laden with new-land fish, being upon their return homeward from the said Newfoundland. Whom the general after some speech had with them (and seeing plainly that they were Frenchmen) dismissed without once suffering any man to go aboard of them.

The day following standing in with the shore again we descried another tall ship of twelve score tons or thereabouts, upon whom Master [Christopher] Carleill, the lieutenant general being in the *Tiger*, undertook the chase, whom also anon the admiral followed, and the *Tiger* having caused the said strange ship to strike her sails, kept her there without suffering anybody to go aboard until the admiral was come up. Who forthwith sending for the master and divers others of their principal men and causing them to be severally examined, found the ship and goods to be belonging to the inhabitants of Saint Sebastian in Spain, but the mariners to be for the most part belonging to Saint John de Luz and the passage. In this ship was great store of dry new-land fish, commonly called with us "Poor John," whereof afterwards (being thus found a lawful prize) there was distribution made into all the ships of the fleet, the same being so new and good as it did very greatly bestead us in the whole course of our voyage. A day or two after the taking of this ship, we put in within the isles of Bayona [southwest of Vigo, Spain] for lack of favorable wind. Where we had no sooner anchored some part of the fleet but the general commanded all the pinnaces with the ship boats to be manned, and every man to be furnished with such arms as were needful for that present service. Which being done, the general put himself into his galley, which was also well furnished, and rowing towards the city of Bayona with intent and the favor of the Almighty to surprise it. Before we had advanced one-half league of our way, there came a messenger, being an English merchant from the governor, to see what strange fleet we were, who came to our general, conferred a while with him and after a small time spent our general called for Captain [John] Sampson and willed him to go to the governor of the city to resolve him of two points. The first, to know if there were any wars between Spain and England; the second, why our merchants with their goods were embarged or arrested. Thus departed Captain Sampson with the said messenger to the city, where he found the governor and people much amazed of such a sudden accident [event].

The general with the advice and counsel of Master Carleill, his lieutenant general who was in the galley with him, thought not good to make any stand till such time as they were within the shot of the city, where they might be ready upon the return of Captain Sampson to make a sudden attempt if cause did require before it were dark.

Captain Sampson returned with his message in this sort. First, touching peace or wars the governor said he knew of no wars and that it lay not in him to make any, he being so mean a subject as he was. And as for the stay of the merchants with their goods, it was the king's pleasure but not with intent to endomage [injure] any man. And that the king's countercommandment was (which had been received in that place some seven nights before) that English merchants with their goods should be discharged. For the more verifying whereof he sent such merchants as were in the town of our nation, who trafficked those parts. Which [message] being at large declared to our general by them, counsel was taken what might best be done. And for that the night approached it was thought

needful to land our forces, which was done in the shutting up
of the day; and having quartered ourselves to our most advantage with sufficient guard upon every strait, we thought to
rest ourselves for that night there. The governor sent us some
refreshing, as bread, wine, oil, apples, grapes, marmalade, and
such like. About midnight the weather began to overcast,
insomuch that it was thought meeter to repair aboard than to
make any longer abode on land, and before we could recover
the fleet a great tempest arose, which caused many of our ships
to drive from their anchor hold and some were forced to sea
in great peril, as the bark *Talbot,* the bark *Hawkins,* and the
Speedwell. Which *Speedwell* was only driven into England; the
others recovered us again. The extremity of the storm lasted
three days, which no sooner began to assuage but Master Carleill, our lieutenant general, was sent with his own ship and
three others, as also with the galley and with divers pinnaces,
to see what he might do above Vigo, where he took many boats
and some caravels diversly laden with things of small value
but chiefly with household stuff. Running into the high country
and amongst the rest, he found one boat laden with the principal church stuff of the high church of Vigo, where also was
their great cross of silver, of very fair embossed work and
double gilt all over, having cost them a great mass of money.
They complained to have lost in all kind of goods above thirty
thousand ducats in this place.

The next day the general with the whole fleet went from up
the isles of Bayona to a very good harbor above Vigo, where
Master Carleill stayed his coming, as well for the more quiet
riding of his ships, as also for the good commodity of fresh
watering, which the place there did afford full well. In the
meantime the governor of Galicia had reared such forces as
he might, his numbers by estimate were some two thousand
foot and three hundred horse, and marched from Bayona to
this part of the country, which lay in sight of our fleet, where
making a stand he sent to parley with our general, which was
granted by our general, so it might be in boats upon the water.
And for safety of their persons there were pledges delivered
on both sides. Which done, the governor of Galicia put himself
with two others into our vice admiral's skiff, the same having

been sent to the shore for him, and in like sort our general went in his own skiff; where it was by them agreed we should furnish ourselves with fresh water to be taken by our own people quietly on the land and have all other such necessaries, paying for the same as the place could afford.

When our business was ended we departed and took our way by the Canary Islands, which are esteemed some three hundred leagues from this part of Spain, and falling purposely with Palma with intention to have taken our pleasure of that place, for the full digesting of many things into order, and the better furnishing our store with such several good things as it affordeth very abundantly, we were forced by the vile sea-gate, which at that present fell out, and by the naughtiness of the landing place, being but one, and that under the favor of many platforms well furnished with great ordnance, to depart with the receipt of many of their cannon shot, some into our ships and some besides, some of them being in very deed full cannon high. But the only or chief mischief was the dangerous sea surge, which at shore all alongst plainly threatened the overthrow of as many pinnaces and boats as for that time should have attempted any landing at all.

Now seeing the expectation of this attempt frustrated by the causes aforesaid, we thought it meeter to fall with the isle of Hierro to see if we could find any better fortune. And coming to the island we landed a thousand men in a valley under a high mountain, where we stayed some two or three hours, in which time the inhabitants, accompanied with a young fellow born in England who dwelt there with them, came unto us, showing their state to be so poor that they were all ready to starve, which was not untrue. And therefore without anything gotten we were all commanded presently to embark so as that night we put off to sea south-southeast along towards the coast of Barbary.

Upon Saturday in the morning, being the thirteenth of November, we fell with Cap Blanc, which is a low land and shallow water, where we catched store of fish, and doubling the cape we put into the bay, where we found certain French ships of war, whom we entertained with great courtesy and there left them. This afternoon the whole fleet assembled, which was a little scattered about their fishing, and put from thence to the isles of Cape Verde, sailing till the sixteenth of the same month in the morning, on which day we descried the island of Saint Iago, and in the evening we anchored the fleet between the town called the Playa or Praya, and Saint Iago, where we put on shore one thousand men or more under the leading of Master Christopher Carleill, lieutenant general, who directed the service most like a wise commander. The place where we had first to march did afford no good order, for the ground was mountainous and full of dales, being a very stony and troublesome passage. But such was his industrious disposition as he would never leave until we had gotten up to a fair plain, where we made stand for the assembling of the army. And when we were all gathered together upon the plain some two miles from the town, the lieutenant general thought good not to make attempt till daylight, because there was not one that could serve for guide or giving knowledge at all of the place. And therefore after having well rested, even half an hour before day, he commanded the army to be divided into three special parts, such as he appointed, whereas before we had marched by several companies, being thereunto forced by the badness of the way, as is aforesaid.

Now by the time we were thus ranged into a very brave order, daylight began to appear, and being advanced hard to the wall we saw no enemy to resist. Whereupon the lieutenant general appointed Captain Sampson with thirty shot and Captain [George] Barton with other thirty to go down into the town which stood in the valley under us and might very plainly be viewed all over from that place where the whole army was now arrived. And presently after these captains was sent the great ensign, which had nothing in it but the plain English cross, to be placed towards the sea, that our fleet might see Saint George's cross flourish in the enemy's fortress. Order was given that all the ordnance throughout the town and upon all the platforms, which were above fifty pieces already charged, should be shot off in honor of the Queen Majesty's coronation day, being the seventeenth of November, after the yearly custom of England, which was so answered again by the ordnance out of all the ships in the fleet which now was come near, as it was strange to hear such a thundering noise last so long together. In this meanwhile the lieutenant general held still the most part of his force on the hilltop, till such time as the town was quartered out for the lodging of the whole army. Which being done, every captain took his own quarter and in the evening was placed such a sufficient guard upon every part of the town that we had no cause to fear any present enemy.

Thus we continued in the city the space of fourteen days, taking such spoils as the place yielded, which were for the most part wine, oil, meal, and some such like things for victual, as vinegar, olives, and some such other trash, as merchandise for their Indian trades. But there was not found any treasure at all, or anything else of worth besides. . . .

But before our departure from the town of Saint Iago we established orders for the better government of the army, every man mustered to his captain and oaths were ministered to acknowledge her Majesty supreme governor, as also every man to do his uttermost endeavor to advance the service of the action and to yield due obedience unto the directions of the general and his officers. By this provident counsel and laying down this good foundation beforehand, all things went forward in a due course to the achieving of our happy enterprise.

In all the time of our being here neither the governor for the king of Spain (which is a Portugal), neither the bishop (whose authority is great), neither the inhabitants of the town or island ever came at us (which we expected they should have done) to entreat us to leave them some part of their needful provisions or at the least to spare the ruining of their town at our going away. The cause of this their unreasonable distrust (as I do take it) was the fresh remembrance of the great wrongs they had done to old Master William Hawkins of Plymouth in the voyage he made four or five years before, when as they did both break their promise and murdered many of his men, whereof I judge you have understood and therefore it is needless to be repeated. But since they came not at us, we left written in sundry places, as also in the spittle-house [hospital] (which building was only appointed to be spared), the great discontentment and scorn we took at this their refraining to come unto us, as also at the rude manner of killing and savage kind of handling the dead body of one of our boys found by them straggling all alone, from whom they had taken his head and heart, and had straggled the other bowels about the place in a most brutish and beastly manner.

In revenge whereof at our departing we consumed with fire all the houses as well in the country which we saw as in the town of Saint Iago.

From hence putting off to the West Indies we were not many days at sea but there began among our people such mortality as in few days there were dead above two or three hundred men. And until some seven or eight days after our coming from Saint Iago there had not died any one man of sickness in all the fleet. The sickness showed not his infection wherewith so many were struck until we were departed thence, and then seized our people with extreme hot burning and continual agues, whereof very few escaped with life and yet those for the most part not without great alteration and decay of their wits and strength for a long time after. In some that died were plainly showed the small spots which are often found upon those that be infected with the plague. We were not above eighteen days in passage between the sight of Saint Iago aforesaid and the island of Dominica, being the first island of the West Indies that we fell withal, the same being inhabited with savage people, which go all naked, their skin colored with some painting of a reddish tawny, very personable and handsome strong men, who do admit little conversation with the Spaniards. For as some of our people might understand them, they had a Spaniard or twain prisoners with them. Neither do I think that there is any safety for any of our nation or any other to be within the limits of their commandment, albeit they used us very kindly for those few hours of time which we spent with them, helping our folks to fill and carry on their bare shoulders fresh water from the river to our ships' boats and fetching from their houses great store of tobacco, as also a kind of bread which they fed on, called cassava, very white and savory, made of the roots of cassava. In recompense whereof we bestowed liberal rewards of glass, colored beads, and other things, which we had found at Saint Iago, wherewith (as it seemed) they rested very greatly satisfied and showed some sorrowful countenance when they perceived that we would depart.

From hence we went to another island westward of it called Saint Christopher's [Kitts] Island, wherein we spent some days of Christmas to refresh our sick people and to clean and air our ships. In which island were not any people at all that we could hear of.

In which time by the general it was advised and resolved with the consent of the lieutenant general, the vice admiral, and all the rest of the captains to proceed to the great island of Hispaniola, as well for that we knew ourselves then to be in our best strength as also the rather allured thereunto by the glorious fame of the city of Santo Domingo, being the ancientest and chief inhabited place in all the tract of country thereabout. And so proceeding in this determination, by the way we met a small frigate bound for the same place, the which the vice admiral took. And having duly examined the men that were in her there was one found by whom we were advertised the haven to be a barren haven and the shore or land thereof to be well fortified, having a castle thereupon furnished with great store of artillery, without the danger whereof was no convenient landing place within ten English miles of the city to which the said pilot took upon him to conduct us.

All things being thus considered on, the whole forces were commanded in the evening to embark themselves in pinnaces, boats, and other small barks appointed for this service. Our soldiers being thus embarked, the general put himself into the bark *Francis* as admiral, and all this night we lay on the sea bearing small sail until our arrival to the landing place, which was about the breaking of the day. And so we landed, being New Year's Day, nine or ten miles to the westwards of that brave city of Santo Domingo. For at that time nor yet is known to us any landing place where the sea surge doth not threaten to overset a pinnace or boat. Our general having seen us all landed in safety returned to his fleet, bequeathing us to God and the good conduct of Master Carleill, our lieutenant general. At which time, being about eight of the clock, we began to march, and about noontime or towards one of the clock we approached the town, where the gentlemen and those of the better sort, being some 150 brave horses or rather more, began to present themselves. But our small shot played upon them, which were so sustained with good proportion of pikes in all parts as they finding no part of our troop unprepared to receive them (for you must understand they viewed all round about) they were thus driven to give us leave to proceed towards the two gates of the town, which were the next to the seaward. They had manned them both and planted their ordnance for that present and sudden alarm without the gate and also some troops of small shot in ambuscado upon the highway side. We divided our whole force, being some thousand or twelve hundred men, into two parts to enterprise both the gates at one instant, the lieutenant general having openly avowed to Captain [Anthony] Powel (who led the troop that entered the other gate) that with God's good favor he would not rest until our meeting in the marketplace.

Their ordnance had no sooner discharged upon our near approach and made some execution amongst us, though not much, but the lieutenant general began forthwith to advance both his voice of encouragement and pace of marching (the first man that was slain with the ordnance being very near unto himself) and thereupon hasted all that he might to keep them from the recharging of the ordnance. And notwithstanding their ambuscados, we marched or rather ran so roundly into them as pell-mell we entered the gates and gave them more care every man to save himself by flight than reason to stand any longer to their broken fight. We forthwith repaired to the marketplace, but, to be more truly understood, a place of very fair spacious square ground, whither also came, as had been agreed, Captain Powel with the other troop. Which place with some part next unto it we strengthened with barricados and there as the most convenient place assured ourselves, the city being far too spacious for so small and weary a troop to undertake to guard. Somewhat after midnight they who had the guard of the castle, hearing us busy about the gates of the said castle, abandoned the same, some being taken prisoners and some fleeing away by the help of boats to the other side of the haven, and so into the country.

The next day we quartered a little more at large but not into

the half part of the town, and so making substantial trenches
and planting all the ordnance that each part was correspondent
to other we held this town the space of one month.

In the which time happened some accidents more than are
well remembered for the present, but amongst other things
it chanced that the general sent on his message to the Spaniards
a Negro boy with a flag of white, signifying truce, as is the
Spaniards' ordinary manner to do there when they approach
to speak to us. Which boy unhappily was first met withal by
some of those who had been belonging as officers for the king
in the Spanish galley, which with the town was lately fallen
into our hands, who without all order or reason and contrary
to that good usage wherewith we had entertained their messengers, furiously struck the poor boy through the body with
one of their horsemen's staves. With which wound the boy
returned to the general and after he had declared the manner
of this wrongful cruelty died forthwith in his presence. Wherewith the general being greatly passioned commanded the
provost marshal to cause a couple of friars then prisoners to
be carried to the same place where the boy was struck, accompanied with sufficient guard of our soldiers, and there presently
to be hanged, dispatching at the same instant another poor
prisoner with this reason wherefore this execution was done.
And with this message further that until the party who had
thus murdered the general's messenger were delivered into
our hands to receive condign punishment, there should be no
day pass wherein there should not two prisoners be hanged
until they were all consumed which were in our hands.

Whereupon the day following he that had been captain of
the king's galley brought the offender to the town's end, offering to deliver him into our hands. But it was thought to be a
more honorable revenge to make them there in our sight to
perform the execution themselves, which was done accordingly.

During our being in this town as formerly also at Saint Iago
there had been passed justice upon the life of one of our own
company for an odious matter, so here likewise was there an
Irishman hanged for the murdering of his corporal.

In this time also passed many treaties between their commissioners and us for ransom of their city. But upon disagreements

we still spent the early mornings in firing the outmost houses. But they being built very magnificently of stone, with high lofts, gave us no small travail to ruin them. And albeit for divers days together we ordained each morning by daybreak until the heat began at nine of the clock, that two hundred mariners did naught else but labor to fire and burn the said houses without our trenches, whilst the soldiers in a like proportion stood forth for their guard. Yet did we not, or could not, in this time consume so much as one-third part of the town. Which town is plainly described and set forth in a certain map. And so in the end what wearied with firing and what hastened by some other respects, we were contented to accept of five and twenty thousand ducats of five shillings sixpence the piece for the ransom of the rest of the town.

Amongst other things which happened and were found at Santo Domingo I may not omit to let the world know one very notable mark and token of the unsatiable ambition of the Spanish king and his nation, which was found in the king's house, wherein the chief governor of that city and country is appointed always to lodge, which was this: in the coming to the hall or other rooms of this house, you must first ascend up by a fair large pair of stairs, at the head of which stairs is a handsome spacious place to walk in, somewhat like unto a gallery. Wherein upon one of the walls, right over against you as you enter the said place, so as your eye cannot escape the sight of it, there is described and painted in a very large scutcheon the arms of the king of Spain and in the lower part of the said scutcheon there is likewise a globe containing in it the whole circuit of the sea and the earth whereupon is a horse standing on his hinder part within the globe, lifted up as it were to leap, with a scroll painted in his mouth, wherein was written these words in Latin: *Non sufficit orbis,* which is as much to say as the world sufficeth not. Whereof the meaning was required to be known of some of those of the better sort that came in commission to treat upon the ransom of the town, who would shake their heads and turn aside their countenance in some smiling sort without answering anything, as greatly ashamed thereof. For by some of our company it was told them that if the Queen of England would resolutely prosecute the wars against the king of Spain, he should be forced to lay aside that proud and unreasonable reaching vain of his. For he should find more than enough to do to keep that which he had already as by the present example of their lost town they might for a beginning perceive well enough.

Now to the satisfying of some men who marvel greatly that such a famous and goodly builded city, so well inhabited of gallant people, very brave in their apparel (whereof our soldiers found good store for their relief), should afford no greater riches than was found there: herein it is to be understood that the Indian people, which were the naturals of this whole island of Hispaniola (the same being near hand as great as England) were many years since clean consumed by the tyranny of the Spaniards, which was the cause that for lack of people to work in the mines, the gold and silver mines of this island are wholly given over and thereby they are fain in this island to use copper money, whereof was found very great quantity. The chief trade of this place consisteth of sugar and ginger, which groweth in the island, and of hides of oxen and kine, which in this waste country of the island are bred in infinite numbers, the soil being very fertile. And the said beasts are fed up to a very large growth, and so killed for nothing so much as for their hides aforesaid. We found here great store of strong wine, sweet oil, vinegar, olives, and other such like provisions, as excellent wheat meal packed up in wine pipes and other cask, and other commodities likewise, as woolen and linen cloth and some silks. All which provisions are brought out of Spain and served us for great relief. There was but a little plate or vessel of silver in comparison of the great pride in other things of this town, because in these hot countries they use much of those earthen dishes finely painted or varnished, which they call "porcellana," which is had out of the East India. And for their drinking they use glasses altogether, whereof they make excellent good and fair in the same place. But yet some plate we found and many other good things, as their household furniture very gallant and rich, which had cost them dear, although unto us they were of small importance.

From Santo Domingo we put over to the main or firmland and going all alongst the coast we came at the last in sight of

Cartagena, standing upon the seaside so near as some of our barks in passing alongst approached within the reach of their culverin shot, which they had planted upon certain platforms. The harbor mouth lay some three miles toward the westward of the town, whereinto we entered about three or four of the clock in the afternoon without any resistance of ordnance or other impeachment planted upon the same. In the evening we put ourselves on land towards the harbor mouth under the leading of Master Carleill, our lieutenant general, who after he had digested [divided] us to march forward about midnight, as easily as foot might fall, expressly commanded us to keep close by the seawash of the shore for our best and surest way, whereby we were like to go through and not to miss any more of the way, which once we had lost within an hour after our first beginning to march, through the slender knowledge of him that took upon him to be our guide, whereby the night spent on, which otherwise must have been done by resting. But as we came within some two miles of the town, their horsemen which were some hundred met us and taking the alarm retired to their townward again upon the first volley of our shot that was given them. For the place where we encountered being woody and bushy even to the waterside was unmeet for their service.

At this instant we might hear some pieces of artillery discharged with divers small shot towards the harbor, which gave us to understand, according to the order set down in the evening before by our general, that the vice admiral accompanied with Captain [Thomas] Venner, Captain [Henry] White, and Captain [Robert] Crosse, with other sea captains, and with divers pinnaces and boats should give some attempt unto the little fort standing on the entry of the inner haven, near adjoining to the town. [They made the attempt], though to small purpose for that the place was strong and the entry very narrow was chained over; so as there could be nothing gotten by the attempt more than the giving of them an alarm on that other side of the haven, being a mile and a half from the place we now were at. In which attempt, the vice admiral had the rudder of his skiff struck through with a saker shot and a little or no harm received elsewhere.

The troops being now in their march half a mile behither the town or less, the ground we were on grew to be straight and not above fifty paces over, having the main sea on the one side of it and the harbor water or inner sea (as you may term it) on the other side, which in the plot is plainly showed. This straight was fortified clean over with a stone wall and a ditch without it. The said wall being as orderly built with flanking in every part, as can be set down. There was only so much of this straight unwalled as might serve for the issuing of the horsemen or the passing of carriage in time of need. But this unwalled part was not without a very good barricado of wine butts or pipes filled with earth, full and thick as they might stand on end one by another, some part of them standing even within the main sea.

This place of strength was furnished with six great pieces, demiculverins and sakers, which shot directly in front upon us as we approached. Now without this wall upon the inner side of the straight they had brought likewise two great galleys with their prows to the shore, having planted in them eleven pieces of ordnance, which did beat all cross the straight and flanked our coming on. In these two galleys were planted three or four hundred small shot, and on the land in the guard only of this place three hundred shot and pikes.

They in this their full readiness to receive us spared not their shot both great and small. But our lieutenant general taking advantage of the dark (the daylight as yet not broken out) approached by the lowest ground, according to the express direction which himself had formerly given, the same being the seawash shore, where the water was somewhat fallen, so as most of all their shot was in vain. Our lieutenant general commanded our shot to forbear shooting until we were come to the wall side, and so with pikes roundly together we approached the place where we soon found out the barricadoes of pipes or butts to be the meetest place for our assault, which, notwithstanding it was well furnished with pikes and shot, was without staying attempted by us. Down went the butts of earth and pell-mell came our swords and pikes together, after our shot had first given their volley, even at the enemy's nose. Our pikes were somewhat longer than theirs and our bodies better armed. For very few of them were armed. With which advantage our swords and pikes grew too hard for them, and they [were] driven to give place. In this furious entry, the lieutenant general slew with his own hands the chief ensign bearer of the Spaniards, who fought very manfully to his life's end.

We followed into the town with them and giving them no leisure to breathe we won the marketplace, albeit they made head and fought a while before we got it. And so we being once seized and assured of that, they were content to suffer us to lodge within their town and themselves to go to their wives, whom they had carried into other places of the country before our coming thither.

At every street's end they had raised very fine barricadoes of earthworks with trenches without them, as well made as ever we saw any work done. At the entering whereof was some little resistance, but soon overcome it was with few slain or hurt. They had joined with them many Indians, whom they had placed in corners of advantage, all bowmen with their arrows most villainously empoisoned, so as if they did but break the skin the party so touched died without great marvel. Some they slew of our people with their arrows. Some they likewise mischieved to death with certain pricks of small sticks pointed, of a foot and a half long, the one end put into the ground, the other empoisoned, sticking past up, right against our coming in the way, as we should approach from our landing towards the town, whereof they had planted a wonderful number in the ordinary way. But our keeping the seawash shore missed the greatest part of them very happily. . . .

We stayed here six weeks and the sickness with mortality before spoken of still continued among us, though not with the same fury as at the first. And such as were touched with the said sickness escaping death, very few or almost none could recover their strength. Yea, many of them were much decayed in their memory, insomuch that it was grown an ordinary judgment when one was heard to speak foolishly to say he had been sick of the calentura, which is the Spanish name of their burning ague. For as I told you before, it is a very burning and pestilent ague. The original cause thereof is imputed to the

evening or first night air, which they term "la serena," wherein
they say and hold very firm opinion that who so is then abroad
in the open air shall certainly be infected to the death, not being
of the Indian or natural race of those country people. By holding
their watch our men were thus subjected to the infectious air,
which at Saint Iago was most dangerous and deadly of all
other places.

With the inconvenience of continual mortality, we were
forced to give over our intended enterprise to go with Nombre
de Dios and so overland to Panama, where we should have
struck the stroke for the treasure and full recompense of our
tedious travails. And thus at Cartagena we took our first resolution to return homewards. . . .

During our abode in this place, as also at Santo Domingo,
there passed divers courtesies between us and the Spaniards,
as feasting and using them with all kindness and favor, so as
amongst others there came to see the general the governor of
Cartagena, with the bishop of the same, and divers other
gentlemen of the better sort.

This town of Cartagena we touched in the out parts and
consumed much with fire, as we had done Santo Domingo
upon discontentments and for want of agreeing with us in
their first treaties touching their ransom, which at the last was
concluded between us, should be a hundred and ten thousand
ducats for that which was yet standing, the ducat valued at
five shillings sixpence sterling.

This town though not half so big as Santo Domingo gives
as you see a far greater ransom, being in very deed of far more
importance by reason of the excellency of the harbor and the
situation thereof to serve the trade of Nombre de Dios and
other places and is inhabited with far more richer merchants.
The other is chiefly inhabited with lawyers and brave gentlemen, being the chief or highest appeal of their suits in law of
all the islands about it and of the mainland coast next unto
it. And it is of no such account as Cartagena, for these and
other like reasons which I could give you, over long to be
now written.

The warning which this town received of our coming towards
them from Santo Domingo by the space of twenty days before

our arrival here was cause that they had both fortified and every way prepared for their best defense, as also that they had carried and conveyed away all their treasure and principal substance.

The ransom of a hundred and ten thousand ducats thus concluded on, as is aforesaid, the same being written and expressing for nothing more than the town of Cartagena upon the payment of the said ransom, we left the said town and drew some part of our soldiers into the priory or abbey, standing a quarter of an English mile below the town upon the harbor waterside, the same being walled with a wall of stone, which we told the Spaniards was yet ours, and not redeemed by their composition. Whereupon they finding the defect of their contract were contented to enter into another ransom for all places, but specially for the said house as also the blockhouse or castle, which is upon the mouth of the inner harbor. And when we asked as much for the one as for the other, they yielded to give a thousand crowns for the abbey, leaving us to take our pleasure upon the blockhouse, which they said they were not able to ransom, having stretched themselves to the uttermost of their powers. And therefore the said blockhouse was by us undermined and so with gunpowder blown up in pieces.

While this latter contract was in making our whole fleet of ships fell down towards the harbor mouth, where they anchored the third time and employed their men in fetching of fresh water aboard the ships for our voyage homewards, which water was had in a great well that is in the island by the harbor mouth. Which island is a very pleasant place as hath been seen, having in it many sorts of goodly and very pleasant fruits, as the orange trees and others, being set orderly in walks of great length together. Insomuch as the whole island being some two or three miles about is cast into grounds of gardening and orchards.

After six weeks' abode in this place we put to sea the last of March, where after two or three days a great ship which we had taken at Santo Domingo, and thereupon was called the *New Year's Gift*, fell into a great leak, being laden with ordnance, hides, and other spoils, and in the night she lost the company of our fleet. Which being missed the next morning by the general he cast about with the whole fleet, fearing some great mischance to be happened unto her, as in very deed it so fell out. For her leak was so great that her men were all tired with pumping. But at the last having found her and the bark *Talbot* in her company, which stayed by great hap with her they were ready to take their men out of her, for the saving of them. And so the general being fully advertised of their great extremity made sail directly back again to Cartagena with the whole fleet, where having stayed eight or ten days more about the unlading of this ship and the bestowing thereof and her men into other ships we departed once again to sea, directing our course towards the Cape Saint Anthony, being the westermost part of Cuba, where we arrived the twenty-seventh of April. But because fresh water could not presently be found, we weighed anchor and departed thinking in few days to recover the Matanças, a place to the eastward of Havana.

After we had sailed some fourteen days, we were brought to Cape Saint Anthony again through lack of favorable wind. But then our scarcity was grown such as need made us look a little better for water, which we found in sufficient quantity, being indeed, as I judge, none other than rain water newly fallen and gathered up by making pits in a plot of marish [marshy] ground some three hundred paces from the seaside.

I do wrong if I should forget the good example of the general at this place, who to encourage others and to hasten the getting of fresh water aboard the ships took no less pain himself than the meanest. As also at Santo Domingo, Cartagena, and all other places, having always so vigilant a care and foresight in the good ordering of his fleet, accompanying them, as it is said, with such wonderful travail of body as doubtless had he been the meanest person as he was the chiefest he had yet deserved the first place of honor. And no less happy do we account him for being associated with Master Carleill, his lieutenant general, by whose experience, prudent counsel, and gallant performance he achieved so many and happy enterprises of the war. By whom also he was very greatly assisted in setting down the needful orders, laws, and course of justice, and the due administration of the same upon all occasions.

After three days spent in watering our ships we departed now the second time from this Cape of Saint Anthony the thirteenth of May, and proceeding about the cape of Florida we never touched anywhere. But coasting alongst Florida and keeping the shore still in sight, the twenty-eighth of May early in the morning we descried on the share a place built like a beacon, which was indeed a scaffold upon four long masts raised on end, for men to discover to the seaward, being in the latitude of thirty degrees or very near thereunto. Our pinnaces manned and coming to the shore, we marched up alongst the riverside to see what place the enemy held there, for none amongst us had any knowledge thereof at all.

Here the general took occasion to march with the companies himself in person, the lieutenant general having the vanguard. And going a mile up or somewhat more by the riverside we might discern on the other side of the river over against us a fort which newly had been built by the Spaniards. And some mile or thereabout above the fort was a little town or village without walls, built of wooden houses as the plot doeth plainly show. We forthwith prepared to have ordnance for the battery; and one piece was a little before the evening planted, and the first shot being made by the lieutenant general himself at their ensign struck through the ensign as we afterwards understood by a Frenchman, which came unto us from them. One shot more was then made, which struck the foot of the fort wall, which was all massive timber of great trees like masts. The lieutenant general was determined to pass the river this night with four companies and there lodge himself entrenched as near the fort as that he might play with his muskets and smallest shot upon any that should appear, and so afterwards to bring and plant the battery with him. But the help of mariners for that sudden to make trenches could not be had, which was the cause that this determination was remitted until the next night.

In the night the lieutenant general took a little rowing skiff and half a dozen well armed, as Captain [Matthew] Morgan and Captain Sampson, with some others besides the rowers and went to view what guard the enemy kept, as also to take knowledge of the ground. And albeit he went as covertly as might be, yet the enemy taking the alarm grew fearful that the whole force was approaching to the assault and therefore with all speed abandoned the place after the shooting of some of their pieces. They thus gone and he being returned unto us again, but nothing knowing of their flight from their fort, forthwith came a Frenchman being a fifer (who had been prisoner with them) in a little boat, playing on his fife the tune of the Prince of Orange's song. And being called unto by the guard, he told them before he put foot out of the boat what he was himself and how the Spaniards were gone from the fort, offering either to remain in hands there or else to return to the place with them that would go.

Upon this intelligence the general, the lieutenant general with some of the captains in one skiff, and the vice admiral with some others in his skiff, and two or three pinnaces furnished with soldiers with them put presently over towards the fort, giving order for the rest of the pinnaces to follow. And in our approach some of the enemy bolder than the rest, having stayed behind their company, shot off two pieces of ordnance at us. But on shore we went and entered the place without finding any man there.

When the day appeared we found it built all of timber, the walls being none other but whole masts or bodies of trees set upright and close together in manner of a pale, without any ditch as yet made but wholly intended with some more time. For they had not as yet finished all their work, having begun the same some three or four months before. So as to say the truth they had no reason to keep it, being subject both to fire and easy assault.

The platform whereon the ordnance lay was whole bodies of long pine trees, whereof there is great plenty, laid across one on another and some little earth amongst. There were in it thirteen or fourteen great pieces of brass ordnance and a chest unbroken up, having in it the value of some two thousand pounds sterling by estimation of the king's treasure to pay the soldiers of that place who were 150 men.

The fort thus won, which they called Saint John's Fort, and the day opened, we essayed to go to the town but could not by reason of some rivers and broken ground which was between the two places. And therefore being enforced to embark again into our pinnaces we went thither upon the great main river, which is called as also the town by the name of Saint Augustine.

At our approaching to land there were some that began to show themselves and to bestow some few shot upon us but presently withdrew themselves. And in their running thus away the sergeant major [Powel], finding one of their horses ready saddled and bridled, took the same to follow the chase. And so overgoing all his company was (by one laid behind a bush) shot through the head; and falling down therewith was by the same and two or three more stabbed in three or four places of his body with swords and daggers before any could come near to his rescue. His death was much lamented, being in very deed an honest, wise gentleman and a soldier of good experience and of as great courage as any man might be.

In this place called Saint Augustine we understood the king did keep, as is before said, 150 soldiers and at another place some dozen leagues beyond to the northwards called Saint Helena [South Carolina] he did there likewise keep 150 more, serving there for no other purpose than to keep all other nations from inhabiting any part of all that coast. The government whereof was committed to one Pedro Melendez Marquesse, nephew to that Melendez the admiral who had overthrown Master John Hawkins in the Bay of Mexico some seventeen or eighteen years ago. This governor had charge of both places but was at this time in this place and one of the first that left the same.

Here it was resolved in full assembly of captains to undertake the enterprise of Saint Helena and from thence to seek out the inhabitation of our English countrymen in Virginia, distant from thence some six degrees northward.

When we came thwart of Saint Helena, the shoals appearing dangerous and we having no pilot to undertake the entry, it was thought meetest to go hence alongst. For the admiral had been the same night in four fathom and a half, three leagues from the shore. And yet we understood by the help of a known pilot there may and do go in ships of greater burden and draught than any we had in our fleet.

We passed thus [northward] alongst the coast hard aboard the shore, which is shallow for a league or two from the shore and the same is low and broken land for the most part.

The ninth of June, upon sight of one special great fire (which are very ordinary all alongst this coast, even from the cape of Florida hither), the general sent his skiff to the shore where they found some of our English countrymen (that had been sent thither the year before by Sir Walter Raleigh) and brought them aboard. By whose direction we proceeded along to the place which they make their port. But some of our ships, being of great draught unable to enter, anchored without the harbor in a wild road at sea, about two miles from shore.

From whence the general wrote letters to Master Ralph Lane, being governor of those English in Virginia and then at his fort about six leagues from the road in an island which they call Roanoke, wherein especially he showed how ready he was to supply his necessities and wants, which he understood of by those he had first talked withal.

The morrow after, Master Lane himself and some of his company coming unto him with the consent of his captains he gave them the choice of two offers. That is to say, either he would leave a ship, a pinnace, and certain boats with sufficient masters and mariners together furnished with a month's victual to stay and make farther discovery of the country and coasts and so much victual likewise as might be sufficient for the bringing of them all (being 103 persons) into England, if they thought good after such time, with any other thing they would desire, and that he might be able to spare.

Or else if they thought they had made sufficient discovery already and did desire to return into England, he would give them passage. But they, as it seemed being desirous to stay, accepted very thankfully and with great gladness that which was offered first. Whereupon the ship being appointed and received into charge by some of their own company sent into her by Master Lane before they had received from the rest of the fleet the provision appointed them, there arose a great storm (which they said was extraordinary and very strange) that lasted three days together and put all our fleet in great danger, to be driven from their anchoring upon the coast. For we broke many cables and lost many anchors; and some of our fleet which had lost all (of which number was the ship appointed for Master Lane and his company) was driven to put to sea in great danger in avoiding the coast, and could never see us again until we met in England. Many also of our small pinnaces and boats were lost in this storm.

Notwithstanding after all this, the general offered them (with consent of his captains) another ship with some provision,

although not such a one for their turns as might have been
spared them before, this being unable to be brought into their
harbor. Or else, if they would, to give them passage into England, although he knew we should perform it with greater
difficulty than he might have done before.

But Master Lane with those of the chiefest of his company
which he had then with him, considering what should be best
for them to do, made request unto the general under their
hands that they might have passage for England. The which
being granted and the rest sent for out of the country and
shipped, we departed from that coast the eighteenth of June.

And so, God be thanked, both they and we in good safety
arrived at Portsmouth the twenty-eighth of July, 1586, to the
great glory of God and to no small honor to our Prince, our
Country, and ourselves.

The total value of that which was gotten in this voyage is
esteemed at three score thousand pounds, whereof the companies which have traveled in the voyage were to have twenty
thousand pounds, the adventurers the other forty. Of which
twenty thousand pounds (as I can judge) will redound some
six pounds to the single share.

We lost some 750 men in the voyage; above three parts of
them only by sickness. . . .

6.

The Voyage Truly Discoursed, Made by Sir Francis Drake and Sir John Hawkins, Chiefly Pretended for Some Special Service on the Islands and Main of the West Indies with Six of the Queen's Ships and Twenty-one Other Ships and Barks, Containing Twenty-five Hundred Men and Boys, in the Year 1595. In Which Voyage Both the Foresaid Knights Died by Sickness.

We broke ground out of the sound of Plymouth on Thursday,
the twenty-eighth of August, and that night anchored again
in Cawsand Bay, where we rode till Friday. Then we set sail
and stood southwest, and about three of the clock the next

morning the *Hope,* wherein Sir Thomas Baskerville went, struck upon the eddy stone and shot off a piece but after cleared herself well enough.

On Monday at six of the clock in the morning the Lands End bare northwest and by north and then we stood away southwest and by south for the coast of Spain.

The eighth of September we took two small Flemish flyboats bound for Barbary, which we carried a while with us and afterward dismissed them without doing them any harm. Only we learned news of them and stayed them from descrying our fleet to the enemy.

The twenty-sixth we saw Fuerteventura, being one of the islands of the Canaries.

The twenty-seventh being Saturday by break of day we had overshot the chief town of Grand Canary to the northeast and then stood about for it again, and by nine of the clock were at anchor fair before the fort to the eastward of the town some league. At one of the clock we offered to land one thousand and four hundred men in the sandy bay betwixt the fort and the town. But by our detracting of the time they had made a bulwark in the sandy bay and planted ordnance, so that by reason thereof and the great breach of the sea that went then on shore we were not able to land without endangering our whole forces, which our general would not do. There were of Spaniards' horsemen and footmen some nine hundred, which played upon us out of their trenches, most of them being shot. At the time of our landing there went by commandment of our general's within musket shot of the shore and rode there at anchor some three hours the *Salomon,* the *Bonaventure,* the *Elizabeth Constance,* the *Phoenix,* the *Jewel,* the *Little John,* the *Delight,* the *Pegasus,* the *Exchange,* the *Francis,* the caravel, and the two ketches. But when the general, Sir Francis Drake, gave over the landing being in his barge, the ships weighed, being in some danger, and stood off again to the great ships. Then we went to the west end of the island and there watered. Where Captain Grimston going up the hill with six or seven in his company was set upon by the herdsmen who with their dogs and staves killed the captain and three or four of his company. The rest were sore wounded. The *Salomon's* surgeon taken prisoner, who disclosed our pretended voyage as much as in him lay, so as the viceroy sent a caravel of adviso into the Indies unto all such places as we did pretend to go to. Howbeit they had intelligence from the king of all our voyage the eighth of August, which was three weeks before we set forth of England, as also by a Fleming that had seen all our provision at London.

The twenty-eighth being Sunday at ten of the clock at night we set sail and stood away southwest and south-southwest some two hundred leagues, until we came in the height of the islands of Cape Verde and then more westerly for Martinique, one of the islands of the West Indies, which we saw the twenty-seventh of October. But the night before we had a storm, in which Sir Francis with four or five other ships bearing on ahead of the fleet was separated. Then we stood for Dominica, an island full of inhabitants of the race of the cannibals, not past ten leagues distant from Martinique. In it groweth great store of tobacco, where most of our English and French men barter knives, hatchets, saws, and such like iron tools in truck of tobacco.

Before we came to Dominica our general, Sir Francis Drake, altered his course and went for Marie-Galante, which we had sight of the twenty-eighth day, and came to an anchor on the northeast side a saker shot off the shore in thirteen fathoms water fair shoaling. There the general went on shore in his barge, and by chance met a canoe of Dominicans, to the people whereof he gave a yellow waistcoat of flannel and a handkerchief; and they gave him such fruits as they had, and the Dominicans rowed to Dominica again. They came thither to fetch some fruits which they sow and plant in divers places of that island, which they keep like gardens.

The next morning by break of day we weighed and stood between the Todos Santos, which are four or five little islands between Guadaloupe and Dominica. There is nothing upon these islands but wood. We came to the southeast side of Guadaloupe and there anchored hard aboard the shore. The southwest side of the island is deep water and good anchorage. Where that day Sir John Hawkins came to us again standing up from the south side of Dominica. There we watered, washed our ships, set up our pinnaces, and refreshed our soldiers on shore.

The thirtieth Captain Wignol in the *Francis*, a bark of thirty-five tons, being the sternmost of Sir John Hawkins' fleet was chased by five of the king of Spain's frigates or zabras, being ships of two hundred tons apiece, which came of purpose with three other zabras for the treasure of San Juan de Puerto Rico. The *Francis* going room with them, supposing they had been our own fleet, was by them taken in sight of our caravel. They left the *Francis* driving in the sea with three or four hurt and sick men and took the rest of our men into their ships, as the prisoners which we took at San Juan de Puerto Rico told us.

The fourth of November we began to unlade the *Richard*, one of our victuallers, which was by the next day unladen, unrigged, and then sunken. Then we stood northwest and by north, and the next morning saw the islands of Montserrat, Redonda, Eustatius, Saint Christopher, and Saba. The biggest of these islands is not past eight leagues long. There is good anchorage in eight, seven, and five fathoms water fair white sand. Then we stood away southwest [i.e., northwest], and on the eighth in the morning, being Saturday, came to an anchor some seven or eight leagues off within certain broken islands called The Virgins, which have been accounted dangerous. But we found there a very good road, had it been for a thousand sails of ships in fourteen, twelve, and eight fathoms fair sand and good anchorage, high islands on either side but no fresh water that we could find. Here is much fish to be taken with hooks and nets. Also we stayed on shore and fowled. Here Sir John Hawkins was extreme sick; which his sickness began upon news of the taking of the *Francis*. The eighteenth [tenth] day we weighed and stood north and by east into a lesser sound, which Sir Francis in his barge discovered the night before and anchored in thirteen fathoms, having high steep hills on either side, some league distant from our first riding.

The twelfth in the morning we weighed and set sail into the sea due south through a small strait but without danger and then stood west and by north for San Juan de Puerto Rico and in the afternoon left the three small islands called the Passages to the southward of us and that night came up to the eastermost end of Saint John, where Sir John Hawkins departed this life. Upon whose decease Sir Thomas Baskerville presently went into the *Garland*. At two of the clock we came to anchor at the eastermost side of the chief town called Puerto Rico in a sandy bay two miles off. Where we received from their forts and places where they planted ordnance some twenty-eight great shot, the last of which struck the admiral through the mizzen, and the last but one struck through her quarter into the steerage, the general being there at supper and struck the stool from under him but hurt him not but hurt at the same table Sir Nicholas Clifford, Master Brown, Captain Stratford, with one or two more. Sir Nicholas Clifford and Master Brown died of their hurts.

Then we set sail and stood to the eastward and at midnight tacked about to the west and in the morning came to an anchor before the point without the town, a little to the westwards by the three islands.

The thirteenth we rode still until night, when in the beginning with twenty-five pinnaces, boats, and shallops manned and furnished with fireworks and small shot we went into the road within the great castles and in despite of them fired the five zabras or frigates, all ships of two hundred tons the piece or more, quite burning the rear admiral down to the water, which was the greatest ship of them all, and also mightily spoiled the admiral and vice admiral, notwithstanding the castles and ships gave us 185 great shot, besides small shot abundance. They had also sunk a great ship in the mouth of the channel and rafted it over with her masts almost to the very forts and castles, so as they thought it impregnable. The frigates had in each of them twenty pieces of brass and a hundred barrels of powder. Their chief lading that they brought thither was silk, oil, and wine. The treasure which they went to fetch, which was brought thither in a ship called the *Vigonia*, was conveyed into the strongest and surest castle of defense; being, as one of the prisoners confessed, three millions of ducats or five and thirty tons of silver. Also they had sent all the women, children, and unable persons into the woods, and left none but soldiers and fighting men in the town. The fight on our side was resolute, hot, and dangerous; wherein we lost some forty or fifty men and so many were hurt. There was also great death of the Spaniards aboard the frigates, with burning, drowning, and killing, and besides some taken prisoners.

The fourteenth we rode still being within shot of the uttermost castle. But they fearing the next night we would come in again, began to warp up the other four frigates, beginning first with the admiral, which whether by chance or their own wills we saw to sink; and, as we suppose, so did they with all the rest, or else by stealth got up farther within their chiefest forces.

The fifteenth also we rode still and at afternoon we espied a caravel from the castle point. But before our pinnaces could fetch her up, she ran on shore, where our boats could not come at her because of the breach, and also many of the islanders came down to guard her with shot. The beginning of this night we weighed and stood one hour to the east and then tacked about to the west.

The sixteenth being Sunday and the seventeenth also we were becalmed.

The eighteenth we anchored a little to the southward of the southwest point of the island, giving the point a berth because of a shoal of sand that lieth some two cables length off. There we rode in four, five, and six fathoms fair white sand, where we set up more pinnaces, washed our ships, and refreshed our men on shore. Here the general took a pinnace of Hispaniola with divers letters, signifying that two English men-of-war had done great hurt along their island.

The twentieth the general rowed to the *Phoenix*, the *Delight*, and the caravel, and caused them to weigh anchor right against the mouth of a fresh river in two fathoms water in oozy sand to the southward of the other ships some league or more. The general went into this river three or four leagues up and took horses in the country. Sir Thomas Baskerville rowed up the river and stayed there all night and went up into the land three or four leagues.

The twenty-third we discharged a bark called the *Pulpit* and burnt her. And at three of the clock that afternoon, when we were ready to set sail, there came aboard the *Defiance*, our admiral, a Spaniard with his wife who feared some great torment for not having repaired to the town according to the general's commandment of that island, who had commanded that all able men of the fleet should repair to the town to defend it against us. Then we stood again west and by north because of a ledge of rocks that lie sunk four or five leagues off the southside of the island.

The twenty-fifth we stood away southwest and saw Mona, being a low flat island between Hispaniola and San Juan de Puerto Rico. That day the *Exchange* of Captain Winter spent her bowsprit; and in the beginning of the night the *Phoenix* was sent back to seek her. Which by God's help that night met with her and kept her company until the next morning, then taking a small cable from her for a tow. But by nine that morning she spent her main mast and split her foreyard, breaking also her tow. So as they were fain to save some trifles out of her and the men and to sink the hull. Then we stood away south and [then] south and by west after the fleet, and the twenty-sixth in the morning had sight of the fleet again.

The twenty-ninth we had sight of the island called Curaçao within eight leagues of the main and on the northwest side came to an anchor in very deep water hard aboard the shore without any danger. But the general weighed presently and stood away northwest and by west and north-northwest for the main, and that night saw Aruba, being somewhat a less island than the other. We left it some three leagues to the southward of us.

On Sunday morning being the last of November we saw three or four little islands called the Monges, betwixt Aruba and the next north point of the main. At twelve of the clock we saw the main, where we saw a great current setting to the westward, and also the water changing very white. The *Phoenix*, the caravel, and one of the ketches kept within and at midnight came under Cape de la Vela and made a fire, whereby the rest of the fleet came to anchor under the cape, where is a very good road, fair shoaling and sandy ground, fourteen, twelve, and ten fathoms near the shore. The cape is a bare land without trees or shrubs and falleth in eight or ten leagues southeast and northwest. And a saker shot off the point standeth a little island like Mewstone near Plymouth, but somewhat bigger. In the morning the first of December we embarked all our soldiers for Rio de la Hacha, which is a town twenty leagues to the westwards, one of the ancientest in all the main, although not very big; but it standeth in a most fertile and pleasant soil.

Our men took it by ten of the clock in the night. The ships bearing all that night and the day before in five and six fathoms, the lesser ships in two fathoms and a half water. The *Phoenix* went so near the shore by the general's commandment that she struck on ground but got off again. There lieth to the eastward of the town a mile or thereabout a shoal of sand, therefore give a berth some half league or more before you come right against the town. There we came to anchor in two fathoms but the great ships rode off in five and six fathoms. There is a fresh river about a bowshot to the eastward of the town, whereinto our pinnaces could scarce enter by reason of a bar of sand in the river's mouth, but within it is navigable for barks of twenty or thirty tons some six or eight leagues up.

The sixth day the Spaniards came in to talk about the ransom of the town, but not to the general's liking. And that night Sir Thomas Baskerville marched up into the country to overrun those parts, and the general the same night with some 150 men went by water six leagues to the eastward and took the Rancheria, a fisher town, where they drag for pearl. The people all fled except some sixteen or twenty soldiers, which fought a little but some were taken prisoners, besides many Negroes, with some store of pearls and other pillage. In the houses we refreshed ourselves and were all embarked to come away and then had sight of a brigantine or a dredger, which the general took within one hour's chase with his two barges. She had in her Indie-wheat, which we call maize, and some silver and pearl but of small value.

On Saturday the seventh Master Yorke, captain of the *Hope*, died of sickness and then Master Thomas Drake, the general's brother, was made captain of the *Hope* and Master Jonas Bodenham, captain of the *Adventure* and Master Charles Caesar, captain of the *Amity*.

The tenth day the Spaniards concluded for the ransom of the town for twenty-four thousand ducats and one prisoner promised to pay for his ransom four thousand ducats.

The fourteenth day they brought in the town's ransom in pearls, but rated so dear as the general after conference with them, misliking it, sent it back again, giving them four hour's respite to clear themselves with their treasure.

The sixteenth the governor came into the town about dinner, and upon conference with the general told him plainly that he cared not for the town, neither would he ransom it, and that the pearl was brought in without his command or consent, and that his detracting of time so long was only to send the other towns word that [they] were not of force to withstand us, whereby they might convey all their goods, cattle, and wealth into the woods out of danger. So the general gave the governor leave to depart according to promise, having two hours to withdraw himself in safety.

The seventeenth Sir Thomas Baskerville with the *Elizabeth Constance*, the *Phoenix*, the caravel with four or five pinnaces went some five leagues to the westward, and landing marched some four leagues up into the country to a place called Tapia, which he took and burned certain villages and farmhouses about it. He had some resistance as he passed over the river, but had but one man hurt, which he brought aboard alive with him. He marched one league farther and burnt a village called Sallamca, and so returned with some prisoners, the soldiers having gotten some pillage.

The eighteenth the Rancheria and the town of Rio de la Hacha were burnt clean down to the ground, the churches and a lady's house only excepted, which by her letters written to the general was preserved. That day we set sail and fell to leeward to meet with Sir Thomas Baskerville.

The nineteenth we weighed and stood to leeward for Cape Aguja, which the twentieth at sun rising we saw. It is a cape subject to flaws by reason it is a very high land; and within the cape lieth an island within the mouth of the sound, which hath a white cliff or spot in the west-northwest part of the island. The land all about the cape riseth all in hummocks or broken steepy hills. A league southwest within that (for so falleth the land thereabout) there standeth on top of a cliff a watchhouse, and a little within that a small island. You may go in between the main and it or to leeward if you lust. And hard within that is the road and town of Santa Marta, which at eleven of the clock we took, the people all being fled, except a few Spaniards, Negroes, and Indians, which in a bravado at our landing gave us some thirty or forty shot and so ran away.

That night their lieutenant general was taken and some little pillage brought in out of the woods. For in the town nothing was left but the houses swept clean. In all the main is not a richer place for gold, for the hops were mixt with the earth in every place, and also in the sand a little to the leewards of the town. In the bay we had a bad road by reason of a small moon, for every small moon maketh foul weather all the main along.

The twenty-first the general caused the town to be burnt and all the ships to weigh and stood out, many of the soldiers being embarked where the general had appointed in the small ships, which rode nearest the shore. We lost that night the company of the *Phoenix*, Captain Austin, Peter Lemond, and the *Garland's* pinnace, which stood along the shore and being chased off by galleys out of Cartagena. Peter Lemond with nine of our men was taken, the rest came safe to our fleet.

The twenty-sixth we came into the mouth of Nombre de Dios and by one of the clock took the town, the people being all fled except some one hundred Spaniards which kept the fort and played upon us, having in the fort some three or four small pieces of ordnance and one of them broke in discharging at us. They gave us also a volley of small shot, but seeing our resolution in running upon them they all fled and took the woods.

The town was big, having large streets, houses very high, all built of timber, but one church very fair and large wrought all of timber likewise. Nothing was left in the town of value. There was a show in their shops of great store of merchandise that had been there. There was a mill above the town and upon the top of another hill in the woods stood a little watchhouse where we took twenty sows of silver, two bars of gold, some money in coin, besides other pillage.

The town was situated in a watery soil and subject much to rain, very unhealthy as any place in the Indies, having great store of oranges, plantains, cassava roots, and such other fruits, but very dangerous to be eaten for breeding of diseases. To the eastward of the town within the bay runneth out a fresh river of excellent good water, with houses, and all about it gardens. Half a league from hence due east into the country was an Indian town, whither as we marched a little before our coming away with a hundred men they had broken down a bridge to hinder our passage, where they lay in ambush with some twenty or thirty small shot and bows and arrows, set upon us and killed Lieutenant Jones, hurt three or four and so fled into the woods, ran before us and fired their own town, and then fled farther into the woods. Our men fired divers other houses in pursuing them and so returned again, our general with Sir Thomas being in the river's mouth with thirty or forty men filling water about some mile from us.

The road of Nombre de Dios is a fair road, but on each side as you come to ride before the town, lieth a ledge of rocks, but there is no danger because they are in sight. You may ride between them in three or four fathom water and without if you will in eight or ten fathoms, where neither castle nor fort can annoy you. The name of Nombre de Dios was greater than their strength. For they had no castle nor fort but only the little fort aforesaid standing on the top of a hill, although they might have made it stronger if they would.

The twenty-ninth Sir Thomas Baskerville with 750 armed men, besides surgeons and provand [mess] boys, went for Panama.

The last of December the general burned half the town and the first of January burnt the rest, with all the frigates, barks, and galliots which were in the harbor and on the beach on shore, having houses built over them to keep the pitch from melting.

The second of January Sir Thomas returned with his soldiers both weary and hungry, having marched more than half the way to the South Sea. The Spaniards played divers times upon us both outward and homeward in the woods, the way being cut out of the woods and rocks both very narrow and full of mire and water. The march was so sore as never Englishman marched before. Having marched some ten leagues in a marvelous strait [narrow] way upon the top of a hill through which we must needs pass, the Spaniards had set up a fort and kept it with some eighty or ninety men who played upon us as we came up, before we were aware of them, and so killed some twenty or more of us, amongst whom was Captain Marchant, quartermaster general, and Ensign Sampson, Maurice Williams, one of her Majesty's guard, besides divers were hurt, as Master Captain Nicholas Baskerville, a valiant gentleman, with divers others. Then Sir Thomas had perfect knowledge that they must pass two such forts more . . . besides Panama —[all] very strong, the enemy knowing of our coming long before.

Also our soldiers had no victuals left nor any means to get more. Which considerations caused Sir Thomas to return and give over his attempt. As he marched thitherward he took an Indian and sent him to Nombre de Dios with letters of his return and proceeding.

The fifth we set sail at twelve of the clock and stood to the westward.

The tenth day we saw an island lying westward some thirty leagues called Escudo [de Veraguas, in Mosquito Gulf], where we came to anchor on the southside in twelve fathoms water, fair sand, and good anchorage. If you come into the eastern point, give it a berth, because of a ledge of rocks that lieth out there from the end of the island. Coming to anchor we saw a roader who, seeing us, set sail, but that night with our pinnaces we took him. He had nothing in him but a little maize. The men being examined by the general confessed him to be an adviser sent from Nombre de Dios to all the ports along the coast westward. This island lieth nine or ten leagues from the main and is not past two leagues long, full of wood, and hath great store of fresh water in every part of the island and that very good. It is a sickly climate also and given to much rain. Here we washed our ships and set up the rest of our pinnaces.

The fifteenth day Captain Plat died of sickness, and then Sir Francis Drake began to keep [to] his cabin and to complain of a scouring or flux.

The twenty-third we set sail and stood up again for Portobelo, which is but three leagues to the westwards of Nombre de Dios.

The twenty-eighth at four of the clock in the morning our general, Sir Francis Drake, departed this life, having been extremely sick of a flux which began the night before to stop on him. He used some speeches at or a little before his death, rising and appareling himself; but being brought to bed again, within one hour died. He made his brother Thomas Drake and Captain Jonas Bodenham executors and Master Thomas Drake's son his heir to all his lands, except one manor which he gave to Captain Bodenham.

The same day we anchored at Portobelo, being the best harbor we found all along the main both for great ships and small. There standeth a saker shot off the shore at the eastern point a little island. And there is betwixt the main and that five and six fathoms. But the best coming in is the open mouth betwixt that island and another island that lieth to the westward with a range of rocks.

In Portobelo were but eight or ten houses, besides a great new house which they were in building for the governor that should have been for that place. There was also a very strong fort all to the water's side with flankers of great trees and stones filled with earth between. And had not our coming disappointed their pretense they would have made it one of the strongest places in all the main. There they meant to have builded a great town. We found there three pieces of brass ordnance sunk in the sea, which we weighed up. All the people were fled and their goods carried away.

Up within this bay there was a little village but of no force, where we found a great fresh river. Our men rowing up some two leagues found pillage, as wine and oil and some small quantity of iron. After our coming hither to anchor and the solemn burial of our general, Sir Francis Drake, in the sea, Sir Thomas Baskerville being aboard the *Defiance*, where Master Bride made a sermon, having to his audience all the captains in the fleet, Sir Thomas commanded all aboard the *Garland* with whom he held a council, and there showing his commission was accepted for general, and Captain Bodenham made captain of the *Defiance* and Master Savill captain of the *Adventure*.

The twenty-seventh died Captain Josias of the *Delight* and Captain Egerton, a gentleman of the *Foresight*, and James Wood, chief surgeon of the fleet out of the *Garland*.

The twenty-eighth died Abraham Kendall out of the *Saker*. At this place we watered again, washed our ships, and made new sails, it being by the general and all the captains agreed that, if we could by any means turn up again for Santa Marta, we should; if not, to go directly for England. Here also we took in some ballast as our need required.

The sixth of February the *Elizabeth* of Master Watts was discharged and sunk and that day the *Pegasus* jolly was going on shore for water carrying no guard. The Spaniards perceiving it came down upon them, killed two of them and took two or three prisoners and so ran up into the woods again.

The seventh the *Delight* and Captain Eden's frigate were discharged and sunk because they were old and leaked and the Queen's ships wanted sailors.

That day our men being mustered we had sick and whole two thousand. And the next day we set on shore all our prisoners as Spaniards and Negroes. But before at our first coming to Portobelo, Sir Thomas sent two of those Spaniards to Nombre de Dios and to Panama to fetch ransom for some of the chiefest prisoners, but they never returned again. As we were setting sail there came one with a flag of truce and told the general that they had taken eighteen of our men and that they were well used, adding that if he would stay eight or ten days longer they should be brought from Panama. We supposed this to have been but a delay to have kept us there while the king's forces had come about by sea, as they daily expected. We set sail the eighth of February, turning up for Santa Marta and the fourteenth day we saw the islands of Barú some fourteen leagues to the westward of Cartagean. The general that night told us he would stand in for the town of Barú in the bay. But that night blew so much wind and continued that small moon that the same night we lost the *Foresight* and the next day standing again to make the land which we had made we lost company of the *Susan Parnel*, the *Help*, and the *Pegasus*. Then the next day we put over for Cape Saint Anthony and gave over Santa Marta.

The twenty-fifth we saw the island of Grand Cayman some thirty leagues to the northwestward of Jamaica, being a low sandy island having many tortoises about it.

The twenty-sixth we saw the high land of Cuba to the eastward of the broken islands to the east of the Isle of Pines and were embayed in among those dangerous places. But perceiving it, we stood out again south-southeast and so got clear and then stood away west and by north for the Isle of Pines, which we saw the first of March. It is a low land with wood and fresh water to the western end. If you come in with the midst of it you shall see rise up above the rest of the land eight or nine round hummocks and the westermost hath three in one.

Being shot forth with the west end and standing in for to water we espied twenty sail of ships about one in the after-

noon. This was a third part of the fleet which the king sent for
Cartagena, the rest of the fleet being gone for the Honduras.
They were in all sixty sails sent only to meet our fleet, being
commanded wheresoever they heard we were to come upon
us with all their three forces. This fleet which we met withal
came standing for Cape Corrientes, and had been refreshed
at Havana.

As soon as they descried us they kept close upon a tack,
thinking to get the wind of us. But we weathered them. And
when our admiral with all the rest of our fleet were right in the
wind's eye of them, Sir Thomas Baskerville putting out the
Queen's arms and all the rest of our fleet their bravery, bare
room with them, and commanded the *Defiance* not to shoot but
to keep close by to second him. The vice admiral of the Spaniards being a greater ship than any of ours and the best sailer
in all their fleet luffed by and gave the *Concord* the two first
great shot, which she repaid presently again. Thus the fight
began. The *Bonaventure* bare full with her, ringing her such a
peal of ordnance and small shot withal that he left her with
torn sides. The admiral also made no spare of powder and shot.
But the *Defiance* in the midst of the Spanish fleet thundering
of her ordnance and small shot continued the fight to the end.
So that the vice admiral with three or four of her consorts were
forced to tack about to the eastward, leaving their admiral and
the rest of the fleet, who came not so hotly into the fight as
they did. The fight continued two hours and better. At sunset
all the fleet tacked about to the eastward. We continued our
course to the westward for Cape Corrientes, supposing we
should have met with more of their consorts. In this conflict
in the *Defiance* we had five men slain—three Englishmen, a
Greek, and a Negro. That night some half hour after, their fleet
keeping upon their weather quarter, we saw a mighty smoke
rise out of one of their great ships which stayed behind; which
happened by means of powder as we think and presently after
she was all on a light fire, and so was consumed and all burnt,
as we might well perceive.

The next day being the second of March, in the morning by
break of day we were hard aboard Cape Corrientes, which is a
bare low cape, having a bush of trees higher than the rest some
mile to the eastward of the cape. All Cuba is full of wood on

the southside. The Spanish fleet which then were but fourteen no more than we were kept still upon our weather quarter but dared not to come room with us although our admiral stayed for them. As soon as we had cleared ourselves of the cape, three of their best sailers came room with the *Salomon,* which was so near the land that she could not double the cape but tacked about to the eastward, and so was both astern and also to leeward of all our fleet. But when we saw the Spaniards working, the *Defiance* tacked about to rescue her. Which the Spaniards seeing, and having not forgotten the fight which she made the night before, they luffed up into the midst of their fleet again and then all the fleet stayed until the *Salomon* came up and so stood along for Cape Saint Anthony, which we came in sight of by two in the afternoon, being a low cape also and to the southwest a white sandy bay where three or four ships may very well water. There is a good road for north and easterly winds. There the Spaniards began to fall astern. That night we stood away a glass [half an hour] or two northwest and northnorthwest and northeast, and in the morning watch south, and in the morning had sight of Cuba about the east part of the Organos, which are dangerous rocks lying eight leagues off upon the north part of Cuba, presently as soon as you pass Cape Saint Anthony. Then we stood to the eastward of the land, the wind at south-southwest and at six at night had foul weather, but after were becalmed all night. The fifth the wind came scant. The seventh we saw a high land like a crown which appeareth so thirteen or fourteen leagues to the westward of Havana, and another place in Cuba called The Table eight leagues to the eastward of the crown. The land over Havana maketh two small mountains like a woman's breasts or paps. Here we found no great current until we came to the gulf of Bahama.

The tenth we saw the cape of Florida, being but a reasonable low land and broken islands to the southward of the cape. And at two in the afternoon we lost sight of the land twelve leagues to the northward of the cape. After we had disemboqued we stood west till midnight and were in twenty-eight degrees and then stood northeast till the thirteenth at night, when we were in thirty-one degrees. And after the wind scanted with a great storm in which we lost the *Bonaventure* and the *Little John,* they bearing on head. Then we stood with our larboard tacked east-southeast.

The nineteenth we were in twenty-nine degrees, our course east-northeast. The twenty-first we had a great stormy gale of wind and much rain but large. And then all the rest of our fleet fell astern except the *Hope,* which bare ahead, so that there kept no more with the admiral but the *Defiance,* the *Adventure,* and the *Phoenix.*

The twenty-eighth we were in thirty-nine degrees and stood away for Flores, which the eighth of April we saw, and the ninth came to an anchor on the southside where we watered because the *Defiance* when we came in had but two butts of water. We bartered with the Portugals for some fresh victuals and set here on shore at our coming away out of the admiral our two Portugal pilots, which Sir Francis Drake carried out of England with him.

The tenth being Easter eve at night we set sail, the wind serving us to lie some slant in our course. That night at northeast we beat it up some thirty leagues to the eastward and then about to the west and so again to the east and tried [lay in a storm with only mainsail set] and the next board [tack] to the west. On Thursday towards night, being the sixteenth, we had sight of Corvo again; we tried all that night. And on Friday towards night we came to an anchor to the westward of the point of Santa Cruz under Flores. But before midnight we drove and set sail the next day standing away northeast. About three of the clock in the afternoon the wind came up again at north. On Sunday the nineteenth [eighteenth] by two of the clock in the afternoon we had made twenty leagues an east way, and then the wind came up a good gale at northwest and so northeast with a flown sheet we made the best way we could. But being dispersed by bad weather we arrived about the beginning of May in the west parts of England. And the last ships which came in together to Plymouth were the *Defiance,* the *Garland,* the *Adventure,* and the *Phoenix.*